THE EXPERIENCE OF ANXIETY
A Casebook

23

THE EXPERIENCE
OF ANXIETY

A Casebook

SECOND EDITION

MICHAEL J. GOLDSTEIN, Ph.D.
Department of Psychology
JAMES O. PALMER, Ph.D.
Department of Psychiatry
The University of California
Los Angeles

NEW YORK
OXFORD UNIVERSITY PRESS
LONDON   1975   TORONTO

Second printing, 1975

To
VIDA AND MINERVA
Whose encouragement and patient editing made this book possible.

PREFACE TO THE
SECOND EDITION

It has been almost 12 years since the first edition of this collection of cases was originally compiled. Feedback, both from our own students as well as colleagues at other universities, concerning these cases has suggested that some of them still prove to be excellent teaching cases, while others have not proved as useful. Therefore, in approaching the revision of this book, we decided to keep those cases which students and faculty still find interesting and educationally sound and to replace those which have proven empirically less valuable.

As we approached the problem of selecting new cases, it was clear that this was not a simple task of selecting more recent cases for old ones of similar form. It has been our experience that the fields of clinical psychology and psychiatry have undergone major changes at multiple levels during the past 12 years. First, the character of those seeking help for emotional disorders appears to have changed markedly. Rarely does one see a classical "neurotic" in clinics anymore. Instead, we see more and more of what might be termed characterological problems, in which it is not the delineated symptoms but the total life style of the individual which causes pain and suffering. Therefore, new cases selected for this edition often do not fit any standard nosological categories, but reflect more honestly the types of cases seen by the clinicians of the 70's—problems of depression, divorce, identity-conflict, drug abuse, adolescent turmoil, and so forth.

Second, probably by virtue of the increasing acceptance of mental health services, we more frequently encounter younger cases—children, teenagers, and young adults—with emotional difficulties. It was our feeling that the second edition of this book required partic-

ular expansion in this area. Thus, we have now included cases of
drug abuse, anorexia nervosa, female identity conflict, ethnic identity conflict, all involving teenagers, a frequently neglected group
in most casebooks. The addition of teenage cases is of particular interest to undergraduates who use this book in courses, as they can
identify readily with these cases just having emerged from adolescence themselves.

Third, there has been a noticeable shift in the mental health field
away from concern with the individual as the unit of study to the
interpersonal network of disturbed relationships. Therefore, all of
the new cases in this book strongly emphasize family interaction
patterns, the disturbances in the family system as well as in the
identified patient within the family. This is reflected in the descriptions of therapeutic intervention as well as the history of the case.
Along similar lines, a greater effort has been made to develop the
social forces operating in conjunction with the familial ones as in
the case, "What it Means to be a Woman," in which problems of
feminine role and identity are seen from a social perspective, and
in the case, "What it Means to be a Man," in which masculine role
conflicts are developed within the context of the Chicano sub-
culture.

As in our prior edition, we have attempted to develop thought-
provoking sequences of questions following each case. These questions are designed for self-study by the student and to take the
student through the case in a systematic fashion. We continue to
use these cases with leaderless groups of students and find this
procedure an effective method for teaching the process of clinical
inference.

Despite additions and deletions we have still adhered to our original goal of providing a representative series of cases within broad
diagnostic groupings. For example, in the area of childhood disorders we have presented cases of hyperactivity, school phobia, obesity, psychotic reactions, and infantile autism representing a typical
spectrum of cases seen in child guidance clinics and child inpatient
units. While good nosologies do not exist for teenage disorders, we
have attempted to sample problems seen frequently such as drug
abuse, sex-role conflicts, acting-out problems, and anorexia nervosa
(self-starvation).

The character disorders represent alcoholism, sexual acting-out with suicide, child molestation, obesity, and a case of the 60's, a counter-culture case involved in a ritual murder.

The neuroses represented are a reactive depression, obsessive-compulsive neurosis, severe phobic neurotic, hysteria with dissociative reaction, and a psychosomatic case involving peptic ulcers.

The psychoses reflect two schizophrenic cases, one reactive and one process, a manic-depressive, and a psychosis associated with aging. Thus, the range of cases selected reflects the types covered in most abnormal psychology textbooks, and the textual material can therefore be readily applied to the specific examples provided by each case.

At times some special issues have been raised by certain cases as in Cal B. in which the role of psychologist as expert witness in court is portrayed. Here, we attempt not only to deal with the problems of the specific case but also with the larger issues which arise when the psychologist attempts to contribute meaningfully to issues of crime and punishment as dispensed by the legal system. We hope that the student will develop a deeper appreciation of the differences between the psychological-psychiatric view of human behavior and the assumptions underlying our legal system and the problems that arise when the two cultures interact.

While there is no formal diagnostic entity for eating disorders, clinicians are becoming increasingly aware of their role as expression of emotional disturbance. If an instructor wishes to focus on this area in his course, three cases in this book illustrate different variations on this theme: the T. Family (obesity), the G. Family (anorexia), and Sally D. in which obesity was a core symptom. Since each of these cases present extensive familial data, it is possible for the student to understand the emergence of eating disorders within the total interpersonal network of family transactions.

Similarly with the issue of suicide, which also is not a formal diagnostic category, three cases deal with this problem: Jack F., who may or may not have committed suicide; Sally D., who clearly did commit suicide after a lifetime of acting-out and despair; and Nancy G. (the G. Family) who could have killed herself through self-starvation if she had not been hospitalized and carefully treated. These cases also illustrate one of the key issues in the new field of suicidology—establishing the degree of intention to die in a suicidal attempt or completion.

While it was not obvious to us, evidently there is a systematic pattern and cadence in our case reports which students recognize. It is evidently a style which lends itself to parody as we learned some years ago when an anonymous undergraduate left a copy of the case of Christopher K. on our desk at the end of a quarter. We enjoyed it so much that we have decided to publish it as the final case in this book so that others can enjoy this student's wit.

We are indebted to a number of people for assistance on this book, but most particularly to Eleanor Walker and Sibyl Zaden for their assistance at many levels. Special thanks are also due Dr. Kathryn West for her excellent contribution of the case of Nancy G. and to Dr. Jean Holyroyd for her review and suggested questions to "What it Means to be a Woman."

September 1974   M.J.G.
                                                        J.O.P.

PREFACE TO THE
FIRST EDITION

This book has developed from our experience in teaching the undergraduate course in abnormal psychology. We have attempted to achieve three objectives in this course: first, to introduce the student to the important theories of psychopathology; second, to review relevant research on abnormal behavior; and third, to provide the student with a variety of case materials illustrating concretely the theoretical abstractions, statistical averages, and experimental analogues read about and discussed.

We were unable to find much published case material that challenged the student's problem-solving ability. Most published case books seem to follow the traditional pattern of clinical teaching; a wealth of clinical detail and invariably, a point-by-point interpretation and analysis of the case by an expert. Such cases serve the purpose of introducing the student to analytic interpretation and to illustrate how case and theory may be integrated.

Our choice of unanalyzed case materials reflects a philosophy worth making explicit. It is our contention that students need direct experience in the process of hypothesis-raising and hypothesis-testing which is so essential to conceptualizing the organization of personality. Cases analyzed by others lead the student to believe that there is *one* correct method for integrating case material. Since we have always supported the view that there are a number of interpretations of a case, some more probable than others, exclusive exposure to interpreted case material seemed to defeat our teaching goals. Therefore, our purpose is to challenge the student with essentially unanalyzed, raw clinical data. By unanalyzed, we mean case descriptions that present a detailed history of a person and his own statements about himself, with little or no inference about the etiology of his condition. For example, it is a fact that a certain person is afraid of trains; it is an inference to assume repressed aggression or castration anxiety as a source of this fear.

This type of teaching requires that the student be provided with an opportunity to use raw material as the basis for defensible inference. In this book a series of essentially "programmed" questions are presented which are designed to encourage the student to develop a consistent and empirically defensible system of hypotheses. In devising these questions, the aim was the achievement of a delicate balance between giving a student guidance and yet permitting him the freedom of his hunches. In most instances, the questions are arranged along a continuum of generality, with the most general questions appearing earliest in the sequence. As the student progresses with the questions, he must deal with specific bits of information essential to the understanding of the case. In addition, we have used questions designed to move the student through a continuous process of hypothesis-raising and hypothesis-testing. If one question in the sequence leads to a consideration of one hypothesis or inference, the next requires him to weigh this against other data and to choose between possible interpretations. As this sequence of raising hypotheses and testing them against subsequent case material continues, the student is gradually forced to account for a larger body of case material. Thus, while two or three hypotheses are equally plausible early in the sequence of questions, some become less and less likely as more material is considered. Ultimately, the student should come up with one series of hypotheses that best accounts for the relevant case material.

It is, in our estimation, a valuable feature of these questions that there need not be only *one* good set of hypotheses which these questions can elicit. We have been amazed at the ingenuity of students in making original integrations of case materials, all of which are adequate but all of which differ markedly in approach. As long as we assume basic agreement that most psychopathology is learned, the questions provided can be answered quite adequately by students varying widely in their theoretical backgrounds.

Despite this flexible quality, it will be readily apparent to the reader that the questions do not arise from a theoretically neutral orientation. They reflect, through unconscious rather than conscious intention, a theoretical position lying halfway between social learning theory and psychoanalysis. Our questions consistently focus upon early family relationships and conflicts and require that the student project forward from these early relationships to later clinical behavior. Our debt to psychoanalysis is further evident in the emphasis in the questioning sequence upon modes of defense mechanisms and the conditions under which they were learned. Social learning theory is reflected on a number of levels. First, our questions frequently force the student to analyze the patterns of social learning reinforced within the family group. Second, our questions imply that the number of learning patterns possible is greater than those originally conceptualized by classical psychoanalysis. Third, and on a more subtle level, we have emphasized the role of learning, rather than innate forces, in shaping motivations and drives.

Those who desire to understand the logic of the questioning procedure should notice that a number of questioning programs exist in the book. The *retrospective pattern* forces the student to consider first in the sequence the pattern of current symptoms and the circumstances under which they originally appeared. From this point, the questions direct the student to project backwards, until he is confronted with questions emphasizing early family relationships. The *prospective pattern* of questioning places initial emphasis upon the early family relationships and then directs attention to the progressive development of the emotional conflict within the individual over the years. The *intermediate pattern,* only rarely used, requires the student to begin the analysis at some earlier period, typically post-puberty, and then requires both forward and backward analysis of data.

In these questions, understanding the dynamics of an emotional disorder is possibly more heavily weighted than symptomatic classification. While we cannot agree with a currently popular view that classification of abnormal behavior is futile and meaningless, we recognize that the fringe of vagueness surrounding most traditional diagnostic categories does not warrant excessive emphasis upon the niceties of differential diagnosis. Where an important diagnostic issue is presented by a case, however, the questions reflect the problem at some point. When the diagnosis is unambiguous, the emphasis in questioning is upon understanding rather than classification of behavior.

Despite the energy and time which have gone into the development of the questions, it is obvious that usage of the cases does not require usage of the accompanying questions. Most instructors will no doubt think of other questions which should be asked and other case data which should be emphasized. The case histories can be used in any fashion that the instructor desires.

The selection of cases for this book was a difficult problem. Puzzling or bizarre cases, however fascinating, are not always the most instructive ones. The cases in this book are intended to represent a wide variety of symptom syndromes and dynamic personality patterns. We have avoided the "classic" cases so common in the psychiatric textbook; these are rarely encountered either in everyday life or in the clinic. It is our hope that the student reading the cases in this book will gain an appreciation of the complexity of people and their lives and of the multiple interrelationships between the various facets of behavior and experience. Each case presents several important problems of psychodynamics and diagnosis and can be used to demonstrate any one of the problems illustrated by a case, while ignoring the others. In addition to presenting a wide variety of symptom and dynamic patterns, we have attempted to select cases that also illustrate special sociological and cultural problems. Thus, different racial and religious groups are represented as well as all phases of the life span. It is our hope that the cases selected are truly representative—representative of all social and ethnic groups as well as the types of cases genuinely encountered in the hospital or clinic.

It may be helpful for the reader to know how we have used these cases as supplemental teaching aids. When enrollments are large, the total class is broken up into discussion groups which meet at various points on campus. The selection of group members is ordinarily done at midterm because it gives the instructor the necessary period of time for introducing whatever general personality theory and theory of psychopathology he is trying to present. The group meetings are leaderless in character and are held once a week. Students are assigned to discuss one case each week, using the programmed questions as a guide. A written report is required following each group session, and typically a different student in the group is picked each week to write the report. This procedure gives everyone a chance to participate in the group discussions and to write at least one case report during the semester. While we have used individual reports by each student on a weekly basis in some instances, the reading time required seriously limits the efficiency of this procedure. It is our impression that these group sessions are extremely lively; discussion is vigorous, and students evidently do a great deal of preparation for them. The discussion is most productive when all students come to the meeting familiar with the case and the questions and use the group to test out their private theories. We have been impressed with the sophistication of these discussions and with the students' desire to check their hypotheses against current research and theory.

When enrollments have been small we have used the materials in this book in a workbook fashion. Students are assigned the task of answering one set of questions each week, and class time is set aside for discussing the various answers.

Material of this sort is always tentative and in need of change. The cases contained herein and the accompanying questions have been pretested in our own classes. However, it is inevitable that other instructors will think of questions that we did not mention which have proved effective with their classes. We welcome comments from both instructors and students who use this casebook so that we can refine and adapt our questioning procedures as indicated.

Our primary indebtedness lies with our patients, who, in turn, have fascinated us, frustrated us, and taught us most of what we know about personality. A wider range of case materials was made possible through the invaluable contributions of our colleagues, Drs. Michael Rosow, Carl Younger, Herbert Eveloff, and Mr. Robert Jones. Our students struggled with us in the initial classroom use of these case materials and supported us with their enthusiasm. Last, but not least, we should like to express our appreciation to the secretaries of the Psychology Department, Alice Vollman, Helen Wiczenski, Valerie Durham, and Deborah Schilling, and to the secretarial staff of the Neuropsychiatric Institute, all at U.C.L.A., who patiently typed the many drafts until this book took final form.

December 1962   M.J.G.
                                                                  J.O.P.

CONTENTS

THE EXPERIENCE OF ANXIETY
A Casebook

PART I EMOTIONAL DISTURBANCES IN CHILDREN

THE CASE OF ALLEN E.

Who Cares If School Keeps

Not only was it difficult to understand why Allen, age 13, had not been attending school regularly for over a year, but it was even more puzzling that neither of his parents were aware of the extent of his absences. It was only during the spring of that year that his parents learned of his absences from school, but they had not been able to enforce his attendance. Part of the problem was a lack of communication between the school and the home, which Allen himself helped to foster. The school records showed that Allen began skipping school shortly after he entered ninth grade. The school did telephone the home, but both parents worked and Allen did not answer the phone. Several times they sent notes home with Allen to inquire about his attendance. Allen never brought the notes home and intercepted the several letters mailed to the home. Twice the school attendance officer made a personal visit to the home, but no one was there. Allen carefully changed his report card so that his days of absence were not shown. Since his grades were dropping off markedly his family did question him, and he replied that he had harder classes and did not understand the work. This was difficult for his parents to understand since he often seemed to be doing homework. Moreover, he had always been a very bright student who enjoyed going to school. In the past he had many friends and was active in sports and student government. In fact, he was president of his 8th grade class. The school authorities finally did reach the parents by phoning Mr. E.'s office, and the parents were most astounded to find that Allen had been absent anywhere from two to five days a week over a period of almost five months. When the parents faced Allen with the school's information he at first denied that it was so serious and then finally broke down in tears and admitted that he hated school, that he could not bear to go, and that he had often come home shortly after his parents went to work. At first he would go to school, stay for an hour or so, and then disappear, usually returning home. Sometimes he would come back in the afternoon with little or no explanation to the school. Other times he would forge notes to the school, excusing himself for illness or family business, signing his parents' name. At other times he would complain of illness, usually nausea, sit in the school nurse's office, and finally disappear for the balance of the day. Sometimes the teacher would be so used to Allen's absence, that she would forget to record it.

After Allen's absences were discovered, his parents were still unable to force him to go to school. He would lock himself in his room, cry, and refuse to come out. At times he would even refuse meals. He seemed very depressed and frightened and declared that he could not go to school, that he was too nervous. Once he was permitted to stay home, he seemed to relax markedly and to be quite at ease. He saw little of his friends after school and displayed none of the previous interest he had in sports. Instead he spent hours pouring over a stamp collection that he had had for many years. During the evenings and weekends when his parents were home he demanded extra attention from them. He would sit close to his mother and follow her around the house. He seemed to need to know where she was every minute and to be no more than a few feet away from her. His behavior toward his father was somewhat similar, but if the parents were not in the same room he would stay close to his mother. In contrast, he seemed more on edge with his older brother, Frank, and they quarreled quite openly, while previously they had only teased one another.

Frank was never quite as good a student as Allen and frequently cut classes in high school to join "the gang." There were considerable difficulties between Frank and his parents over his long hair, his alleged use of marijuana, and the hours he kept. Mr. E. was very critical of what he called Frank's "playboy" attitude toward life. On the other hand, Allen had always been praised for his excellent performance at school, his achievement in sports, and his general compliance and obedience at home. The parents remarked that they did not understand why it was Allen who stayed away from school, since they could understand if Frank had dropped out.

Despite the fact that the parents were well aware that Allen was not attending school throughout the balance of the school year,

they had not taken any action to obtain any help regarding his behavior until the school threatened several times to prosecute the parents for keeping Allen out of school. In the initial intake interview
both parents were quite embarrassed at having to come to a Psychiatric Clinic. They had thought that Allen's behavior was only a
"phase" he was going through; they hoped he would be markedly
improved by the end of the summer and would report to school in
the fall. But by the end of September Allen still had not returned for
his second year in junior high school. The parents now agreed that
the situation was quite serious, and they admitted with considerable
reluctance that he must be quite emotionally disturbed. At first they
both felt that something very bad must have happened at school.
They had gone to the school with many questions but learned of
no particular incident there. Allen, at one point, complained that his
shop course teacher had been quite critical of him, but when the
parents met with him they were not at all convinced that Allen's
complaint was justified. In fact, the school counselor reported that
the shop teacher had been one who had taken special interest in
Allen and had long been aware that something was disturbing the
child. Allen admitted that he was fond of the shop teacher and
could not say why he had initially complained about this teacher.

Allen's parents also wondered if there had been some incident
with the other children. The previous year Allen had been very
angry at a bully who had been in his class for quite a few years and
who continually upbraided him. However, Allen, who was a fair size
boy, had finally turned on the bully and knocked him flat in the
school yard. Allen was punished for this by the principal, but only
lightly, and everyone at the school felt that Allen was justified in his
attack on the bully. The incident was passed over and forgotten.
Allen agreed that the incident with the bully had no relationship to
his dropping out of school. He could not explain what it was about
the school that made him uncomfortable, yet he felt physically ill
and nauseous whenever he spent more than an hour or so at school.
Only at home in his own room did he feel at ease and in peace. Nor
could he remember exactly how it began. He was vague about the
first times that he started to return home from school and could not
cite any particular incident either at home or at school that he
could think of that started the whole series of events. He could not
think of any one thing at school that he disliked the most or any one

thing that was going on to disturb him. It is "the whole bit," he would say, "I hate *all* of school."

The parents tried to think of anything that had disturbed Allen outside of school. He had seemed quite happy during the summer vacation prior to this particular school year. He had even looked forward to returning to school at the end of the vacation; he talked about the new sports program that was being initiated at school, where competitive sports between other schools were to be allowed for the first time. The family had had a very pleasant vacation together for a longer period than they usually could afford. The boys and their father had taken up water skiing and came home in high spirits.

In the initial sessions in which the family met together in the clinic, they discussed the fact that they had been upset with Frank's behavior the previous year, but both parents felt that this should not have concerned Allen. They denied that they had been unusually disturbed by Frank's behavior, instead regarding it as part of the teenage scene, albeit one of which they disapproved. Allen too said that he thought Frank was "awful" but did not seem to be very concerned with Frank's behavior. However, during these initial sessions the boys made verbal and physical attacks on one another. Allen could not seem to sit near Frank without kicking him or hitting him, and Frank quickly retaliated. Also, they made joking remarks about one another which sometimes passed over the threshold of humor into verbal bitterness. When the parents discussed Frank's "playboy" attitudes, Allen would remark, "Yeh, you're a bum." In turn, when the fact was mentioned that Allen could not seem to be at any physical distance from his mother whenever she was home, Frank would refer to Allen as "prissy" and a "mother's boy." This would make Allen fly into a rage, and he would start to physically pummel on Frank, and the two boys would have to be separated by their father.

As part of the initial assessment of Allen's difficulties, the clinic psychologist administered a series of psychological tests (Rorschach Inkblot Test and Thematic Apperception Test, TAT), and Allen proved to be extremely bright and seemed to enjoy the intellectual challenge. However he was not nearly as productive and creative as one might think on the Rorschach Inkblot Test, nor on the storytelling test, the Thematic Apperception Test. However, the psychologist noted that Allen frequently saw inkblots to be shaped as monsters about to attack or devour a victim. Where such responses are fairly common in boys half Allen's age, they are not nearly as frequent from the teenager. Allen's responses suggested that he was extremely tense and almost ready to explode. However, the psychologist explained that the general pattern of Allen's responses to the inkblots suggested that he kept a very tight lid over his feelings and was unable to let anyone know how he really felt.

It was Allen's fantasy productions to the TAT that were most astounding and seemed to give some initial clue as to what was disturbing him. In story after story the central theme was one of infidelity and jealousy. Again such a topic is inappropriate for a fourteen-year-old boy. As far as anyone knew, Allen had almost no interest in the opposite sex and was never known to watch the television plays or read stories about such topics. Thus, these themes seemed to come from Allen's own feelings rather than from any stimulus in his environment. And the psychologist and clinic staff were puzzled as to what may have stimulated Allen to have such fantasies. Such fantasies are relatively uncommon among adolescents, perhaps with the exception of the late teenage girl.

Allen's responses to the psychological tests suggested that he might have many more fantasies of even more open sexual nature which he could not immediately discuss, and certainly which he could not discuss in front of his family. Thus it was decided to abandon a family therapy approach after the initial sessions and to treat Allen alone for a while. The therapist decided to begin by exploring with Allen his relationship with Frank, partly because Allen seemed most concerned about this and most willing to talk about it and partly because the therapist guessed that Frank's "playboy" behavior might have sexual implications for Allen. The latter did prove true. Allen revealed that what disgusted him most was Frank's sexual promiscuity. He thought his parents were not nearly strict enough with Frank. "I know many things that he did that my parents did not know about." Frank had frequently boasted to him about his sexual activity with girls, which upset Allen considerably. However, Allen had never revealed Frank's confessions to his parents because Allen said he didn't want to be thought of as "tattling" and because Frank had threatened to "really give me the business" if I ever said anything to anybody. As Allen's discussion with his therapist progressed, it seemed that Frank's adventures were Allen's first knowledge about sex in any way. Frank had kidded him about his sexual innocence and filled him with many details of an assorted nature, using the street vulgarities. Subsequently Allen admitted that he had heard these terms and other references to sexuality before Frank had revealed them. Allen was most upset when Frank taunted him with the fact that their parents were sexually active. Frank had taken Allen to his own bedroom which was next to their parents and had told Allen that if he put his ear to the wall, he could hear his parents engaged in intercourse. Allen was not quite sure what he heard, but he was very angry at Frank for intimating that his parents were involved in something so "dirty." Frank seemed to realize that talk about sex upset his younger brother and continued to tease him with further sexual references. Frank had intimated that he knew that Allen masturbated, and Allen was extremely angry at him for saying this, especially when Frank did so in front of his parents. When Allen denied to Frank that he had ever engaged in masturbatory activity, Frank said that he must be a "queer" since "all guys do." Allen asked anxiously if what Frank said about masturbation being normal was actually true. When the therapist asked Allen what he thought, Allen agreed that this was very probable, but was still quite uncomfortable about it.

Throughout this discussion, Allen seemed quite ambivalent as to whether to continue discussing the topic or not. He obviously wanted or needed more information about sex, but was very uncomfortable in discussing it further. At times he sat in silence, but could think of nothing else to talk about when he did start talking again. One day Allen sat silent during most of the hour and seemed quite uncomfortable. When the therapist asked what he might be thinking about, he said "oh the same old thing," but refused to say anything further about it. The therapist reflected that the two of them had discussed sex quite a bit and wondered if Allen were somewhat uncomfortable about it and did not want to explore it further at that point? Allen agreed that it had become an old topic and that he really didn't want to think about it anymore and maybe they should talk about something else. However, he couldn't think of what else he wanted to talk about or do and became silent again. When the therapist suggested that the topic of sex might be on his mind a great deal, Allen got quite upset and said that he had not really thought about it at all until he came to these therapy hours and that it really was the therapist's interest. The therapist agreed that this was a topic that he had thought was important to Allen. Moreover, he repeated that, of course at Allen's age, sex was very much on most boys' minds. Allen disagreed that he thought about it very much but did go on to say that there was a lot of talk about it at school all the time. Allen remarked that the boys were often making very "dirty" cracks about the girls and their sexual availability or their sexual habits. When the therapist suggested that by the time one reached the ninth grade most girls' bodies were changing and were attractive to the boys, Allen tentatively agreed and remarked that he supposed that the girls were thinking all these things too. When the therapist asked Allen whether he thought thinking about sex was in itself "dirty" Allen replied that he "guessed not" but he did wish that it wouldn't come up all the time. The therapist responded that he understood that it was difficult to keep one's mind on classroom assignments, on work, or on doing other things when sexually pro-vocative thoughts or actions were being discussed around him. The therapist asked Allen if one of the things that he disliked about school was his thoughts about sex when he saw girls or the talk about sex when he was with the boys. Allen reluctantly agreed but said that he supposed that he could avoid this if he wished. The therapist added that probably one could avoid it if he wished but for many people thinking about sex and joking about sex was con-sidered fun. Allen shrugged and said that he really did not like to have to think about it all the time.

During the next several sessions Allen was still unable to talk very much or express his thoughts but seemed to be quite concerned and worried. The therapist repeated that maybe there were many diffi-cult things to talk about but that he certainly would wait until Allen felt more comfortable. Allen was unresponsive. When the therapist suggested that perhaps there were still things that Frank might be saying or doing that disturbed Allen, Allen agreed but seemed most tense. After a while Allen finally said that Frank had said something that made him extremely angry. Frank apparently had suggested that their father might have had sexual adventures outside of his marriage. Allen physically attacked Frank who repelled him by laughing and teasing again. Allen became more upset when he over-heard his parents discussing his father's secretary. It seemed obvious that his mother was jealous of his father's secretary and his father was always teasing her about having a pretty and vivacious woman in the office. Allen said that he was pretty sure from the way his father talked that "nothing was going on," but he was angry that his father teased his mother. This incident brought back to Allen's mind times when he had observed his father kissing other women at parties, although, Allen said, "he only kissed them goodby." Allen always felt that his father was more openly affectionate with other women than most of the other men he had observed. He also remembered his mother being quite angry when the father had spent considerable time with the neighbors next door because the mother felt that the father was admiring the next door neighbor's wife. Allen agreed with the therapist that maybe he was overly surprised to find his father had sexual interests and that perhaps it was quite natural "for men."

When the therapist asked if Allen had ever considered that it might be equally true for women to have sexual interests, Allen again grew quite silent and worried. When the therapist inquired about why Allen was so very worried and depressed for the moment, Allen shrugged and turned away. The therapist then asked Allen directly, what he later described as risky questions, that is, if he ever thought that his mother had sexual interests. Tears rolled down Allen's face, and he then finally told the therapist that he thought maybe his mother was also unfaithful. He said that he came home from school one day several years ago, "before I started staying home from school," and had gone in the back door and had discovered that his mother was in the living room. He remained quiet in the back of the house for a moment since he thought he heard her talking to some man. He watched through a crack in the door and saw his mother and a man in the living room and finally saw them drive off in a car together. He was surprised to find his mother home in the middle of the day and to be going out with a strange man. Later when he began staying home from school he would often telephone his mother to see where she was without letting her know that he was at home. At first he denied that he stayed home to see what his mother might be up to but later admitted that he frequently had fantasies that she was unfaithful to his father. He admitted that he had never again seen his mother with any other man nor had he seen this particular man come back to the house. The

therapist again remarked that thinking about sex was a very natural
thing for a boy to do as his body changed and made him more aware
of sexuality. He added that when one begins to think about sex one
wonders about everybody else and whether they might also be thinking about sex or having sexual activities. Allen nodded agreement
with this, and the therapist then asked if Allen wondered if he, the
therapist, was also interested in sex and sexual activities. Allen's
eyes really grew round and he agreed that he had wondered this,
all the while smiling and looking at the therapist. The therapist
asked Allen what he had imagined that the therapist might do in
the way of sex. Allen said that he didn't know because he didn't
know whether the therapist was married but that he had often believed that the therapist must be sexually active because the therapist
didn't mind talking about sex.

As the therapist remarked later, he again took a risk by directly
asking Allen if he had a lot of dreams about how he might be sexually active and what it might be like to have sexual intercourse. To
the therapist's surprise, Allen seemed to be able to discuss these
fantasies quite easily. He told the therapist about his original fantasy
before he had any idea that a woman had both a vagina and an
anus. At that time he thought that intercourse would involve having
one's penis covered with feces and that the whole thing would be
"dirty." He still was uncomfortable about sex even after he had discovered that women had a vagina because they "pee'd through it."
However, when he thought about that, he realized that the same
was true for the men who pee'd through their penises.

The therapist then asked him if he thought that the experience of
having sexual climax (using the street terms for Allen's understanding) might be the same as urination. Allen agreed that he often experienced it that way and then blushed to realize that he admitted
to the therapist that he had masturbated. The therapist comforted
him explaining that this was probably the way most people at first
learned about and experienced any kind of sexual sensations. "It's
probably best that a person gets to learn about his own sensations
before he starts sharing them with someone else," the therapist explained. Allen then remarked that he had at times felt that he
needed to urinate when he masturbated and for a while thought that
his ejaculation was a form of urination. He admitted that he worried
a great deal as to whether he might be harming himself by mastur-

bating since some of the boys at school had intimated this. He said he worried also because he found himself masturbating far more than he thought he should. He was quite frightened that someone else might discover his masturbation, although he agreed that he felt somewhat relieved telling the therapist about it. His fear of being found out had started at school where another boy had been caught masturbating in the boys' room by a group of boys. Allen explained that he had never been comfortable about going to the bathroom since "they took the doors off the toilet stand." As he continued to discuss this, it seemed obvious that Allen's discomfort at school was greatest when he felt like masturbating for he could not really control himself completely and would have to return home to masturbate three or four times in the middle of the day. Yet he would feel badly about not being at school and would return for the afternoon. However, at other times, especially in the most recent months, Allen could go several days without masturbating, or even "without thinking about it."

The next week the therapist received a rather strange phone call from Frank. Frank seemed quite angry and asked the therapist what "the hell" he had been telling Allen. When the therapist inquired about what he meant, Frank said Allen didn't seem to think about anything except sex. The therapist tried to find out what was disturbing Frank, but he became very embarrassed and hung up. When the therapist mentioned the phone call to Allen, Allen smiled very broadly and said that he had been thinking again about his mother having had an extra-marital affair. He decided that the only way to satisfy his anxiety was to "find out the truth," and so he had revealed his "imagination" to Frank and asked Frank's opinion. Much to Allen's surprise, Frank became extremely angry and upset. He accused Allen of having an "evil mind." Allen smiled as he thought about this incident and admitted that he was glad that Frank could become upset about something rather than always upsetting Allen. The therapist agreed that one could become quite upset when one thought of one's mother having any sexual interest, but if one could look at it objectively one would realize that it was probably true that mothers and women had sexual urges just as men did. Allen brightened and said that he realized that if his mother didn't have sexual urges he wouldn't be here. The therapist then inquired if Allen had other thoughts about his mother having any continued sexual relations, especially when he had come home and wondered if the man and his mother would come back. Allen said that he had spent many hours watching the streets for the man's car and admitted that he had thought up plans of what he might do if the man did return. Allen had discovered a gun in his father's dresser drawer but had never been able to find any bullets for it. He said he could imagine himself shooting this man or getting rid of the man or "even" himself as well as the man in other ways. The therapist remarked that this was something many boys thought of when they imagined their mothers having any sexual impulses. In fact, remarked the therapist, we often become very jealous. Allen was quite thoughtful after this interpretation but did not seem to be terribly disturbed by it.

The therapist then decided to become even bolder. He remarked that part of the reason that we are so upset about thinking of our mothers having sex is because as little boys we are often very close to our mothers and love to be held and comforted by them. Allen's eyes brightened, and he said that he had often wondered what his mother and father did in bed together even before he was quite aware of what intercourse might be. He had tried at various times to see his mother dress or undress or take a bath, but "the door was always slammed in my face." He had often enjoyed being allowed into his parents' bed on Sunday mornings, at which times his mother read the comics to him while his father "pretended to sleep." At other times, "when I was a little boy," his mother would go to his bed, read him a story, and fall asleep beside him while he remained awake. He could also remember being brought to the parental bed when he had awakened with nightmares. He remarked that he had been called "mother's lover" by his father and brother when he was little because he would love to climb into his mother's lap and cuddle up against her rubbing her arm or her breasts; he could still remember the smell of her perfumed soap. Allen shuddered when he mentioned the term "mother's lover." At the time he had thought it was "a fun name," but now it made him very uncomfortable.

During the eight months Allen was in treatment, the parents had been only minimally involved. Both the father and mother had been interviewed separately and together on intake. Both of them seemed to be fairly emotionally stable people, and their backgrounds did not seem to bear in any way on Allen's current symptoms and disturbance. Therefore, the clinic did not continue to see either of them regularly, but the clinic social worker conferred with them from time to time about Allen's behavior at home. Nor did Allen's early life seem to have been the cause of his current disturbance. His birth was fairly normal, and his mother had suffered no ill effects during her pregnancy. He appeared to be a very happy baby who grew rapidly and seemed to develop normally. His mother could remember no particular disturbances during his early childhood. She remarked that he was probably better behaved than Frank but added with a smile that Frank had been her first and she had worried more over his behavior. She did remember Allen as being more affectionate than Frank. She said that he did love to cuddle with her, and she enjoyed this. Only later, when asked specifically, did she remember about the term "mother's lover" but laughed when this was brought up and said that this had happened but she had thought little of it. She did not remember Allen as having many nightmares, but agreed that she recalled one or two times when he had awakened and come to their room and she had allowed him to sleep next to her. She remembered that he had tried to do that more than once or twice, but she had "marched him back to his own bed." All of this happened when he was about "four to five." At that time, also, he had wet the bed for a brief period but had stopped soon after he started kindergarten. Thinking about this, the mother remarked that she had really not had to do anything about the bed wetting since it had embarrassed Allen a great deal. He had in fact placed undue emphasis on being neat and clean. Allen was upset when his clothes got dirty or if his hair were not brushed correctly. Unlike Frank, he enjoyed taking a bath. His room was neat, and he "picked up after himself." In this respect Mrs. E. said that Allen was very much like his father who had to have everything right in order all the time and always had to be dressed correctly. She laughed when she said that in contrast, she regarded herself as "sloppy." In fact, her husband often criticized her housework much to her annoyance, but she had learned to laugh it off and to do what she pleased about it. The final example she cited was that the previous Christmas Allen had saved most of his money to buy her an expensive dressing gown. Her husband had criticized her because she "often looked like a tramp" in the morning, wearing a comfortable old but stained dressing-gown, while cooking or sitting around reading the morning paper.

After the Christmas vacation and at beginning of the new semester, Allen decided to return to school. He was a bit uncomfortable initially but was determined to "sit it out." He found himself more and more at ease. He began to talk about some of the girls in the class whom he thought were attractive, but he also continued to be repelled by the talk of the boys boasting of their sex role adventures and reciting in detail how easy it was to "make-out" with girls. He was invited to a party by one of the girls whom he liked but was too inhibited to accept the invitation. However, in a couple of weeks he did accept one invitation and said he enjoyed himself tremendously. He was a bit upset when they played kissing games, and he was particularly angry at one of his close friends whom he thought was quite fresh in "making-out" with one of the girls. He regretted that he did not know how to dance but decided to be quite brave and go to another party where a girl whom he did like helped him learn to dance; and he really enjoyed it. By this time he was looking forward to the parties and school affairs that would accompany his upcoming graduation. He was also very excited about the possibility of going on a long summer trip with a group of his classmates which was going to be conducted by a few of his teachers. He noted, with a grin, that one teacher was a man and another a woman, and "they aren't even married." He was unhappy, however, to realize that quite a few of his friends were using marijuana and even stronger drugs. He resolved that he would stay away from these people since "they can get you in trouble." Since he seemed to be making so much progress, it was decided that therapy would stop at the end of the school year. At Allen's request another appointment was made at the time he started high school the following September. At that time he reported that he had enjoyed the trip across the United States with his friends and teachers very much. He said that he now thought that he had a permanent girl-friend. He had not felt too bad "when he kissed her" and even agreed that maybe he wouldn't mind "making-out" a little. However, he said very solemnly, he didn't think that he was "ready" for intercourse. The therapist assured him that it wouldn't be enjoyable to try intercourse at all before one felt ready for it and that being able to hold hands and kiss and be comfortable about it was really the first step. Allen seemed to look forward to high school and was eagerly planning his courses there. He thought he might like to take up dramatics but was worried whether or not people would think it was all right for a boy to do this. Later in the hour he mentioned that several of his new friends were also interested in dramatics, and he decided he would join them.

Questions for Allen E.

1. School phobia may result from:
    a. a morbid dread of some aspect of school life
    b. a dread of what may happen at home while he is away

What aspect of school life did Allen fear? Why did he confine himself to the house?

2. The most common psychic conflicts thought to contribute to school phobia are ambivalence and aggression. Explain how these were demonstrated.

3. The development of sex-role identification is affected by the family of an individual as well as his peer culture and society as a whole. Discuss Allen's preparation for his adult sexual role.

4. Why do you think Allen was unable to resolve his conflicts without resorting to a phobic reaction?

5. In view of your answers to Questions 3 and 4, can you understand why Allen would have difficulty in openly expressing certain feelings and impulses? Explain your answer.

6. Can you suggest some hypotheses that would explain why Allen's parents were unaware of his skipping school for over a year. Describe the type of reaction they exhibited at the time of the initial interview. Why do you think the parents avoided recognizing the problem for so long? What needs of theirs did this avoidance meet?

7. During a series of projective tests Allen revealed a source of his problems to a therapist. Describe what happened and how this affected Allen's subsequent treatment at the clinic.

8. What prompted the therapist to begin treatment by discussing Allen's relationship with Frank?

9. Why did Allen's relationship with Frank change rather dramatically during the course of Allen's treatment?

10. Both behavioral techniques and interpersonal psychotherapy can contribute in different ways to treatment of phobias; defend or contest the therapist's approach to Allen's problem.

11. Allen's problems seemed to reflect a temporary period of developmental stress. Do you agree or disagree? Discuss the interviews which took place with each parent separately during the course of Allen's treatment.

References

BANDURA, A. Influence of models reinforcement contingencies on the acquisition of imitative responses. *Journal of Personality and Social Psychology,* 1965, **1**: 589–595.

BELL, R. R. Parent-child conflict in sexual values. *Journal of Social Issues,* 1966, **22**: 34–44.

COOLIDGE, J. C., TESSMAN, E., WALDFOGEL, S. & WILLER, M. L. Patterns of aggression in school phobia. *Psychoanalytic Study of the Child,* 1962, **17**: 319–333.

DOUVAN, E., & ADELSON, J. *The adolescent experience.* New York: Wiley, 1966.

EISENBERG, L. School phobia: a study in the communication of anxiety. *American Journal of Psychiatry,* 1958, **114**: 712–718.

FREUD, S. Three essays on the theory of sexuality. *Standard Edition,* 1953, **7**: 125–243.

HARRINGTON, C. C. *Errors in sex-role behavior in teenage boys.* New York: Teachers College Press, 1970.

JOHNSON, A. M. School phobia: discussion. *American Journal of Orthopsychiatry,* 1957, **27**: 307–309.

LEVY, D. M. Hostility patterns in sibling rivalry experiments. *American Journal of Orthopsychiatry,* 1936, **6**: 183–257.

SOBEL, R. Adolescence and family stress: a clinician's approach. In SCHOOLER, J. C. (Ed.) *Current Issues in Adolescent Psychiatry.* New York: Brunner/Mazel, 1973, pp. 53–64.

WALDFOGEL, S. COOLIDGE, J. C., & HAHN, P. B. The development, meaning and management of school phobia. *American Journal of Orthopsychiatry,* 1957, **27**: 754–780.

WEINER, I. V. Psychological disturbance in adolescence. New York: Wiley, 1970, Pp. 203–243.

THE CASE OF RONALD W.

The "Hyperactive" Child

On the recommendation of the pediatric neurologist, Mrs. W. brought Ronnie, age six, to the clinic for psychological study. She claimed that she was very concerned because the school had advised her that they would not admit Ronnie to the first grade unless his very high activity level was controlled. According to his teachers, throughout kindergarten Ronnie was constantly on the move, never sitting still for more than a few seconds, even to have a snack. He refused to relax in the rest period. He always seemed to be talking, and sometimes what he said did not make sense. If he were not talking, he was usually making some other kind of racket, either verbally or physically by knocking or hitting something. He seemed to be impervious to injuring himself or others. He would ride his tricycle against the wall and hurt himself but only cry for a minute and then be back into some kind of activity. He similarly would smash into others either by accident or in anger. When crossed, even slightly, he would have a temper tantrum and attack the next person he saw, whether or not that person might be to blame. Several times during the year, the school authorities had sent him home and had even threatened to expel him. He had almost blinded one child by throwing sand in the child's eye. Another time he knocked a child unconscious. The climax came about two weeks before the end of school, when in a rage he tore a toilet from the wall. The school specified that he should be put on an amphetamine drug which the school doctor was then advising for any child who was unable to sit still in the classroom.

Under this pressure, Mrs. W. had consulted her pediatrician who then sent her to a pediatric neurologist. The report from this neurologist showed that Ronnie had no marked neurological defect. Several EEGs (electroencephalograms) had been done with questionable results. One did seem to indicate that the child had some "mild generalized abnormality." However, the neurologist noted that the EEG was not a reliable instrument for children of this age since approximately 40 per cent of children under the age of six showed some kind of wave pattern that would be considered abnormal in older children or adults. The pediatrician was also very reluctant to prescribe the amphetamine drug which the school had advised because he said, "these drugs are still in an experimental stage and have been given far too wide publicity." He pointed out that there had been no control studies and that amphetamines and amphetamine-like drugs are highly addictive. He advised a further study of the child's actual behavior and psychological development.

Although Mrs. W. had emphasized chiefly the school's complaint, she also readily admitted that she had long been worried about Ronnie's high activity level at home. She said that she and the neighbors and friends were concerned that he always seemed to be on the move and into everything. She remembered that once before he was age one he had actually crawled up on top of the piano and knocked everything to the floor. As soon as he was walking he seemed to want to have, to touch, and to grab everything. She at first deplored this behavior but had been told by her husband that his activity was not abnormal, that he was merely being a very active boy. However, it seemed that everything that Ronnie touched was broken or marred or misplaced. Everything in the house had to be put out of his reach, often, however, without avail.

He seldom fell asleep easily and often got out of bed four or five times before he was asleep. He slept very poorly, often awakening in the night and wandering around the house. Sometimes he seemed to be awakened by nightmares and to be frightened, at which time he would crawl into her bed for comfort. He also arose early in the morning clambering through the house, looking for food, and waking up other household members for company.

Ronnie had a violent temper when crossed and would strike out at anything. His mother at times was at a loss over how to discipline him; the only thing that seemed to stop him was to grab him tightly and to hold him until he relaxed. He was constantly in a struggle with his little brother, two years younger, and the two boys always had to be separated. He also once "accidently" injured his baby sister, age nine months, when he threw a heavy toy into her crib.

Mrs. W. and the boy's father disagreed completely on how to discipline Ronnie. The father maintained that nothing was wrong and that Ronnie would outgrow his behavior. He pooh-poohed Mrs. W.'s complaints to the pediatrician, who also originally assured Mrs. W. that nothing really was wrong. Thus, she had done very little about any method of controlling Ronnie and hoped that once he was in school and out with other children he would "behave himself." However, she became more and more concerned when neighbors would not permit Ronnie to come to their homes. Even his grandparents were reluctant to babysit or otherwise care for Ronnie. In fact, while riding in a car with his grandparents, Ronnie had been so active jumping up and down that his grandfather had smashed his car into the back of another car. Thereafter the grandparents refused to let Ronnie come to their home.

According to Mrs. W., Ronnie's development had been rather normal. He was a large child at birth, weighing almost 10 pounds, but she had no difficulty in delivering him, and her pregnancy was relatively smooth. He grew rapidly, seemed to be a happy child, and she was delighted with him. She breast-fed him and had a slight difficulty in weaning him to a cup; even at age six he would ask if he could be breast-fed when he saw her breast-feeding his baby sister. She first described him as a cuddly child but then remembered that he also had been very wiggly and hard to hold at times. His development proceeded at a normal pace: he walked at about 12 months of age with no difficulty; he began talking at approximately 18 months, with definite short sentences soon after he became two years old. Because he was her first child she had kept a baby book on him with pictures, which showed that he was active. In every photograph he was in some kind of motion or making some kind of gesture or face. She did not try to toilet train him until he was almost three, when she said "I got tired of having two boys in diapers." He was not easy to toilet train since he would not sit still on the potty very long, but he did respond somewhat to her admonishments and to her praise and was in effect very well toilet trained when he started nursery school at age three-and-a-half. However, even to this day he had "small bowel accidents" largely because he would not stop his play or activities to go to the bathroom. He did not wet the bed or otherwise soil himself at night.

After hearing this description of Ronnie's behavior and background the staff at the clinic decided to observe Ronnie and administer psychological testing and to have some further interviews with Mrs. W. about the family. Ronnie was a sturdily built youngster who did not immediately appear to be overly active. He sat in the waiting room and cuddled up to his mother and was reluctant to leave her. He did show some signs of the injuries she had mentioned: his knee was scarred from old wounds and there were fresh lacerations. Scars were also on his elbows and across the bridge of his nose. On the way to the examining room the psychologist asked him about his bruises and scars, and Ronnie seemed to have enjoyed getting each one, as if that had been part of the fun. Throughout the examination Ronnie was up and out of the chair quite frequently, wanting to grab at the test materials and play with them before the psychologist could get them out of the case. Nevertheless, at the examiner's request, he did return to his chair and wait relatively patiently for the psychologist to put the materials on the table and give him instructions. He often was impatient with his own work. When he could not immediately draw exactly what he wanted, he would scribble across the page; when the blocks would not stack according to his own satisfaction, he would throw them into the air with a whoop. He grew more restless as the hour proceeded, and on the final test, where he was to tell stories to a picture, he crawled under the table and told his stories to the examiner from there.

The test results showed that Ronnie had an IQ of 118 and was developing intellectually at a fairly fast rate. His responses indicated no intellectual deficits nor any difficulties in his fine motor activities. He stacked the blocks with fair agility despite his own disappointment in the activity.

Ronnie's free associations to the Rorschach Inkblot Test and to the story-telling to pictures suggested several themes. First, his characters were in constant action and one thing happened after another. His fantasies were fairly elaborate and prolonged. He seemed more preoccupied with destruction and violence than most children his age (some acts of violence occurred in nearly every fantasy), although this is an age where monsters and shoot-outs are common themes in fantasy. However, the really bizarre responses had to do with Ronnie's open and free discussion of sex. He began telling stories in which adults' sexual acts were described in four letter words. He watched the examiner carefully as he uttered these vulgarisms. He seemed to be poking fun at the examiner and was delighted to find that he was not immediately cautioned to watch his language. He admitted that he could not say these words to other adults. He seemed quite preoccupied with finding various anatomy parts on the Rorschach Inkblot Test, hinting broadly that these body parts either were genitals or had other sexual connotations. On another projective technique (Make a Picture Story Test) which involves making up stories using cardboard doll figures, Ronnie was immediately attracted to the undressed dolls and made up plays involving sexual interaction between the boy and girl dolls and the adult dolls. For example, he had the naked boy doll kiss the girl doll's vagina, or he had the adult dolls go to bed together and do "you know what." When asked if he had ever observed people doing "you know what," Ronnie replied, "of course, my father and his girlfriends do it all the time." When questioned further, Ronnie reported that his family often went around in states of undress and indicated that he was very fascinated by what he had observed and the whole topic of sex. As he was telling about this, Ronnie's face was flushed, and he seemed to be masturbating as he rubbed his leg; he was jumping up and down and his voice was rising in volume and pitch.

Family Background. Mrs. W. was a tall, voluptuous woman whose posture and gestures and voice all suggested a considerable amount of sensuality. The staff observed immediately how she held Ronnie close to her large breasts whenever they were together. When they parted she leaned over to kiss him directly on the mouth, as if she were kissing a lover. Asked about the current family milieu, Mrs. W. replied that there were herself, the three children, Mr. R., her current lover, and Bobby, her teenage brother, who was spending the year with her. Because of their limited finances and the difficulties in finding an apartment that would take children, they were all crowded together in a two-bedroom apartment. She and her lover shared one bedroom, the three children shared the other bedroom, and the teenager slept on the living room couch. However, Ronnie raised a fuss about having to share a room with his younger siblings, and for most of the past year he would spend the night with his young uncle in the living room. Mrs. W., a professional dancer, usually danced in the evenings at various night clubs, and the children were under the care of either Bobby or Mr. R. However, Mr. R. had only been present in the home for a few months and was not happy about having the responsibility for child care and discipline. In fact, Mrs. W. complained, Ronnie had often attacked her boyfriends more viciously than anyone else and had succeeded in driving away several men whom she had thought might make prospective husbands. Mr. R. was the first one to at all tolerate Ronnie's behavior, but he too tried to spend as much time away from the house as possible. She admitted that Ronnie often embarrassed her by calling attention to the possibility of her sexual relationships with other men; she was very angry at him about this and had washed his mouth out with soap, but to no effect. She wondered if Bobby had taught Ronnie these "filthy" words since she remembered that Bobby had behaved in a similar fashion when their parents had been divorced and her mother had had a boyfriend. At this conjecture she noted that Bobby, although almost 17, seemed to show no interest in females. Moreover, she remarked, she would have to "do something" about Bobby who masturbated about the house almost publicly. She was worried lest Bobby be teaching Ronnie to masturbate as she observed that Ronnie easily had an erection "whenever I give him a bath. He seems so cute." She added that she thought that Ronnie had extra large genitals for a child of his age.

Ronnie's parents first had separated shortly before the birth of his younger brother. The separation occurred because Mrs. W. could not endure further Mr. W.'s flagrant infidelity. In fact, Mrs. W. reported, Mr. W. would bring other women to the house and entertain them there even if she were home. Although this had occurred several years ago, Mrs. W. became furious as she described her ex-husband's behavior and called him several vulgar names. After about three years of marriage with her husband behaving in this manner, she left him and moved, with the children, into her mother's home. At this time her mother was also divorcing her father, who she had known for a long time to have "another woman on the side." Mrs. W. remarked that she really believed that most men were unreliable and unfaithful and cited as further proof that most of the men that she saw were either married or had just separated from their wives. She began to weep and remarked, "I really hate them all; they are all dogs and animals. I wish I could live without them, but I can't." After the separation Mr. W. visited the home several times a week, often staying overnight. He ostensibly came to visit the children, but Mrs. W. admitted that they were still sexually involved. In fact, her second child was fathered by Mr. W. after the separation. However, for the past year Mrs. W. had not permitted Mr. W. any sexual relationships and tried to keep him out of the house except to pick up the children and bring them back. Even before this final year, there were several other men she was interested in having sexual relationships with. One of these lovers had moved into the house briefly, but could not stand Ronnie who physically attacked him. Ronnie's father continued to take him to various entertainments for a few hours mid-week and then to pick him up again either Friday night or Saturday morning and keep him until late Sunday evening. Mrs. W. knew little about Mr. W.'s living situation, other than that he had a small apartment. He had not married, but she surmised that there was usually a woman living with him.

After these initial interviews and examinations, the clinic staff agreed that some kind of emergency measures were necessary. Although no one believed that Ronnie was "psychotic" it was agreed fairly unanimously among the staff that he should be separated from the family, and he was placed in a residential treatment center. In this hospital-like setting, Ronnie calmed down immediately. He occasionally would have a temper tantrum when disciplined by one of the nursing staff but soon found that the structured environment was easier to live in than the chaos at home. One male nurse was assigned to Ronnie's continuous care, and Ronnie easily attached himself to him. He continued to vent a great deal of sexual curiosity, but this was largely ignored by the staff and Ronnie's fascination and excitement died down rather quickly. He began to pay much more attention at school and was making marked progress.

In the meantime, his mother was encouraged to enter into a counseling situation at the clinic which then gradually involved both Mr. R. and Mr. W., whom it was adjudged would be somewhat responsible for Ronnie's care also. In this counseling it was emphasized that it would be quite necessary to have well-structured controls, agreed upon by all adults for Ronnie, and that the high level of sexual stimulation in the homes needed to be cut back. After six months of residential treatment for Ronnie and supportive counseling for father, mother, and lover, Ronnie was discharged to his mother's home. The situation at home had improved considerably as the family now had a three-bedroom house in which Ronnie had his own room. Serious efforts were made to reduce the level of sexual stimulation in both the mother's and father's homes, which aided Ronnie in instituting proper controls over his behavior. Shortly thereafter Ronnie was able to return to public school where he completed the first grade very successfully showing little evidence of hyperactivity.

Questions for Ronald W.

1. Discuss the difficulties that Ronnie was manifesting at the time that he was referred to the clinic. Consider:
   a. his activity level
   b. his attention pattern
   c. his emotional control or lack of it
   d. his preoccupations.
What pattern do you see in all these areas?
2. Consider what factors during early development are considered important in stimulating
   a. delay of immediate gratification
   b. emotional impulse control and sustained attention to external stimuli.
Which of these factors were present in Ronnie's early home environment and which were absent? Can the absent factors account for some of the behaviors shown by Ronnie which you cited in your answer to Question 1?
3. Many theories of child development emphasize the interrelationships between innate temperamental factors and parental handling.
   a. To what extent did Ronnie manifest what appeared to be a high activity temperament in his very early months?
   b. How was this pattern responded to by his parents?
   c. To what extent was this high anxiety level reinforced or accentuated by the parental handling received by Ronnie during his first three years of life?
4. At least some of Ronnie's symptoms can be seen as reactions to chronic problems existing within the home. Consider the hypothesis that some of Ronnie's symptoms represent reactions to frustration arising from incompatible impulses being aroused constantly. What role have the following played in frustrating Ronnie by arousing impulses which were exciting and frightening at the same time?

a. Mother's manner of cuddling Ronnie

b. father's exhibitionistic sexual acting-out behavior

c. mother's flagrant sexual behavior

d. Bobby's behavior patterns

e. Ronnie's abandonment by both father and mother at different points in time.

5. The birth of a sibling is always a difficult experience for a young child. What made this experience particularly frustrating for Ronnie? How did he express this frustration?

6. What conditions existed in Ronnie's home environment which reinforced his poor impulse control? Consider:

a. the crowded living conditions

b. mother as sole breadwinner

c. lack of parental supervision and nurturance.

7. Why was Ronnie unable to establish an inner system of controls? Which learning conditions were absent which are necessary for this system to develop? Consider the models reflected in:

a. Mrs. W.'s relationship with Ronnie

b. Mr. W.'s relationship with Ronnie

c. Mr. and Mrs. W.'s relationship to each other

d. the presence of Mr. A. in the home

e. the effect of Bobbie on Ronnie.

8. How would you explain Ronnie's preoccupation with destruction and violence as shown by the Rorschach Test and by his behavior in school? What stimuli appeared to be eliciting these responses?

9. Ronnie's treatment appears to have been successful. What changes in attitudes and behavior might have occurred? Discuss the importance of

a. the therapist who treated Ronnie

b. the male nurse who cared for Ronnie during his stay in the guidance center.

10. If Ronnie were never treated, what sort of behavior would you expect from him ten years later? Support your prediction.

11. Ronnie's mother said "the only thing that seemed to stop him was to grab him tightly until he relaxed for a moment." What can you interpret from this statement?

12. A clear-cut distinction is not always made between the hyperactive child who is evidencing minimal brain dysfunction (MBD) and the child whose hyperactivity is the result of crowded classrooms,

anxiety, depression, or a pathogenic home situation. Which characteristics of MBD were present in Ronnie and which were not? On
what basis was it decided that Ronnie's problems were psychological?
13. Cerebral stimulants (amphetamines) are often administered to
hyperactive children like Ronnie because of their ability to reduce
motor activity while increasing attention span and concentration.

a. How can you account for the fact that a stimulant appears to
calm children who appear behaviorally over-stimulated? (Refer
to Satterfield and Dawson.) What models of behavior might explain this behavioral effect?

b. Do you feel that the pediatrician's decision *not* to administer
amphetamines to Ronnie was a wise one? Defend your answer
and consider what might have happened if Ronnie had been
given this medication and shown behavioral improvement.
Would this have been good or bad for Ronnie's total development?

References

Burks, H. F. The hyperkinetic child. *Exceptional Children,* 1960, **27**:
18–26.
Campbell, S. F. Cognitive styles in reflective, impulsive and hyperactive
boys and their mothers. *Perceptual and Motor Skills,* 1973, **36**: 747–752.
Chess, S. Diagnosis and treatment of the hyperactive child. *New York
State Journal of Medicine,* 1960, **60**: 2379–2385.
Chess, S., Thomas, A., Birch, H. G., & Hertzig, M. Implications of a
longitudinal study of child development for child psychiatry. *American
Journal of Psychiatry,* 1960, **117**: 434–441.
Clements, S. D. Minimal brain dysfunction in children. Identification
and terminology. *Public Health Service Publication. No. 1415,* 1966.
Eisenberg, L. Principles of drug therapy in child psychiatry with special
reference to stimulant drugs. *American Journal of Orthopsychiatry,* 1971,
4: 371–379.
Freedman, D. X., & Members of Drug Panel. The use of stimulant drugs
in treating hyperactive children. *Children,* 1971, **18**: 111.
Ladd, E. T. Pills for classroom peace? *Saturday Review,* November 21,
1970: 66–68, 81–82.
Morrison, J. R., & Steward, M. A. A family study of the hyperkinetic
child syndrome. *Biological Psychiatry,* 1971, **3**: 189–195.

RUTTER, M. Parent-child separation: psychological effects on the children. *Journal of Child Psychology and Psychiatry*, 1971, **12**: 233–260.

SATTERFIELD, J. H., & DAWSON, M. E. Electrodermal correlates of hyperactivity in children, *Psychophysiology*, 1971, **8**: 191–197.

WARREN, R., KARDUCK, W., BISSARATID, S., STEWART, M., & SLY, W. The hyperactive child syndrome. *Archives of General Psychiatry*, 1971, **24**: 161–162.

WEISS, G., MINDE, K., WERRY, J. S., DOUGLAS, V., & NEMETH, E. Studies on the hyperactive child. VII. *Archives of General Psychiatry*, 1971, **24**: 409–421.

THE CASE OF ROSA C.

Possessed

When Rosa's father called the psychologist his first question was whether all matters were kept entirely confidential. He did not want anyone to think that any member of his family would need any type of psychological attention. He said he was bringing his daughter Rosa, age 9, to a psychologist only because he had been strongly advised to by his sister-in-law who was also the child's pediatrician. He arrived at the appointed time with Rosa and her older sister, Theresa, and made both girls sit quietly in the waiting room while he talked to the doctor. He was a white-haired gentleman with a heavy Italian accent. He first made sure that all doors were closed and then spoke to the doctor in a very secretive fashion. He began by saying that he thought the whole trouble lay in the fact that the child might never have had recovered from the death of her mother approximately four years ago. He thus regarded most of her behavior as part of a prolonged grief. On the other hand, he admitted that he could not understand why the child could not recover from this death and agreed that her behavior was out of the ordinary. He had become most disturbed recently when she would not stay at school but returned home and stayed around the house most of the day. He tried to scold her, but she would sob endlessly. He found himself trying to comfort her, but she was inconsolable. Often she would cry herself into an exhausted state in his arms, and he would take her up to bed where she would continue to sob softly until she fell asleep.

Rosa, complained often that many things were "poisoned." There were chairs in the house which she said were contaminated and in which she could not sit, and she often could not use certain dishes or touch certain utensils. She would complain that her whole room was contaminated and that she could not sleep in her bed; she would come to sleep in her father's bed. He would try to scold her, but again she would start to sob, and he would retreat. He regarded part of the problem as coming from the television; she was preoccupied with the morbid stories and pictures which would fascinate her for many hours unless he disturbed her. As he described the child, he himself began to weep and begged the doctor for some kind of help. He said he refused to believe that she was "mad" but sometimes thought perhaps that she had been possessed by the Devil "even though I do not believe in such things."

Family Background. Upon further questioning, Mr. C. said that he was not sure how long the situation had existed. He explained that he was a very busy man and was away from the house many hours of the day and evening. He had come to the United States at a young age, very impoverished, and had worked very hard to amass a small fortune, mainly in apartment houses and business properties which he rented out. Mr. C. was over 50 when he returned to his native Tuscany where a marriage was arranged for him with a young distant cousin, almost half his age. He purchased a beautiful home in the most expensive part of the city and was ecstatically happy with his young bride. They had many friends, and they loved to entertain, and he was exceedingly proud of her. They were very happy at the birth of their first child, Theresa. Soon they planned a second child which they hoped would be a boy. Mrs. C. was pregnant with Rosa when it was discovered that she had a fast-developing cancer of the bone marrow. Nevertheless, the baby was born completely healthy. Mrs. C. became bed-ridden soon after Rosa's birth. For the next four and one-half years her condition waxed and waned. There were many times when it was not expected that she would live for more than a few days, when she seemed to make some gradual recovery, only to be deathly ill again. Both children were kept out of the room because it was feared that they would become depressed when they saw their mother so ill. However, they were usually ushered into her bedroom at least once a day when she would press them to her bosom and weep with them. Rosa had seldom seen her mother other than in bed. During Rosa's early years she was cared for by a Negro servant who was with the children day and night. However, this housekeeper was killed in an automobile accident, almost in front of the children's eyes, about three months before their mother's death.

The children's aunt and pediatrician and several other female relatives tried to care for the children during the ensuing months because it proved difficult to find any housekeeper who would stay for more than a few weeks. Each child seemed to have some way of annoying or disturbing housekeepers. At first it was Theresa's violent temper. She would resent and resist any kind of discipline from the housekeepers and became so angry that she would go on destructive binges, smashing the furniture and glassware throughout the house. Despite the aunt's advice to the father that Theresa was severely emotionally disturbed, nothing was done about Theresa's behavior. It seemed to quiet down within a few months after the mother's death. Tessa then became a very serious student at school and a relatively well-behaved child at home. Yet occasionally she would become angry at her father or at one of the housekeepers and again go on a destructive binge, during which time Rosa would hide in the back rooms of the house and not appear until hours after quiet ensued.

Thus, in the past four years there had been no one housekeeper who had stayed more than two or three months, and very often there were months where there was only Mr. C. and the two girls in the big house. He was very devoted to his children and would make sure that they were fed and clothed and bedded down for the night, but he felt helpless about any other parts of their care. The girls would sometimes spend many hours at neighbors where the mothers of other children would take pity on them and invite them in for dinner or ask them to stay overnight. Tessa seemed to enjoy these social exits from what must have been a very sad and morbid home, but Rosa became less and less able to leave her own surroundings. She would sit for hours in the house, in one chair or another, those that she decided were not contaminated at the moment, staring at the walls, unable to respond to anyone. Sometimes the old man would have to walk through the gardens and up the hillside behind the house until he found her crouched behind a tree, shivering in fright and mute. Tessa would unmercifully tease her sister, declaring that certain ghosts and goblins would get her if she did not immediately do what Tessa wanted. Thus Tessa had commandeered the best bed, the best closet and dresser, and all the prize possessions. At the time that Rosa was brought to the psychologist, she would sleep only in her father's bed, sit only in one chair in the house, and eat off of only one plate and with one spoon. Her father had given in to all of her demands. He slept fitfully on the sofa and served her dinner to her wherever she wanted it.

Rosa was a beautiful, slight-built, pale-skinned child with dark eyes and jet black hair. She greeted the doctor rather formally and solemnly, calling him Sir. She seemed quite willing to talk about her problems and situation, being much less reticent than her father had described her. She readily admitted that she regarded many objects in her home to be "poisoned" and dangerous. She believed one might die if one sat in certain chairs or touched certain objects. She said she felt it was evil to eat meat and could not touch a knife. Thus she restricted herself largely to cereals and vegetables which she consumed only with a spoon. She explained that she thought her mother was a vegetarian. Her mother had become a Christian Scientist before she died, but Rosa was not quite sure what it meant to be a Christian Scientist. She only knew that her father and her aunt disapproved of this religion and told her never to mention it to the priest. Rosa spoke of her mother in a rather matter-of-fact tone, almost as if she were still alive. She said that they had many pictures of her mother in the house including a large painting over the fireplace in the living-room and that she liked to sit and watch her mother. She said that her mother often looked back at her and spoke to her "not really spoke, you know, but I can hear her." She explained that the portrait seemed to look at her and to know what she was thinking.

Although Rosa spoke of her fears and fantasies about her mother. she seemed most anxious to talk about her relationship with Tessa. She complained bitterly that Tessa, who was two years older, much taller and heavier, and more athletic, often physically abused her. She pulled down her dress shoulder to show a black-and-blue mark where she said Tessa had hit her. She complained to her father, but her father did not really believe her because Tessa usually seemed to be "a good girl." She said that her father had told her that it was just another one of her imaginings. However, when the father was away Rosa said that Tessa would strike out at her, grab things away from her, and otherwise abuse her verbally and physically. She felt it little use to try to strike back and could only run out of the house and hide. She said that she frequently dreamed that Tessa was dead and in her coffin and they were attending Tessa's funeral. At this point she left the chair that she was sitting on since it had become an evil spot where the Devil was. She could not talk anymore about her feelings and looked very frightened.

In the subsequent interview she avoided the chair where she sat the first time, often giving it furtive glances and then turning her head away. She talked again about the abuse that she received from Tessa, saying that Tessa had been the one who had really contaminated much of the house. She could not sleep in the same room where Tessa slept; if Tessa sat on her bed, it became contaminated; if Tessa touched her clothing, Rosa could not put it on; if Tessa came to the table Rosa could not eat there. She mentioned that Tessa might die, "just like my mother died." At this point Rosa got up and looked around the room, avoiding the chair on which she had been sitting. As the office only contained these two chairs and the one on which the psychologist was sitting, Rosa retreated to the corner of the room for a while saying that both chairs were now poisonous. She asked then if she could sit in the chair with the psychologist; she was offered his chair, and seemed a bit more comfortable, but became quite afraid when the psychologist occupied one of the "contaminated" chairs.

Assured that he felt no discomfort, she became a little more bold and began discussing her mother's illness and death. She said that she was sure that her mother must have been very brave to have endured so much pain and that she had tried to be a very good girl so as to please her mother and to make sure that God knew that she loved her mother. She said that she knew that God knew this because her mother now smiled on her from Heaven. She began to weep slightly saying that she hoped the psychologist could tell her that her mother knew that she, Rosa, loved her so much. When the psychologist asked why Rosa doubted that her mother knew this, Rosa began to sob more violently. At this point she decided the psychologist's chair was contaminated and sat on the floor under the edge of the table. She seemed unable to talk very much during the rest of that hour, although she did stop crying.

At the third hour Rosa again asked for help with her sister. She said that her sister had accused her of killing her mother, and she wanted the psychologist to tell God that this was not true. She said that Tessa had told her that she said out loud that she did not care whether her mother had died. She wanted the psychologist to tell God that Tessa was a liar. She said that if God knew that Tessa were a liar that God would send Tessa to Hell. There were now very few spots in the psychologist's office where Rosa could sit comfortably; as she began to weep she climbed into the psychologist's lap and clung to him, such as she often did with her father. Once she was comforted a bit, she exclaimed that she felt her father did not understand what troubled her at all. She said that God knew that she loved her father very much and that she was safe only when she was in her father's arms.

A few days after this third interview the father called the psychologist very excitedly to say that he had come home to find the two girls quarreling violently, and it was only with a great deal of effort that he had wrested a knife away from Rosa who was threatening to kill her sister. He asked for some help and was advised that it would probably be necessary at this point to put Rosa in the hospital for at least a brief period so that her condition could be studied a bit more and she could be separated from her sister. He adamantly refused this advice saying that he again did not believe that his child was crazy and that he would not let her be admitted to a mental hospital. He subsequently did allow the pediatrician aunt to place Rosa in the pediatric ward but said that he felt that the psychological treatment was doing her no good whatever. The aunt strongly advised him to return the child to the psychologist's care, but he continued to state strongly that he believed treatment had only made her worse.

Subsequently the psychologist learned through the aunt that the father had allowed the aunt to take Rosa home with her and to find another psychologist who continued to treat Rosa. Two years later Rosa was placed in the children's section of the local state hospital where she remained for the next five years.

Questions for Rosa C.

1. Summarize Rosa's symptoms at the time that she was first brought to the psychologist.
2. What do they suggest about her view of her world at that point?

3. To what extent was this world view reflective of the way things actually were in her life and to what extent did it reflect distortions of reality?

4. Consider Rosa's first year of life:

    a. What critical losses did she experience?

    b. What compensatory nurturant figures were available?

    c. To what perceptions of death and dying were Rosa exposed?

5. Try to estimate the effect of each of the above on Rosa's:

    a. personal sense of security

    b. sense of responsibility about maternal death

    c. her ability to control her emotions.

6. How did Theresa deal with these same life events? How did her coping pattern affect Rosa?

7. Whenever Rosa expressed certain feelings to the psychologist she then indicated that certain objects were contaminated in the room.

    a. What were these feelings that preceded the sense of contamination?

    b. What defense mechanism is suggested in the fear of contamination, and how did it operate to reduce Rosa's anxiety?

    c. Are these mechanisms usually associated with neurotic or psychotic development?

8. What aspects of Rosa's behavior are compatible with the current literature on maternal deprivation?

References

BARNES, M. J. Reactions to the death of a mother. *The Psychoanalytic Study of the Child*, 1964, **19**: 334–357.

BIRTCHNELL, J. The possible consequences of early parent death. *British Medical Journal*, 1969, **42**: 1–12.

BOWLBY, J. Separation anxiety. *International Journal of Psychoanalysis*, 1960, **41**: 89–93.

CHILDERS, P., & WIMMER, M. The concept of death in early childhood. *Child Development*, 1971, **42**: 299–301.

ENGEL, M. Psychopathology in childhood. New York: Harcourt, Brace & Jovanovich, 1972, Pp. 73–94.

LESTER, D., & TEMPLER, D. J. Resemblance of parent-child death anxiety as a function of age and sex of child. *Psychological Reports*, 1972, **31**: 750.

MAHLER, M. S. On sadness and grief in infancy and childhood: loss and restoration of the symbolic love object. *The Psychoanalytic Study of the Child*, 1961, **16**: 332–357.

MILLER, J. B. M. Children's reactions to the death of a parent: a review of the psychoanalytic literature. *American Psychoanalytic Association Journal*, 1971, **19**: 697–719.

YARROW, L. J. Separation from parents during early childhood. In HOFFMAN, M. L. & HOFFMAN, L. W. (Eds.) *Review of Child Development Research Vol. 1.* New York: Russell Sage Foundation, 1964, Pp. 89–106.

THE CASE OF PAULA O.

What's in a Name?

When Paula O., a sixteen-year-old high school student, confessed to her teacher that she intended to commit suicide, her parents decided to bring her directly to the hospital that evening, without waiting for an appointment. However, this decision was reached only after intense discussion. Her father, Mr. O., scornfully skeptical, believed that the school was exaggerating the situation. Mrs. O. was more obviously concerned for her daughter, particularly since this was not Paula's first suicidal threat. The parents' confusion and ambivalence made the situation a difficult one to assess. Paula, white-faced and tense, sat silent and refused to answer any questions. The admitting psychiatrist advised that a brief period of immediate hospitalization was warranted because of the danger of further suicidal attempts. Mr. O. protested vigorously that the doctor was making far too much of Paula's threats. In response, the psychiatrist pointed out that Mr. O.'s inability to recognize the seriousness of the situation was probably part of the problem, and that if Mr. O. refused to follow his advice, then neither he nor the hospital could assume any responsibility in the eventuality of Paula's death. The father continued to argue with the psychiatrist. Mrs. O. broke into tears at this point and hurriedly left the office with the two younger children. The psychiatrist walked out and Paula followed him. Finally, after several minutes, Mr. O. came out and joined his family.

Paula's over-all appearance suggested a child closer to ten years of age than an adolescent. She wore no make-up and her dark hair hung in twin braids down her back. Her chubby figure was exaggerated by a simple, childlike frock closed at the collar. At the time of arrival, Paula carried with her three worn pocket books: Plato's *Dialogues,* Dostoevsky's *Crime and Punishment,* and a biography of Mozart. It was impossible to interview her. She sat rigidly upright in the chair, staring at the interviewer. When she did answer, it was mostly in monosyllables and frequently in a manner which made it difficult to assess whether or not she comprehended the question. Paula's face was generally expressionless, but on occasion her eyes would narrow and she would quickly look away. Whenever the interviewer made a particularly strong effort to get her to discuss what had happened, Paula would fidget in her chair and pull at her dress.

In the interview with the mother, she stated that Paula had been unusually upset two months ago, when she brought home a report card with a B in Science, instead of the A she had been striving for. During the following months, Paula became listless and careless with her homework, although up until then she had been a straight A student. At home, it was noticeable that she paid little attention to the family conversation, and she was very slow to respond to any question or request. In subsequent interviews the parents dated the onset of Paula's difficulties to approximately three years before, when she was thirteen. At that time, Paula began to withdraw more and more into herself; isolated in her room, she would either read or listen to music. The only activity that brought her out of her room was her piano practice. At the time, her parents saw nothing unusual in this behavior pattern, since they themselves enjoyed all three of these activities. However, it gradually dawned on them that Paula had no close friends. In fact, their daughter avoided her peer group entirely.

Currently, Paula spent all of her spare time behind the locked door of her room. When her father ordered her to leave her door unlocked, an angry tearful scene ensued. Mr. O. was astounded, for Paula had always been respectful of his wishes. Her father, in going over her school work, which he was in the habit of doing rigorously, discovered that the margins of her books and papers were filled with bizarre and morbid notes which he could not comprehend. When Paula sloughed off his questions about these notes, he decided she was deeply involved in her studies and decided to ignore them. The psychiatrist recognized that these notes contained broad hints of suicide.

In the middle of March the school guidance counselor called Mrs. O. to report that she was disturbed by Paula's behavior; particularly, she was uneasy about the essay on suicide that Paula had written for her English class. Although excellently composed, with many scientific references, it impressed the teacher as exceedingly morbid. The teacher also had noticed that Paula had no associations with any of her classmates, but sat silently by herself in the classroom during period when the class was not in session. Previously, Paula had recited easily, often volunteering material, but during the past month and a half she had been almost completely silent during class periods. When Paula went to this same teacher to discuss the easiest way to commit suicide, the school authorities finally demanded that the parents remove Paula from school and seek psychiatric help. Mr. O. admitted that two weeks earlier, he had been looking for Paula to call her to dinner and discovered her in his workshop over the garage. She was standing on a chair, with a noosed rope flung over the rafters. He asked what she was doing; when she replied, "Nothing," he responded, "Well, then, come in to dinner." Mr. O. denied that he saw anything of import in this incident and maintained that his off-hand response to her at that time was appropriate, since he considered that nothing was amiss; the whole thing was probably "a childish fantasy."

Family Background and History. The O. family consisted of Mr. O., age forty-two, Mrs. O., thirty-eight, Paula, sixteen, Karen, twelve, and Paul, three. They lived in an upper-middle-class district of an urban community. Their spacious but older house sat isolated on a knoll above the new homes of a recently built-up community. Each child had his own room, and in addition to the usual living quarters there was a library and music room. The O.'s had very little association outside of their own family. They did not belong to any club, they did not attend PTA, and they had few friends and no relatives in the community. Only on rare occasions did Mr. O.'s business require him to be away from home other than during working hours. Mrs. O. did not enjoy shopping; she seldom left the home except for direct purchases, and even these errands she tried to save for Saturday morning when she could be accompanied by her husband. Thus, there was always someone home during the day, and during the evening the entire family were always together.

THE FATHER: Mr. O. was assistant director of a large, commercial, scientific laboratory. He immediately informed the interviewer that, despite limitations in his education, he was enjoying a very responsible position in the laboratory, directing the activities of scientists with doctoral degrees. The elder son of a small town New England judge, he was brought up in an environment in which conformity to "proper" standards of behavior was emphatically enforced. Although not generally a superior student, he obtained outstanding marks in science courses in high school.

Throughout his childhood, he had yielded unquestioningly to the autocratic domination with which his father ruled the family. However, in his late teens he became more sullen and finally rebelled by refusing to attend college as his father demanded. Instead, he left home and obtained a job in a chemical laboratory. All during high school, he had had very little social life. It was on his first date, away from home, that Mr. O. met his wife-to-be. They were married two months later. The United States had just entered World War II and almost immediately Mr. O. was inducted into military service and shipped overseas, where he remained for two and a half years without furlough. On the basis of his civilian interest and employment, Mr. O. was assigned to a chemical warfare unit, where he received a commission and was assigned administrative duties. Thus, upon discharge from the army, despite his lack of a college education, he was able to obtain a managerial position in an industrial firm. In appearance Mr. O. was a tall, lean, rangy man, casual but not untidy in his dress. He loved to talk and to argue; he admitted he often took the opposite position at any point "just for the fun of it." A chain smoker, he never seemed to relax, and always gave the impression of being in a hurry.

THE MOTHER: Mrs. O. was born and reared in a rural New England community, the only daughter of the owner of a small restaurant. She had always been a very timid person who was dominated by her complaining and overbearing mother. She could not remember her father well since he died at sea when she was still very young. During her early childhood, she spent many long hours alone in the apartment behind the restaurant while her mother waited on customers. Mrs. O.'s attempts at courtship were strongly resisted by the mother, who had constantly warned her daughter about the unreliability of men. Mrs. O. continued to live with her mother after her husband went overseas. Soon after her husband left for overseas, Mrs. O. discovered that she was pregnant with Paula. Friction with her mother increased during her pregnancy and continued after

Paula's birth. However, Mrs. O.'s mother found Paula such a charming baby that she changed her attitude, and she gradually began to show off the infant to her customers.

On Mr. O.'s return, the postwar housing shortage made it difficult for him to find a place of their own. Thus, the following year was one of mounting hostility between Mrs. O.'s mother and her husband. Each made constant demands upon her and each blamed the other when she failed to live up to their demands. Mr. O. began to put pressures on his wife to move away from her mother. This prospect frightened her, as she had never been separated from her mother even overnight, except for the time she spent in the hospital giving birth to Paula. Mr. O. was finally able to find a flat nearby and insisted that his wife move away from her mother. About the same time as this move was made their second child, Karen, was born. The new home was unsatisfactory, and Mrs. O.'s mother continued to interfere in their marriage. It was partly for these reasons that the couple moved to the Pacific coast.

On the surface, the balance of the O.'s marriage was most peaceful—chiefly because Mrs. O. deferred to her husband's every wish and opinion. During her therapy she admitted that she was always tense whenever her husband became amorous, even though this was infrequent. Having been brought up in a home where the "dangers" of sex were frequently emphasized, she had no sexual experience prior to marriage and was always frightened by it afterwards.

When first seen in the clinic, Mrs. O. gave a rather dowdy appearance. She was dressed in an unassuming tweed suit with white lace blouse buttoned up to the collar; she wore no make-up, and her dark, graying hair was tied up in a low bun at the nape of her neck. With her lips pursed and her hands folded in her lap, she usually sat rigidly upright at the edge of the chair, staring straight ahead, very much like a frightened animal. Often she had to clear her throat several times before speaking and then her voice was so low as to be nearly inaudible. At times, however, when tense or excited, her voice broke into a high pitch. She seldom volunteered anything except when questioned, and her answers tended to trail off into generalities. "Oh, you know," was one of her favorite responses.

PAULA: At birth, Paula seemed in every way a normal infant. Her mother's pregnancy had lasted almost exactly nine months and despite a prolonged labor, there had been no difficulty at her birth. Her weight and length were fairly average. She breathed immediately and fed at the breast readily and without difficulty. Mrs. O. was able to continue breast-feeding of Paula for over three months, at which time she gradually shifted Paula onto a formula in the bottle. Paula's development during the first year of life was fairly regular and uneventful. She grew rapidly and, if anything, was somewhat precocious in the development of her motor and social functioning. She was sitting up before age three months, standing in the crib by five months, and was taking her first steps before she was a year old. Mrs. O. had nothing to do but care for Paula and poured a great deal of affection and attention upon her during these first three years of her life. Paula began to speak her first words shortly after her first birthday; she never talked any baby-talk and was combining words into two- or three-word combinations and sentences by the time she was eighteen months old. Mrs. O. reported that Paula "almost toilet-trained herself." Paula's development continued uneventfully until her father's return three years later. At their reunion, Mr. O. grabbed her and overwhelmed her with a "bear-hug." Paula was terrified and for the first two weeks after his return ran screaming from the room at his appearance. His pride was injured and he kept making remarks about the fact that he had hoped for a boy, and "What did you expect from girls anyhow." Soon afterwards, however, Paula and her father made up, and very quickly she became known as "daddy's little girl."

During Mrs. O.'s pregnancy with their second daughter, Karen, Mr. O. cared for Paula in many little ways, brushing her hair, toileting her, and putting her to bed. His attentions to her continued unabated even after the birth of the younger sister. Paula was obviously very bright, and her father was able to teach her to read and write before she started school. He let everyone know how proud he was of her intellectual development. Paula read everything she could lay her hands on, started playing the piano as soon as she could sit up to it, and by the time she was eight she had helped her father build a ham-radio set, which they both operated. She seldom participated in any of the housework but was always there ready to help her father with the gardening.

Paula appeared to have little in common with Karen; they shared no friends and usually played separately. Although they were disdainful of one another's opinions and sarcastic toward one another, they seldom openly quarreled, as this was forbidden sternly by their parents. At school, Paula made excellent progress, usually had all outstanding or A grades and was twice given a double promotion. She had no intimate friends and even her casual acquaintances seldom numbered more than two or three. She did not seem to be interested in little girls' games, and her friends were uninterested in her scientific prowess. Thus her friends seldom returned to her home after one visit and she seldom visited them. She had no interest in sports and several times the teachers reported to the parents that Paula was reading instead of playing on the playground during recess. Since the school was nearby, Paula usually came home for lunch.

Paula began to take on some weight and the secondary sexual characteristics of womanhood at about age twelve and had her first menstrual period the week of her thirteenth birthday. Her mother had been completely unable to give her any sex instruction, but her father was doggedly determined that she should be informed and the year before had given her books, chiefly medical, regarding the facts of life, and had discussed them with her, including the fact of her onset of menses. He even provided her with her first supply of sanitary napkins! In junior high, Paula withdrew more and more from her classmates. She had several admirers among the boys but kept them at a distance. Her intellectual interests and her formal manners and speech tended further to isolate her from the other children. In contrast, her teachers praised her intellectual achievement and her creative writing. She was fascinated by the prospect of her brother Paul's birth and offered to care for him at every opportunity. However, she proved to be quite clumsy with the baby, almost dropping him several times, and was never really able to dress him or feed him properly. Her father was quite upset by her inability to care for her brother and made remarks about how unfeminine she was.

KAREN: Little was known of Karen other than the behavior mentioned above. She apparently was of no general problem to the family other than that she adopted typical teen-age ways which were disapproved by her father. She was more able to ignore her father's disapproval than Paula, who became tearful whenever her father glowered. Karen enjoyed helping her mother and made fun of Paula when she did not join in the housework. She rivaled with Paula for the attention of their father, but maintained more of a teasing, provoking relationship with her father, while Paula tended to treat her father with deference. Whereas Paula failed in her attempt to help her mother with the new baby, caring for an infant came rather naturally to Karen, who had always "played house" with dolls much more than had Paula.

PAUL: Little data were obtained regarding Paul's development and insofar as Paul was discussed with the parents, both described him in idealistic terms as the "perfect baby," who gave them no trouble. Mr. O. was obviously delighted to have a son. During the one occasion when Paul accompanied his parents to the clinic, he constantly interrupted them, ran noisily up and down the hall, and grabbed at any thing he wanted! Mr. O. smiled benignly and made no effort to control him; Mrs. O. was manifestly uncomfortable, looked pleadingly at her husband, but said nothing.

When queried why they had decided to name the baby *Paul* when they had already named the oldest daughter *Paula,* Mr. O. smiled and nodded to his wife, indicating (for one of the few times) that she should answer. Mrs. O. demurely replied that she liked the name as both her husband and father were named Paul. When the interviewer persisted and asked how Paula had reacted when the baby was given the masculine equivalent of her name, Mr. O. replied sternly, "She was honored!" Later, in an interview separate from her husband, Mrs. O. acknowledged that her husband had hoped that their first born would be a boy and had made it clear to her that he assumed she would name him Paul. She felt she had failed him by having a girl and hoped to appease him by naming her after him anyway. When he decided to name the baby Paul, she did not voice her disagreement, even though it occurred to her that Paula might feel hurt or confused. As far as Mrs. O. could observe, Paula appeared to ignore the contamination of names. Questioned further, Mrs. O. became flustered and denied hotly that the subject was ever discussed. When the topic was broached later with Mr. O. he attempted to debate the interviewer; assuming a mock injured air, he accused the interviewer of the *argumentum ad hominum,* adding slyly that the interviewer was unfairly using "Freudian tactics." When the psychiatrist asked Paula her feelings about the similarity of the names, she suddenly became completely impassive, turned away, and would answer nothing else for the rest of that hour. She remained immobile in her hospital room the rest of that afternoon, unresponsive to anyone or anything. That night she slashed both of her wrists.

Progress in Treatment. During the next three weeks, Paula sat in her room as much as possible and was unresponsive to everyone. She continued to read Dostoevsky and Plato or to listen to the radio. Occasionally, she would play the piano. She would not respond to any questions, and would sit in silence with the psychiatrist for the entire hour if permitted. Nor did she respond to any of the psychological tests. She was very tense when urine specimens were taken and ran and stood in the corner in obvious terror when the physical examination was begun. She would not disrobe for the physical examination which was abandoned because she seemed so upset. Later it was thought that Paula would be less embarrassed by a woman physician, but Paula seemed terrified even when a woman physician attempted to examine her. The nurses and occupational therapists made efforts to include Paula in the ward activities, but it was extremely difficult to get her to leave her room. She ate sparsely but there was no noticeable drop in her weight. Her parents visited almost daily; she would come out to see them but said very little to them, which upset her father.

At the end of three weeks, despite interviews with the parents, Mr. O. signed the patient out of the hospital against medical advice. This was his vacation and he had decided months in advance to take the family on a trip. Four days later, the parents returned with Paula and reported that she had refused to go camping and that after her father had raged at her, she had gone to her room crying. Later, after everyone was in bed, she had slipped out of the house and walked down a main boulevard, where she was picked up by the police in her nightwear. Sometime during the evening, she had again slashed both of her wrists with a piece of glass. Paula was readmitted to the hospital on the understanding that both parents would come regularly to interviews with the social worker and psychologist. Gradually Paula began to talk to her therapist, at first mainly about irrelevant topics, e.g. her interest in music, what she was reading, her poetry. At the end of another six weeks, it was felt that Paula could be seen on an outpatient basis and she continued coming into the clinic three times a week. Meanwhile, Mrs. O. was seen regularly by the social worker once a week. More of the history of the family was obtained. A beginning was made in helping Mrs. O. to explore her feelings, first about Paula, and gradually about her husband. Mr. O. was also seen in therapy.

Approximately four months after outpatient treatment Paula appeared still to be making little progress in her individual interviews with the psychiatrist. She had made several further suicidal threats, though less definite than before. Then one morning on the way to school, she came across a pre-school child, entirely a stranger to her, and suddenly she began throttling him. His mother rescued him and called the police, and Paula was brought in to the hospital.

During the ensuing year, both parents continued in treatment in the outpatient clinic. Paula's homicidal attack on this child sobered the father and made him realize, finally, the necessity of looking at what was going on in his family. He argued less and less with his therapist, talked increasingly more about himself, his wife, and his daughter. The changes in Mrs. O. were even more dramatic. One day after a brief holiday, her therapist looked for her in the waiting room, but did not at first see her, for she had cut her hair, was wearing make-up, and a very modish dress. Mr. O. was irritated that his wife was talking back to him, was spending a lot of money on clothes, and wanted to be taken places at night. On the other hand, he allowed his wife to take the lead in handling Paula on her visits home from the hospital and to take Paula shopping, which she had not done before. Mr. O. reported with some pride that he was able to be less critical of Paula. During this second stay in the hospital, Paula's behavior swung to the opposite extreme. She lost about 35 pounds, smeared make-up across her face in an amateurish fashion, dressed in shorts and a dirty blouse, and tried to avoid wearing her glasses. She behaved in such a seductive and almost vulgar fashion toward the male patients that it was at times necessary to restrict her behavior. Her father was scandalized when he saw her and was prevented from writing a letter of protest to the governor only by the quick work of the hospital social worker. However, on his wife's insistence, he began to accept a little of the change in Paula and at the end of the year, when she was returned home, he was able to accept her greater freedom in talking back to him, and her general

THE CASE OF PAULA O.

independence. When the clinic's contact with the family ended, Mr. O. was reporting that he could accept Paula's first date, even though he felt very tempted to bring the young man in from the hallway and cross-examine him. However, Mrs. O. had foreseen that Mr. O. might do this and had warned him against doing anymore than saying good evening to Paula's date. A year later, Paula wrote a brief letter to her therapist in which she indicated that she was completing high school and had no further problems.

Questions for Paula O.

1. What are the significant symptoms which are to be understood in this case?
2. Identify the stresses which, over the preceding three years, may have acted to precipitate Paula's illness.
3. On the basis of the evidence available evaluate the role of the following in producing Paula's illness:
    a. the separation from her father during her first two years
    b. the relationship between Mrs. O. and her mother
    c. Paula's relationship with her father
    d. Paula's relationship with Karen and Paul
4. What psychological defenses do we see operating in Paula? Why did these defenses fail to stabilize her anxiety level?
5. What are some possible underlying reasons for *attempting* suicide and which of these seems most appropriate in Paula's case?
6. Paula showed a marked departure in her behavior after her second hospitalization. She changed from a prim, asexual girl to a seductively behaving, less controlled woman. Was this change predictable from Paula's past history? Defend your answer.
7. Why, do you think, did the interviewers press the O.'s so closely about Paula's name? What might have been the significance of her name in:
    a. her relationship with her father
    b. relation to her "lack of femininity"
    c. her feelings about Paul
8. What might be the significance of:
    a. Paula's drive toward intellectual achievement
    b. her dress and appearance

    c. her dread of physical examination

    d. her attack on the neighbor child

9. What two diagnostic classifications suggest themselves to you? Attempt to choose between these two classifications by weighing the evidence for each one.

References

DEUTSCH, H. *The psychology of women.* New York: Grune & Stratton, 1944. Read Chap. 3, Puberty and adolescence.

JACKSON, D. Theories of suicide. In SCHNEIDMAN, E., & FARBEROW, N., *Clues to suicide.* New York: McGraw-Hill, 1957.

LIDZ, T., et al. The intrafamilial environment of the schizophrenic: the father. *Psychiatry,* 1957, **20**: 329–342.

LYNN, D., & SAWREY, W. The Effects of father absence on Norwegian boys and girls. *Journal of Abnormal and Social Psychology,* 1959, **59**: 258–262.

THE CASE OF MERRY L.

The Model Child

Even before Merry was four, her pediatrician had expressed concern over her emotional and social development and had advised her mother, with increasing urgency, to seek a psychological evaluation. Mrs. L. did not believe there was really anything wrong with Merry, but was disturbed by the pediatrician's insistence. She agreed that Merry's development could be considered slow, but she was not worried. It was her opinion that Merry would develop at her own pace and would eventually be quite normal. She believed "in letting children develop at their own pace rather than pushing them," but could not convince the pediatrician that Merry would "grow out of it." The confident manner with which Mrs. L. voiced her opinions made it clear that she expected the psychologist to support her point of view.

Asked to describe Merry's slowness, Mrs. L. first mentioned that Merry did not seem to "talk clearly." As Mrs. L. explained further, the problem was not that Merry could not express herself in words, for she had been using brief sentences since approximately the age of two, but rather that Merry talked to herself when she played and did not seem to converse with anyone else. She repeated words over and over in sing-song fashion, and did not seem to pay attention to what other people said. In fact, Merry's parents had suspected that she might be hard of hearing, but an examination by the pediatrician had revealed no auditory defect. Furthermore, Merry had not responded to efforts to toilet-train her until age three and continued at age four to have "accidents" during the day and to wet the bed at night. This rather puzzled Mrs. L. since, in other ways, Merry seemed excessively concerned with neatness and would become almost panic-stricken if she got her hands dirty or if something were spilled or dropped. Otherwise, in Mrs. L.'s eyes, Merry seemed to be an ideal child. She was quite independent; she seemed to be able to get many of the things she wanted and seldom was any bother to her mother or others. Although occasionally she would inexplicably burst into tears, she was comforted easily with some favorite doll or her blanket. She had several such objects, the favorite of which was a small blanket, but she was also very attached to a hair brush which she had brought home from her grandmother's, and a couple of small stuffed animals which were always in her bed or crib. To illustrate how "well behaved" Merry could be, Mrs. L. cited an incident of the previous New Year's Day: she and her husband had been out most of the night before and when she awakened the next afternoon, Mrs. L. suddenly realized that Merry had not been fed or taken care of in any way. To her surprise she discovered Merry at the other end of the house by herself in her play pen; in the kitchen was evidence that Merry had helped herself to cereal and milk. Merry seemed undisturbed by the fact that her parents had slept through most of the day.

Merry knew how to feed herself fairly well and even was quite independent in bathing herself. However, a great deal of Merry's care was given over to a Negro housekeeper, who usually fed and bathed Merry, and, if the parents were not home in the evening, saw that Merry got to bed. Mrs. L. thought that perhaps some of Merry's slow development was due to the fact that there were no other children her age in the immediate neighborhood with whom she could play. She had hoped to put Merry into a nursery school class, feeling that the example of the other children would be helpful, but the nursery school would not accept Merry until she was completely toilet-trained.

Petite, blonde, blue-eyed, and dressed in an immaculate crinoline skirt which stuck out stiffly, revealing several petticoats underneath, and wearing patent leather shoes, Merry looked like a very beautiful little doll. During the interview with her mother, Merry at first clung to her mother's coat, but Mrs. L. pushed her toward another chair. Merry promptly climbed up and knelt on the chair, facing away from her mother and the examiner. There she stayed for the entire hour of the interview, rocking up and down, rhythmic fashion, and making small cooing noises to herself. Mrs. L. paid no attention to Merry throughout the interview. At the end of the hour, when the examiner asked to see Merry in the playroom, Mrs. L. spoke to Merry, but

Merry did not move. Merry looked up when Mrs. L. touched her, but did not respond to Mrs. L.'s introduction to the doctor. The examiner reached out his hand and Merry took it and followed him down the hall for a short distance. She did not look at the examiner but seemed to be staring at the ceiling. She walked on her tiptoes in an odd dancing fashion. Finally, she broke loose from the examiner's hand and began to whirl around in large circles, up and down the hall, still on her tiptoes. When the examiner neared her and reached out his hand, she again grasped it and then clung to him for a moment, all the time silent. She permitted herself to be led into the playroom, where she once more whirled about the room for a few moments. She did not respond to the examiner's directions or voice, and seemed to be almost unaware that he was in the room. Finally she stopped in the corner and began to repeat the cooing noises that she had made previously. Occasionally there would be words interjected in these noises, which would be repeated over and over again. Only two of these words were distinguishable; the first was "darling," and the second was her name. She did not respond to any offers to play with the toys nor otherwise pay any attention to the examiner. However, if the examiner came close to her, she would move to another part of the room. She began to move her hand up and down in front of her face, sometimes touching various parts of her body. Finally she crouched in the opposite corner from the examiner and began rocking back and forth. She permitted the examiner to come closer to her and sit down beside her. When she was touched, she reached out her hand and rose to her feet as if expecting to be led from the room. Taken back to her mother, she continued to gesture in front of her face and make her cooing noises as she left the clinic.

Prior History. Mrs. L. reported that her pregnancy with Merry had been entirely uneventful. She mentioned that she had been very pleased since she had gained very little weight during this pregnancy and had been able to continue her work as a model in a dress shop until the last three months. Even during these final three months, she had continued to work as a saleslady in the office. Merry's birth was without complication; Mrs. L.'s labor was quite brief and parturition was achieved with only an ordinary anesthesia. Although, as far as could be determined, the pregnancy had lasted nine months,

Merry, who weighed less than four pounds at birth, was considered "premature" and was put in an incubator for five days.

Mrs. L. left the hospital before Merry but fell ill shortly thereafter and returned to the hospital again, remaining in the hospital for three months. At first, she passed over the details of this illness, saying that she had a mild, but persistent fever of unknown origin. Later, however, she admitted that she had had "a nervous breakdown," and had been treated with electric shock. She claimed that the electric shock had erased from her memory her feelings and experiences during this "nervous breakdown," but agreed that perhaps she had been quite depressed. During this interval, Merry remained in the hospital for another month and was then sent home in the care of a practical nurse. When Mrs. L. returned home from her hospitalization, she was still too weak to care for Merry. It was difficult to find a permanent nursemaid and there was a succession of people taking care of the child. Mrs. L. reported with pride that Merry seldom cried; she would lie for hours in her crib often without moving. However, she readily adapted to a routine feeding. Mrs. L. never did breast-feed Merry, partly because a special formula was recommended to help Merry gain weight, and secondly because, after she returned home, she had no lactation. All in all, she could recall very little about Merry's development during the first two years of her life. She could not remember when Merry sat up or began to stand. Merry did seem quite different from her eight-year-old brother, Mark, in that Merry lay so inert in her playpen. She remembered Mark as climbing out of the playpen and getting "into everything." She described Mark as making many more demands upon her for attention. She went on to describe how Mark was a very cuddly baby whom she loved to hold. On the other hand, she remarked, "Sometimes I would just forget for the whole day that Merry was there."

THE MOTHER. Mrs. L., age twenty-eight, was a beautiful shapely blonde, chic in dress and appearance. As she sat, she seemed to pose in the chair in a slightly seductive fashion. She wore a slight, set smile as if it were part of her stylish costume and lacquered coiffure. About the only change in her facial expression occurred when she began to talk about some of her own personal problems—then her smile changed to a pout.

Prefacing her remarks with a denial that she had any difficulties in adjustment, Mrs. L. seemed to enjoy talking about her background. She was an only child. Her father had deserted her mother soon after Mrs. L.'s birth, and her mother was forced to work to support them. In her early years, Mrs. L. was cared for by her maternal grandmother, whom she remembered with considerable fondness. There was more than occasional dissension between her mother and grandmother, as her grandmother repetitiously insisted that she had warned Mrs. L.'s mother about her father's unreliability before they were ever married. Mrs. L.'s mother did not deny her mother's accusations against Mrs. L.'s father, but resented being reminded of her marital mistake. Mrs. L.'s mother also tried to quiet the grandmother, saying that this topic should not be "brought up in front of the child." Mrs. L. was quite curious about her father, but her grandmother would tell her nothing about him, saying only that she hoped that Mrs. L. never made such a mistake. In Mrs. L.'s words, her mother "devoted her life to me," providing "everything that I ever wanted." Although they were not well-to-do, Mrs. L. always had all the playthings and all the clothes that she ever needed. As a dressmaker, Mrs. L.'s mother was able to provide the finest clothes for Mrs. L. She also began music lessons and dancing lessons for her at an early age. Mrs. L.'s mother was disappointed when Mrs. L. did not turn out to be talented; about the only frustration Mrs. L. could remember in her childhood was the many long hours of practicing her piano or ballet lessons. Otherwise, she said her childhood was quite happy. She made average to above-average grades in school and had many playmates. In junior high and high school, she was quite popular, went to many parties, and always had dates.

Both her mother and grandmother continually warned her in rather vague terms about "watching herself" with boys. She laughed, as she remembered feeling guilty when she was first kissed by a boy at age fourteen. However, despite her mother's warning, she began to pet heavily on her dates and had her first sexual experience at age sixteen. She completed high school at age seventeen, took a brief course in modeling clothes, and obtained a job as a model. She met her husband shortly thereafter and became pregnant by him at age nineteen. Her mother and grandmother were very upset but became mollified by the fact that her husband came from a wealthy family and that his parents agreed to their marriage. Her husband was one of the most handsome boys in the high school class, a basketball star, and one of the top students. His father was a leading physician in the community, and it was he who paid for the extravagant and elaborate wedding. Although Mrs. L. felt a little uncomfortable about the fact that she was pregnant at the time of the wedding, she had gained no noticeable weight and she believed that no one, other than her immediate family, was aware of the pregnancy. It was understood that her husband's plan to go on to university and medical school was not to be interrupted and her father-in-law agreed to pay for his education. She saw little of her in-laws as they never invited her over or spoke to her. Her father-in-law occasionally dropped by their apartment, but only to make financial arrangements with her husband. During her ensuing pregnancy with Mark, she suffered considerable illness, with continual nausea and vomiting. She also had prolonged labor and continued to be weak and depressed after Mark's birth. Nevertheless Mark seemed to be a healthy baby and she enjoyed caring for him and devoted a great deal of attention to him. During the next eight years, Mr. L. was forced to devote all of his energies to his studies and there was little opportunity for them to have a good time, to do much together, or to go anywhere. However, having a baby to care for at least partially compensated Mrs. L. for the isolation from her husband. She also spent considerable time visiting her mother and grandmother.

The year before Merry's birth, her grandmother died. Mrs. L. was again depressed and her depression seemed to increase when, six months later, her mother remarried. She denied that she was disappointed that her mother was not near her when she became pregnant and gave birth to Merry, saying that since she had been through this once before with Mark and since Merry's birth was so easy, she really did not miss her mother. When Mrs. L. was asked about the aspects of her environment which could have produced her nervous breakdown following Merry's birth, she smiled wanly, remarked again that she did not know the nature of this "nervous breakdown," and said she regarded the whole incident as unimportant and probably merely resulting from fatigue.

Soon after recovering from this "nervous breakdown," Mrs. L. decided to go back to work and had been steadily employed nearly ever since. She hired a nursemaid to care for Merry, and Mark was enrolled in a private school, where he stayed most of the day. There were frequent changes in nursemaids, probably because Mrs. L. expected them to do all of the housework in addition to caring for Merry. She expressed considerable dissatisfaction with these maids, complaining that they were sloppy and disobedient. Critical as she was about their inability to keep the house exactly as she required, she made no mention about their care for Merry. Exactly why she decided to go to work at this time was not clear, except that she had enjoyed her work as a model and had, for a long time, been determined to return to it. This decision seemed even more inexplicable because by this time Dr. L. had completed his medical training and was beginning his practice. Thus, their income no longer depended upon the father-in-law and was much larger than it had been throughout the previous nine years of their marriage.

Regarding their marriage, Mrs. L. maintained that she and her husband had an ideal relationship. Although he had seldom been free from his studies, whenever they did have a little money he would make sure that they went someplace together. He was always buying her little presents, and encouraged her to buy the clothes that she wanted, and praised her for her beauty and taste. She did intimate that she had hoped that when he finished his medical education they would have a great deal more time together, but while building up his practice he had many night calls, was off early in the morning for operating schedules, and seldom seemed to be available for personal contact, let alone social activity. She might not see him from morning to night. They used to play golf together but since he began his practice they did not have the same day off. She expressed considerable annoyance with his friends, since all they talked about was medicine and she could not endure the wives of the other physicians. She considered them all snobs who talked about nothing but their husbands and children. Asked about her sexual relations with her husband, she responded with her oft-repeated "wonderful" and declined to discuss the topic further.

THE FATHER. Doctor L. was a tall, blondish man with an athletic build. He expressed considerable willingness to come in and discuss his daughter's condition, but it proved difficult to arrange an appointment because of his busy schedule. When he finally came, he seemed quite relaxed and jovial, in an expansive mood. Offering the therapist a cigar, he proceeded to describe his daughter and wife as if they were cases of his own he was discussing with a colleague. He began by stating, with a laugh, that he was afraid he was a very poor informant since, because of his extremely busy practice, he was not home enough to really say much about Merry's development, and "I don't even know what my wife is up to these days." He said that he also had been unaware that Merry presented any particular difficulties until he was advised of it by their pediatrician. Even then he was inclined to disregard the pediatrician's advice because "All of us knew that this guy is off on a psychiatric jag in his ideas." However, he did observe that Merry seemed somewhat slow in development and that many of her mannerisms were annoying to him. He had one of his colleagues in neurology examine her, but there were no findings indicative of any neurological defects and her electro-encephalographic record was normal for this age. His colleague also advised that Merry's difficulty was probably some sort of emotional disturbance, which Dr. L. said that he accepted although he could not immediately see what the nature of the disturbance was or the possible causes of it.

With only slightly more questioning, Dr. L. began to express considerable dissatisfaction with his wife. He started by saying that he now realized that, in many ways, she did not seem to be "well-adapted to being a mother." He felt that she was very unhappy with her first pregnancy with Mark, that she continually complained that Dr. L. had ruined her life, and, to this date, really never let him forget that their marriage had been forced by the fact of her pregnancy. In neither her pregnancy with Mark nor with Merry had Mrs. L. worn maternity clothes and, indeed, Dr. L. had been concerned because Mrs. L. had made many efforts to hide the fact of her pregnancy by wearing tight undergarments and by going on a much more severe diet than was recommended by the obstetrician. During her pregnancy with Merry, Mrs. L. ate almost nothing, to the point that she was often weak and he feared she would become anemic. She appeared extremely tense during her pregnancy with Merry. Since she was always on edge, he constantly had to avoid upsetting her. "We never really quarrel, but that's only because I shut up and get out of the way." When asked about Mrs. L.'s "nervous breakdown" following Merry's birth, Dr. L. said that she had been extremely depressed, unable to talk to anyone, and wept constantly. She was hospitalized in a private sanitarium and given a brief series of electric shock treatments. Following these treatments she improved rapidly but seemed to have no memory of her experience. He could not account for her depression, adding with a laugh, "There's a great deal I cannot account for in my wife's behavior." Questioned further about their marital relationship, Dr. L. became a little sad and said that originally he had been very much in love with his wife and considered himself extremely lucky to have had such a very beautiful "doll," but things had really not turned out as well as he had hoped. He said that he himself felt somewhat guilty in that he had devoted so much of his time to his studies and had so little time for his wife. On the other hand, he felt she always seemed extremely wrapped up in herself and her own needs, and had really never understood his educational or vocational goals. He agreed she seemed "attracted to" Mark when he was a baby and had attempted to take care of Mark, but that this seemed to be largely a matter of "pride in her production"; when Mark grew into "a naughty little boy" she quickly made plans to put him into a day school. He did not believe that she wanted to have any more children after Mark's birth since she so resented being pregnant. Their sexual relations had never been very frequent and never really satisfying to either of them. He was very surprised when she became pregnant with Merry since he thought that she was preventing pregnancy by use of contraceptives. Since Merry's birth, sexual relations between them had been almost nonexistent. He agreed that he felt extremely frustrated and often wondered if their marriage was going to continue. He hinted that he found his sexual satisfaction outside of marriage, but when questioned on this, laughed, held his hands up in front of his face, and protested that he saw no connection between Merry's disturbance and his own sexual problem.

Course in Treatment. Merry was placed in a psychiatrically oriented nursery school which she attended daily for a two-hour period along with other children of her age who had similar disturbances. In this setting, the teacher, a person specially trained in work with emotionally disturbed preschool children, directed her efforts chiefly toward helping Merry to find a relaxed atmosphere in which it was hoped that she could establish emotional relationships with others. At the same time, Mrs. L. was seen in individual, periodic interviews with the psychologist and attended a group discussion with other mothers whose children were in the nursery school. In the individual interviews Mrs. L. spent most of her time reporting on Merry's current behavior at home and resisted any attempts to encourage her to talk about herself or her own feelings. In the group, she sat silent, posed, and staring straight ahead. She protested that she got nothing out of the group discussions. Often she missed these sessions or came quite late. Several times, the other women in the group remarked on her silence and one woman in particular, kept remarking that she did not understand how anyone who seemed as poised, calm, and beautiful as Mrs. L. could possibly have a child that was disturbed. This remark did not seem to faze Mrs. L.

Merry very gradually became more and more attached to the teacher. At first there was little change in her behavior in the nursery school playroom; she stuck to her own corner, continuing her gestures and noises. From time to time, however, she began to accept things from the teacher or bring over toys to show the teacher, but would permit very little interaction with the teacher or with the other children. She became attracted by the teacher's coat and loved to sit and rub the teacher's coat or the teacher's arm. At first she seemed unwilling to handle any of the materials which would at all soil her hands or her clothes, but one day she became fascinated by the sandbox and, thereafter, seemed almost to enjoy getting messed up, much to the annoyance of her mother. The teacher encouraged Mrs. L. to dress Merry in playclothes, to which Mrs. L. finally acceded. Then Merry seemed a little more relaxed and willing to paint or play with the toys in the yard. After approximately three months, Merry seemed to be running and playing fairly well, although she remained verbally uncommunicative. Her rocking and whirling behavior was much less frequent.

About this time, Dr. L. called to report that his wife had disappeared and had notified him that she was in Las Vegas to obtain a divorce. He would not discuss the conditions of the break-up of their marriage but seemed relatively cheerful. He requested that Merry be continued in the playschool, but said that he did not have time to come in and discuss Merry's behavior, suggesting that perhaps the maid would be a better informant. Although the clinic felt that, under these conditions, it was improbable that Merry would continue to progress, they saw no other possibilities and agreed to continue Merry in the nursery school.

During the following several months Merry reverted to much of the behavior she had shown when she began treatment. Dr. L. was called in for an interview and advised that it was quite probable that Merry would need hospitalization. Again, he begged that the clinic continue to work with Merry, saying that the only progress he had ever seen in her development had occurred during Merry's stay there. He agreed that Merry's relapse probably was related to the fact that her mother had left, but said that he hoped to rectify the situation soon as he planned to marry again. A week later he called and asked for a further interview and requested that his fiancée be seen also. The second Mrs. L., who looked very much like Merry's own mother, had previously been the nurse in Dr. L.'s office. She expressed considerable interest in Merry, saying that she had discussed the situation with Dr. L. and that she planned to take an active part in Merry's treatment and rehabilitation. Dr. L. remarried within the month after the divorce and Merry's stepmother began to attend the mothers' group. She had left her job and stayed at home caring for Merry and Mark. She often came and observed Merry in the playroom along with the teacher. She seemed to be a fairly warm-hearted woman who was quite disturbed at first over Merry's behavior and puzzled by it. During the group sessions, she expressed her feelings of uneasiness about taking over the care of the children of her husband's previous wife, but apparently was quite attracted by Merry and determined to help out with Merry's recovery, motivated by her devotion to her new husband. Very gradually Merry seemed to accept her stepmother and a second period of improvement in Merry's behavior ensued. At the end of a year and a half, Merry was playing quite actively, talking a little bit, and showed very few of her old mannerisms. It was agreed to try Merry in a public kindergarten, continuing the nursery school treatment in the afternoon. Merry's problem was discussed briefly with the kindergarten teacher and she was accepted. Her interaction with the other children, at nursery school and the kindergarten increased markedly during her year at kindergarten. She remained a silent and somewhat withdrawn child but was able to start school at age six in the first grade. At this point her attendance at nursery school was dropped.

Questions for Merry L.

1. What aspects of Merry's early development appear unusual according to any set of developmental norms? Group these deviant trends according to the following categories:

   a. motor development
   b. development of personal habits
   c. responses to people in her environment
   d. verbal development.

2. What aspects of Merry's early life, particularly during the first year, could provide a fertile ground for learning each of these categories of behavior?

3. Which categories of behavior listed in response to question 1 do not seem to follow from the pattern of Merry's early environment? How might we account for the appearance of these other classes of behavior?

4. What needs and conflicts present in Merry's parents made it difficult for them to perform their parental roles comfortably? In particular, what aspects of Mrs. L.'s early life situation set up conditions which made it difficult for her to assume the role of the mother?

5. How can one account for the fact that one child in this family was ostensibly normal and the other seriously emotionally disturbed?

6. Escalona (ref. 4) has suggested, on the basis of her research with children like Merry, that at times, we may be confusing cause and effect in understanding this type of child. Her research indicates that children like Merry are deviant from birth and that much of the parent-child friction grows out of the parents' frustration in not receiving the normal response that they need from a child. What support for this point of view is present in the case of Merry? How would you reconcile Escalona's point of view with the changes shown by Merry in the preschool?

7. In studying this case, what questions arise in your mind that you would like to see attacked by research? List these questions and summarize how we might go about finding the answers to them. (Don't let your lack of experience hinder you!)

References

EISENBERG, L. The autistic child in adolescence. *American Journal of Psychiatry*, 1956. (Also reprinted in REED, C. F., ALEXANDER, E. E., & TOMPKINS, S. S., *Psychopathology*, Cambridge: Harvard Univer. Press, 1958. Pp. 15–24.

EISENBERG, L., & KANNER, L. Early infantile autism—1943–1955. *American Journal of Orthopsychiatry*, 1956. (Also reprinted in REED, C. F., ALEXANDER, I. E., & TOMPKINS, S. S., *Psychopathology*, Cambridge: Harvard Univer. Press, 1958. Pp. 3–14.)

ESCALONA, SIBYLLE. Some considerations regarding psychotherapy, with psychotic children. *Bulletin of the Menninger Clinic*, 1948, 12: 127–134.

GOLDFARB, W. Effects of psychological deprivation in infancy and subsequent stimulation. *American Journal of Psychiatry*, 1945, 102: 18–33.

SPITZ, R. A., & WOLF, K. M. Anaclitic depression: an inquiry into the genesis of psychiatric conditions in early childhood. *The psychoanalytic study of the child*, Vol. II. 1946. Pp. 313–342.

THOMPSON, W. R., & HERON, W. Effects of restriction early in life on problem solving in dogs. *Canadian Journal of Psychology*, 1954, 8: 17–31.

THE CASE OF THE T. FAMILY

"Eat, My Children!"

Initially, Mr. and Mrs. T. came to the clinic for help with their daughter Sharon, age nine. They were troubled by the fact that Sharon could not be separated from her mother even for a short while. If Mrs. T. had to leave the house to run an errand, Sharon had to be taken along. Sharon refused to go to school unless her mother accompanied her every morning; even then, she was likely to raise a fuss about entering the classroom. She would hang on to her mother and beg to return home. Mrs. T. had to arrange her daily schedule in order to pick up her daughter after school.

Although the I.Q. tests showed that Sharon had superior intelligence, she was inattentive and unco-operative in the classroom and consequently made mediocre grades. At school and at home Sharon was a very demanding child; if she did not immediately get her own way she would throw a screaming tantrum.

During the interview with Sharon, she stated that her main problem was her brother Jerry, who was almost thirteen. According to Sharon, Jerry always got everything he wanted; yet whenever she asked for anything, her parents would say no. Her brother also teased her constantly, particularly about her weight, and he was always doing things just to annoy her. Jerry, in turn, had almost identical complaints against his sister. She was always into his things, she was a big cry-baby, and she was always getting him in trouble by "tattling." Both parents said that Jerry was also a discipline problem although in a different manner. Jerry procrastinated; he would forget to do things they wanted him to do, and in general, passively resisted their authority. For example, he would forget to bring his homework from school or he would forget when he had a music lesson or when it was time to go for his religious training. Jerry complained that his mother was always after him for something, "She'll jump down your throat before you have a chance to open your mouth."

Mr. and Mrs. T. had many complaints against one another, particularly in regard to rearing their children. Sylvia T., age thirty-two, said that since her household was in such a constant turmoil of bickering, it was no wonder that she had frequent headaches. She felt that her husband did not appreciate the immense amount of responsibility and pressure he left to her. She made bitter complaints that he made no attempt to discipline the children. For example, the children could be screaming and pommeling one another and he would ignore it completely, "once he gets his nose in the newspaper." Sidney T., age forty, retorted that his wife "makes a mountain out of everything." He said that Sylvia was a constant worrier and that he felt the children were merely resisting her "nudging." Mrs. T. responded that if Sid were ever home he would see what she was up against. She explained that Sid was a salesman who was frequently "on the road" and even when in town he seldom came home until late in the evenings. In addition, he was very active in community and church affairs and was currently the treasurer of the synagogue, which he had helped to found. He also "had to" have his night a week with the "boys" bowling. On top of everything, Sylvia worried over the fact that Sid had suffered a coronary attack three years before. After the attack he had been unable to work for almost six months. His physician had advised that he cut down on all activities except work and had put him on a strict dietary regimen.

All four members of this family were obese. Sharon, tall for her age, was almost thirty pounds overweight. In appearance, she seemed to be bursting out of her clothes, her face was pudgy, and she wore a constant pouting expression. Jerry was always getting into scrapes at school over the nickname "Tubby." He had always been at least fifteen to twenty pounds overweight. Sidney usually weighed about 225 pounds although he was only five feet, nine inches tall. After his coronary he lost seventy-five pounds, and he stayed on his diet for about two years; however, during the past year he had gradually started gaining, so that he now hovered around 200 pounds. Sylvia, who was only five feet, one inch, weighed 170 pounds. Even before Sid's coronary, the entire family had tried various diets, but without noticeable results. Sylvia complained that the children used their allowances to buy candy. Sid pointed out that his wife bought herself sweets which she hid in the top kitchen cupboards, but the children knew of this and helped themselves. He agreed that he was not consistent about keeping to his own diet, but he shrugged his shoulders and said that "life wouldn't be worth living if you couldn't eat."

It was really Sylvia who seemed to feel the most miserable. In addition to her frequent headaches, she suffered from periods of excessive fatigue and occasionally had to take to her bed for twenty-four-hour periods. On these occasions, she always felt guilty, because "there are so many things to be done." From her husband's description and her own account, Sylvia must have been a meticulous housekeeper. Sid joked that you could scarcely finish eating before she had the table cleared. She was always nagging the children to pick up their things. Daily she vacuumed the entire house and scrubbed her kitchen. She kept a strictly kosher house, which meant extra cooking and special sets of containers and dishes. She did all her own laundry and ironing and even the major part of the gardening. Her main complaint was not about the amount of housework, only that she got absolutely no co-operation from her children or husband. They never put anything away and they seemed to ignore her efforts to keep an immaculate house. Sylvia tried to get Sid to supervise Jerry and take over the heavy work of the gardening, but Sid always seemed to be busy with something else. Jerry was pretty fair about keeping his room reasonably neat, but Sharon's room was always in shambles. Sylvia readily agreed with her husband that she was fast becoming a "nag," but she argued that if she weren't, the children would never learn to take care of themselves. It was true that she seldom left anything for the children to do; it always seemed easier for her to go ahead and do the necessary chore. She worried a great deal about whether or not she was a good mother, and she always felt guilty after she had scolded her children. Because of her husband's heart condition, she tried to shield him from the minor household worries, but as a result she felt resentful and neglected.

Sylvia also was left with the responsibility of managing the complicated family finances. Sid was given an expense account, but there were always items on the monthly sheet for which he was not compensated by his company. Sylvia felt that Sid had no conception of the household budget; for example, they were already in debt, yet in the past year Sid traded in his two-year-old car for a new one, and bought an expensive air conditioning set for their home. On the other hand, she felt that her weekly food budget was much too low. She mentioned that she had had no new clothes other than what her mother had bought for her the previous summer. She also made Sharon's clothes, but Sharon outgrew them so fast that it was discouraging. Besides, Sharon was very careless with her clothes. Although Sid had encouraged his wife to join him at the synagogue in his activities, or in bowling, Sylvia often felt too tired. Moreover, if she did leave the children at home, Sharon was likely to raise a fuss, or the two children would start a fight, so that Sylvia would find it necessary to return home. The few times that she went to the synagogue with her husband, she received constant phone calls from home; one time, Sharon even appeared at the synagogue in her pyjamas, weeping loudly and greatly embarrassing her parents.

A typical day at the T. family home began at six in the morning when Sid would arise as "I have done all my life every day of the week whether I was working or not." Sylvia, on the other hand, always had great difficulty in waking up and would have liked to stay in bed half the morning but felt terribly guilty in doing so. In recent years Sid had tried to reassure her by getting his own breakfast, particularly mornings when Sylvia wasn't feeling well. He was frequently joined by Jerry, who seemed to enjoy a few minutes with his father before the women appeared. Sylvia, from her room, would worry whether or not they were getting the proper breakfast, and she would become even more upset if she should hear any word of dissension between them. Since this was one of the few moments that Sid and Jerry had together, Sid would attempt to inquire about Jerry's progress at school or his social life, and there were times he would preach at his son. Jerry would become sulky and sometimes he would talk back. By this time, Sylvia would be up, fussing over Jerry's lunch, his homework, and criticizing his attire, all of which would irritate her husband so that he would slam out of the house.

Ordinarily, Sharon would not arise until just before Jerry left for school, but even during this short interval, the two managed to argue over trifles. Then there was a daily fuss over Sharon's breakfast. Getting Sharon dressed was also a constant struggle, during which Sylvia felt she had to return to Sharon's room every few minutes to make sure she had pulled on the other sock, buttoned her dress correctly, combed her hair, and so forth. Before they started off for school Sharon had to be reassured that she would be picked up at noon and brought home for lunch. Sylvia then returned home exhausted, attempting, however, to get her house cleaned before lunch. The whole problem with Sharon was repeated at lunch time, sometimes so unsuccessfully that both became exhausted and spent the afternoon sick in bed. On the days Sharon returned to school, Sylvia would try to get her daily shopping done before school was out so that she would not have Sharon dogging her heels in the market. Very often, however, Sylvia's routine was interrupted by some other business or a caller and she could not always accomplish everything on schedule. Whenever possible, she tried to be home at the time the children got home from school to prevent another fight over the afternoon snack. Then there would be laundry and gardening and the attempts to get the children to help her. Jerry was not so much of a problem after school as he had his religious training three times a week and was involved in after-school sports, and, for a while, also had a paper route. Sharon, though, had absolutely nothing to occupy her time. She had no friends; she would not leave the house to go play with any of the children on the block, and when any of the neighbor children came over to play she was so possessive with her toys and so resentful of any demands that they might make that she soon drove them away. Thus Sylvia was left with the chore of keeping Sharon entertained; Sharon would whine for the rest of the afternoon that she was bored. Sometimes she begged to watch television, but Sylvia tried to limit this.

By the time Sid came home from work it was usually past six-thirty. Sylvia had spent the last hour before her husband's arrival arbitrating between Sharon and Jerry over which TV program, if any, they were allowed to watch. Both children would immediately demand some attention from their father, often by creating a fuss which Sylvia would then turn over to him to settle. Sid considered the evening meal a family gathering and would not brook his wife's suggestion that the children have an earlier dinner by themselves. Here at the dinner table, all the problems of the day would reappear with Sid trying to play the role of judge and lecturer. Very often Sylvia would become so upset that she was unable to eat dinner; as a result she would raid the icebox later. After dinner, there were the children's homework and more TV programs to arbitrate. Getting the children off to bed was the final battle. Even after Sylvia finally got the children off to bed, she continued with the housework, catching up on her ironing, mending, or sewing. Many of the evenings, Sid would go out after dinner, leaving Sylvia feeling rejected and lonely.

Their sexual life was also a matter of dissension. Sylvia was often too tired and irritable to have sexual relations with her husband. Although she might be quite tired, unable to sleep, often she would get up from bed to read for another hour in the living room. Sid had long felt frustrated by his wife's denial of his sexual needs and from time to time tried to make some demands on her but to no avail. Only rarely did they desire sexual relations simultaneously or find any satisfaction. Sylvia admitted that she had long been sexually inhibited, but defended herself by pointing out that her husband had a need for a great deal of sexual play prior to intercourse, which disgusted her. Furthermore, she argued that in view of his heart condition, she was afraid that the strain and excitement of sexual intercourse might be dangerous.

In addition to their immediate family problems both Sylvia and Sid had extrafamilial stresses. Sylvia, who had always been exceedingly attached to her parents, worried a great deal about them and her siblings, none of whom lived close to her. She wrote daily to her mother; if she so much as missed one day, her mother would telephone. She was particularly worried about her father who had had a coronary about the same time as her husband. She heard frequently from her brothers, mainly about their marital problems and their problems with their children. She had no immediate relatives where she was living and felt quite homesick. Because of their many debts and Sid's illnesses, it had been necessary for the T.'s to borrow several times from Sylvia's parents. Although the money they received from Sylvia's parents was technically a loan, they were never pressed for repayment. Sylvia was determined to repay her parents in monthly payments, but Sid regarded this as unnecessary. On the other hand, Sid's mother was always writing to ask for money. His brothers and sisters also wrote to Sid, criticizing him for not contributing to his mother's support. Sylvia was disgusted; she felt her mother-in-law did not really need the support from them. She pointed out that the elder Mrs. T. had all the necessities provided by the older bachelor brother, whose home she was sharing. Moreover, Sid's mother was an inveterate gambler; hence the constant requests for money. Sid felt guilty about the situation; from time to time, he would resolve that he was going to "do something" for his mother, but he seldom even wrote to her.

Sid's personal worries were chiefly occasioned by his job. He had worked for the past five years for the same company selling plumbing supplies to retailers. He earned a good base salary, and his commissions were above average. His company had been most considerate of his illness, keeping him on salary during the entire period, despite the fact that they had no definite sick-leave plan. Nevertheless, Sid knew that if he were to have another attack it was unlikely that the company would be so generous again. Lately, he had begun to feel very discontent with his job; in his eyes he was "getting nowhere." It was a very conservative company which had not turned out any new products, and Sid knew that salesmen from more progressive companies were making sales where he was not. He considered his company very tight-fisted with their expense account. He wished that he had made a shift to another company when he had first felt dissatisfied with his present job. However, Sylvia was opposed to his changing jobs because she feared that he might lose out, particularly if he had another heart attack. More and more Sid found himself idling time away rather than pushing his sales.

In addition to this daytime stress, Sid found his position as treasurer of the synagogue a strenuous one. It provided him with considerable social status, but it demanded a great deal of time and energy. He was responsible for the fund-raising affairs of the synagogue as well as keeping the accounts. His phone, both at home and at the office, constantly rang with calls regarding the synagogue's business.

He was very concerned that Jerry get a complete religious training, which was an additional financial burden. The family was currently trying to scrape up enough money for Jerry's Bar Mitzvah, which was planned for the coming summer. It was hoped that both Sid's and Sylvia's parents would come from New York to California, since Jerry was the oldest grandson. Sid openly voiced the hope that his parents-in-law would make a sizeable contribution toward the cost of Jerry's Bar Mitzvah because a large catered party was planned, but Sylvia was set against asking her parents for any more money, especially for this event. She pointed out that the Bar

Mitzvah symbolized the relationship between father and son, and therefore Sid should stand the major cost.

Past History. Sylvia was born and reared in Brooklyn, New York. Her father was owner of a small dressmaking factory, which he had inherited from his father. He always made a fair living, even during the depression years. Sylvia had two older brothers, three and five years her senior. The family lived in a spacious, old-fashioned flat in an older part of the city. In an upstairs flat lived Sylvia's maternal grandmother and uncle. Sylvia described her family as a very tight-knit group in which everyone was concerned with everyone's else business. Sylvia was always extremely attached to her mother. As she began to talk about Sharon's school problems, she remembered that her behavior in grade school was almost identical. She cried desperately when she was taken to kindergarten, and her mother stayed with her in the classroom for many weeks. She always hated to go to school and was otherwise afraid to leave her mother. She described her mother as "the most wonderful person in the world," who "always did almost too much for everyone." She described how her mother was almost a martyr-like slave to her father and brothers, and how she tended to their every need, even to the extent of polishing their shoes. She could not remember that her mother ever scolded her for anything, or that she had been denied anything. "I guess I was dreadfully spoiled." She described her father as a very kindly man, whom she adored. At the same time, she admitted that he was a quite tyrannical disciplinarian with his sons and that the only time she saw any dissension between her parents was when her mother occasionally tried to interfere with her father's domination of her brothers. In general, however, Sylvia's mother was able to keep peace in the family. She was always a little over-anxious that Sylvia and her brothers had the proper food or that they were warmly dressed. The boys teased her affectionately about her overprotection, and they nicknamed her "Queeny," a name that was soon adopted by everyone. Even as an adult, Sylvia alternately referred to her mother as "Queeny" or "Mommy." Although Sylvia did not regard her mother as dominating or overprotective, she openly was critical of her grandmother for being excessively dominating. Her maternal grandmother ran her mother's life and would have dominated her father had he permitted it. She depicted her maternal uncle as being so cowed that he had no life of his own; even as an adult he was unable to function without his mother telling him every step to take.

The weight problem was an early one for Sylvia. Periodically she was overweight; yet other times she could actually be underweight. She was frequently told that she was prematurely born and considered a feeding problem as an infant. The family tried special formulas and special foods which were either prescribed by the pediatrician or based on the folklore of her maternal grandmother. "If any problem occurred, my grandmother had some old remedy for it, usually something to eat. 'Kinder ess!' was her motto." By the time Sylvia started school, she was tubby. Then came alternating periods of dieting and stuffing. When Sylvia turned thirteen and her menses and secondary sexual characteristics began to appear, she suddenly became conscious of and concerned with her weight. She went on a very strict diet, starving herself so that she rapidly lost a considerable amount of weight. Afterwards she could no longer eat regularly and she suffered such a loss of appetite that her weight fell far below normal. She was hospitalized for a short time at age fourteen when it was considered that her life was in danger because of her loss of weight. She was force-fed for a brief period and then placed under the care of a psychiatrist. She remembered very little about the nature of this psychiatric treatment except that she talked to the doctor. Her appetite returned and she regained weight, but she remained slim throughout the rest of her adolescence.

At school Sylvia was an above-average student. She had many playmates but preferred to have them come to her house; rarely did she go to their houses. During adolescence she became more and more socially isolated. She did not learn to dance nor did she enjoy parties where there were boys. She never accepted a date. Her mother and grandmother began to worry about her and tried to encourage her to take some interest in boys, but whenever they started on the subject Sylvia would burst into tears and run to her own room. While relating her adolescent fear of boys and sex, Sylvia remembered that as a growing child she had somehow gained the impression from her grandmother and mother that sex was extremely painful, and possibly even dangerous. She was aware that her mother had become pregnant when Sylvia was about ten and had had an illegal abortion. The abortion left her mother quite ill for some time, and disrupted the entire household. When Sylvia had her first menstrual period, her grandmother slapped her face, which greatly frightened the child. Her mother explained that this was an "old country" custom, considered necessary in order to restore color to the girl's face because of the loss of blood. Thus, Sylvia understood her menstruation in terms of "the curse," a painful and embarrassing period to be endured. No other explanation regarding sex was ever given her, and she recognized the topic was entirely taboo in her family. One time when her father discovered that her older brother had a collection of pictures of nude women, he upbraided him for hours, and her brother had to destroy the pictures in the fireplace in front of the family.

Sylvia was nineteen and had finished high school and one year of business college when she met her husband. Her family had known Sid's family for many years but regarded the T.'s as beneath them socially. Sylvia met her husband through a girl friend who was going with Sid's younger brother. Sylvia's family was torn about the possibility of Sylvia and Sid getting married. Her grandmother and mother were very eager that she should marry, but they wanted the marriage to be a "good one." They disapproved of Sid because he was older and had been previously married and divorced, and also because his family had no social status. On the other hand, it was considered in his favor that Sid was presently making a good living. Sylvia, herself, did not know at the time what she actually wanted to do. The whole possibility of their getting married was discussed for many weeks by her parents and brothers and grandmother, shortly after Sylvia and Sid met, and long before Sid gave any indication that he was interested in marrying Sylvia. Finally her mother and grandmother decided that this could be a good marriage, and, thereafter, they encouraged Sid. Sid, in reporting his version of their courtship, laughed, saying he knew very well that he was being pulled into the marriage by Sylvia's mother and grandmother, but he enjoyed it as he was very much in love with Sylvia and liked Sylvia's mother. "It probably was really Sylvia's mother I was in love with, as she is a wonderful warm-hearted person and a topnotch cook." Sid would have preferred to have a quiet, civil ceremony, but his in-laws would have none of it, and planned an elaborate social wedding. Sid had made arrangements to rent an apartment, but on their wedding day Sylvia broke down in tears and confessed that she would be unable to leave her mother's home. Sid was almost ready to drop the whole marriage, but he was persuaded by Sylvia's mother to try the arrangement for a short while. For the next year-and-a-half Sid and Sylvia lived with her parents, using the bedroom Sylvia had as a child.

From the very start the couple had considerable difficulty sexually. Sylvia had had no sexual instruction or experience whatever; she reported that she does not believe that she even masturbated, although she later did remember that she was very much afraid that she might be caught masturbating. On the other hand, Sid readily admitted that he had had considerable sexual experience from the time of early adolescence and, of course, there was his previous marriage. He said that one of the most difficult problems of the first months of their marriage was that he could not really initiate his wife into such relations because of the lack of privacy in his mother-in-law's home. Not only was he afraid that they might be overheard, but he also knew that Sylvia would run and report everything to Queeny. He acknowledged that he always got along well with Queeny and with his father-in-law, but gradually, he began to feel that his in-laws were dominating his entire marital life. They inquired kindly but firmly about his business affairs and about personal expenses. Many times Sidney urged Sylvia to move into separate living quarters, but Sylvia would stubbornly refuse. The usual result was that she would become tearful and develop a headache. Despite their sexual difficulties Sylvia became pregnant approximately three months after their marriage, a pregnancy which resulted in Jerry's birth. Shortly after Jerry's birth Sid decided that once and for all they must make the break with Sylvia's parents, so he rented a separate apartment. With the help of his father-in-law he moved Sylvia's furniture into the new apartment. Sylvia was led by her mother from her home to the new apartment, both of them weeping all the while. Even after the couple was settled in the new apartment, Queeny continued to visit Sylvia daily; she helped to take care of the baby and did most of the housework. The hours that Sylvia's mother was not at her home, Sylvia was back at her parents' house. Sid found the situation intolerable but did not really know how to free her and himself from his in-laws. This situation continued for four more years until Sharon's birth.

Formerly, Sid had scarcely qualified as a social drinker, but now he started the habit of stopping in at the neighborhood bar after work. It was at the bar that he met a woman who confided to him that she was unhappy with her marriage, and coincidentally, she also lived in the same apartment house. Shortly after they began an affair, Sylvia learned of it from the neighbors. Indeed, neither Sid nor the other woman made any effort to cover up the relationship. Sylvia was extremely angry and depressed and threatened to return to her mother. Sid became contrite and guilt-ridden. Finally he convinced Sylvia that he had been unfaithful only in desperation and that he really wanted to continue with their marriage. Their rabbi advised Sylvia to forgive her husband and he supported Sidney in his determination to leave New York City to get away from Sylvia's parents. Very reluctantly Sylvia agreed, and the couple and their two children used the last of their savings to make the move to California. Almost immediately Sid found his present job, and soon he was earning enough for them to live quite comfortably. They bought a new development home and furnished it in the standard style. For a year or two they were busy and happy, although Sylvia remained depressed about the separation from her mother. New problems arose concerning the children and the extra demands of Sid's jobs. The final crisis in their family life was Sid's heart attack which threatened Sylvia extremely. She became very apprehensive that she might be left with two children to support, and she had no idea how she could ever manage to earn an income.

Sid was also born and reared in Brooklyn, also the youngest of three children, all boys. He remembered practically nothing of his early childhood. He had very little memory of his father, who died of tuberculosis when Sid was six. The family lived in extreme poverty, subsisting on government relief and also help from friends, neighbors, and the temple. His mother worked as a seamstress in one of the nearby clothing factories. Sid could not remember a period when he was not attempting to supplement the family income. He shined shoes, sold newspapers, ran errands, at times he even stole. He was often absent from school; by the time he was thirteen he had already made several appearances in juvenile court for being truant or for disobeying the curfew. At one time, he was convicted of petty theft in company with a gang of boys but was given in probation to the youth director of the neighborhood youth house. Both of his older brothers also had police records for minor delinquencies. "How we ever grew up without permanently becoming criminals I don't know." For the most part, Sid and his brothers were left to shift for themselves, for his mother was not home to cook meals or take care of the house. By the time she returned home late in the evening she was often too tired to do anything. She began to gamble with friends and often spent her weekends at the racetrack. She frequently came out ahead in her gambling, and on these occasions the family would be able to have extra clothing or have a small celebration. Otherwise Sidney had very little family life.

Sidney began having heterosexual relationships at a very early age, first with the neighborhood girls and later with prostitutes. He married a neighborhood girl when he was eighteen and left high school to get a job. Shortly thereafter, he was drafted into the army, just before the beginning of World War II. It was while he was overseas that his first wife wrote him that she was obtaining a divorce in order to marry someone else. Sid was embittered and, upon his return to civilian life, resolved to have nothing more to do with women. He went to night school and completed his high school education. Through some army buddies he obtained a fairly good job as a salesman in the plumbing business. He was thus earning a fair living at the time he met Sylvia. Although he was determined to remain single, he found that he was very attracted to Sylvia. He was very lonely and was happy to be welcomed into her home, which he readily admitted was the kind of family he had always dreamed of having. Regarding his own overweight, he reported that he had been excessively thin as a child and was extremely underweight when he went into the military service. He gained a considerable amount of weight in the service; "It was the first time I had good food and regular hours." He continued to gain weight on Queeny's and Sylvia's cooking.

Course in Treatment. Although the focal point of the T. family's complaints was Sharon, both Sylvia and Sid readily admitted that they themselves needed direct help with their own problems. They half-recognized that their own obvious anxieties were a strain on the children. At first Sid and Sylvia were treated by separate psychotherapists. In his treatment Sid began by trying to maintain that his behavior needed very little change, but that his wife was the one who was really "neurotic." However, in his behavior toward his therapist he was very much like a little boy, constantly asking for advice and making extravagant promises. As he described first his marital history and then his childhood, he began to understand how he was using his wife and family to satisfy some of his own emotional needs, without providing anything in return.

Sylvia spent most of her initial treatment hours reciting her complaints against her husband and children. Gradually, however, she began to realize that she was repeating much of the pattern with them that she had experienced in her own childhood. She denied vigorously that she had any resentment toward her mother for her overprotection, but then she remembered nightmares where she had dreamed of her mother's death, which had always made her feel guilty. Furthermore, when she recalled her grandmother's extreme overprotection of her uncle and her mother, she began to feel that perhaps in some way her mother's overprotection might have not been the "wonderful" thing that she really longed for. She began to admit that she had considerable hostility toward Sharon and she wished at times, secretly, that she had never had Sharon. At one point while she was admitting this, she wondered whether her mother had felt this way when she was born. Shortly after the time that she began to recognize some of these factors, she became quite resistant to treatment but was able to overcome her resistance, with some support. She recognized that there was a realistic problem of finances in the family and on her own initiative took the step of finding a job in a nearby manufacturing plant—the first time in her life she had worked outside her home. Her children were left a little more on their own and the housework seemed less important to her. She also began to share the responsibility of determining the budget with her husband; much to her surprise he proved very adequate to the job.

Sharon's psychotherapy was most stormy. She resented having to come at all. She refused to talk to her therapist, and at first it was even difficult to get her to enter the playroom. She played by herself in the corner, ignoring the doctor, spending considerable time with doll play. She spent many hours rearranging the doll furniture and taking care of the baby doll. When the therapist noticed that Sharon made use of the baby, father, and boy doll but no use of the mother doll, Sharon became very angry and said that she could not come back for further treatment. Later, Sharon picked up the mother doll and tried to drown it in the sink. She dropped it on the floor and "accidently" stepped on it. One day after "accidently" kicking the mother doll across the room she began to weep and then built an elaborate mausoleum in which to bury the mother doll. Sharon gradually began to talk to her doctor; she raised many side questions which indicated that she had an intense sexual curiosity. Sylvia was then encouraged to discuss some sexual matters with Sharon which Sylvia had ignored previously. Sylvia was made very anxious by this and was helped only by further discussion of her own sexual fears. At the end of the first year of treatment Sharon went on a voluntary diet and lost about fifteen pounds. Sylvia, remembering her own diet as a child, became fearful for Sharon, but she helped to support Sharon and watched closely the nature of the diet. Sid also returned to the diet prescribed for him. Sharon's school reported improvement in her behavior. At the end of the year of treatment Sharon's doctor left the clinic. Although Sharon's behavior had not altered to the point that her parents were completely satisfied, it was decided not to continue further treatment at that time. For the following year Sid and Sylvia were seen jointly by the same therapist as a means of permitting them to work out some of their common problems. At the end of this year, much of their marital tension had abated and both of the children seemed to be adjusting at home and school without any serious difficulties. Sylvia calculated that the four of them had successfully lost a total of one hundred pounds in weight, without discomfort.

Questions for the T. Family

1. Make a list on a sheet of paper with two headings, one for Sidney and one for Sylvia as follows:

       Sidney T.   Sylvia T.

Under each heading list the treatment experienced by each individual during their early home environment with regard to:
     a. gratification and frustration of dependency needs
     b. handling of aggressive expression
     c. training and introduction to sex
2. Which needs or drives appear to you to have been excessively

gratified for each individual and which appear to have been frustrated and associated with anxiety? Can you, from your answer, explain the eating behavior of the T. family?

3. If we look exclusively at the area of dependency (i.e. satisfaction of the need for help and support while young), what contrast do we see between Sidney and Sylvia?

4. How did these contrasting experiences shape the personalities of each individual? (*Hint:* Seek out material in your text or in the research literature which contrasts the effects of excessive dependency gratification with the effects of deprivation of dependency needs on personality development.)

5. Looking at their marital relationships, in what way could you say that these contrasting childhood environments provided a crucial source of conflict for Sylvia and Sidney?

6. In what ways might Sidney's and Sylvia's conflicts have influenced their treatment of Jerry and Sharon?

7. From your reading in the text or in other sources, what three hypotheses can you raise about the basis for maternal overprotection? (See Levy's article "Maternal Overprotection" for a good summary of the basis for maternal overprotection.) Which of these hypotheses best accounts for Sylvia's treatment of Sharon?

8. How can you account for the fact that Sylvia and her daughter demonstrated similar behavior patterns when they were young?

9. From the brief descriptions of Sylvia's and Sharon's psychotherapy as well as the background history, what hypotheses can you raise to account for Sharon's school phobia?

10. When attempting to understand the dynamics of family relationships, it is helpful to spell out the needs of each individual and the degree to which they are gratified by the significant individuals in their family. In an attempt to integrate all of your previous answers, fill in the blank in the following pairs of incomplete sentences. When you finish, if done correctly, the incompatibility in need-gratification within the T. family should be clear. Feel free to use more than single word answers in doing your completions.

1.   *a.* Sylvia desired .... from her mother.
     b. Sylvia received .... from her mother.

2.   *a.* Sidney desired .... from his mother.
     b. Sidney received .... from his mother.

3. *a.* Sylvia desired .... from Sidney.
   b. Sylvia received .... from Sidney.

4. *a.* Sidney desired .... from Sylvia.
   b. Sidney received .... from Sylvia.

5. *a.* Sharon desired .... from her mother.
   b. Sharon received .... from her mother.

6. *a.* Sharon desired .... from her father.
   b. Sharon received .... from her father.

11. In psychoanalytic theory, the T. family would be considered "oral" personalities.
   a. List the behavior of each of the T.'s (in addition to excessive food consumption) which might be classified as "oral."
   b. What factors in each of their lives led them to "regress to oral" behavior in the face of stress?
   c. What aspects of their culture promote use of this defense?

12. Although this report dealt almost exclusively with the conflicts *within* the T. family, it is very likely that their anxieties impinged on their relationships outside their home. Imagine, if you will, how each of the following might have reacted to the T.'s. What might these other persons do to exacerbate or ameliorate the T.'s anxieties, within the limits of their respective social roles?
   a. Sid's employer
   b. the T. family's rabbi (at present)
   c. Sid's physician
   d. Sharon's schoolteacher

References

Baam, I. Psychic factors in obesity: observations in over 1000 cases. *Archives of Pediatrics,* 1950, **67**: 543–552.

Bowen, M. The family as the unit of study and treatment: I. Family psychotherapy. *American Journal of Orthopsychiatry,* 1961, **31**: 40–60.

Levy, D. *Maternal overprotection.* New York: Columbia Univer. Press, 1943.

Parloff, M. The family in psychotherapy. *Archives of General Psychiatry,* 1961, **4**: 445–451.

THE CASE OF JACK F.

This Boy Will Self-Destruct

Jack, age sixteen, was brought to the clinic by his parents on the advice of Jack's probation officer. He had been arrested for the third time for possession of marijuana, and his parents were furious. The court at this time was almost adamant that Jack be removed from the family and placed in a correctional camp for delinquents. However, the probation officer and the family attorney had argued with the court successfully that if the family were willing to seek psychological help for Jack, the probation would be continued rather than having him put in the camp.

Jack, a slim blond youngster with a fairly severe case of acne, greeted the psychologist with a silent scowl. His jeans were ripped and his shirt food-stained, his bare feet were caked with dirt. In contrast his father was in a formal business suit, and his mother wore an expensive knit dress.

The parents began by reciting a lot of accusations against the boy as if they were his prosecutors in court. He had never been well behaved; he was always sullen; he didn't carry out the garbage; he wouldn't do anything; he wouldn't speak to anybody; he wouldn't eat with the family; and, worst of all, he was always in trouble. He had a record of five arrests: three for possession of marijuana and two for "trespass." The father at times threw up his hands and said he didn't know what to do with Jack anymore and maybe it really would be better if he went to "camp." However, they would give him this "one last try." The father said he had been to every expense and he didn't know what else to do. Jack then spoke up and said, "You can buy me a car," at which time the father exploded and left the room. The mother was also quite angry, near tears, biting her lip, and saying very little. She mentioned that she was very hurt that Jack paid no attention to her needs or her demands. She was hurt that he would not eat her cooking, even though she went to extra steps to try to please his appetite. He also fought constantly with his younger sister, hid in his room with food and dirty dishes all over the place, and would not let her into his room.

Jack said he didn't want to be there, that he might as well be in "camp." He refused to talk about anything further at that time. To any question he replied, "Ask my parents . . . they'll tell you . . . they know everything . . . I'm not going to say anything."

The parents were then seen individually. Each of them readily admitted that Jack was not their only problem. The father said that he was about to divorce his wife because she was a "neurotic." He blamed everything on his wife saying that it was her depression, her neurosis, her ill temper that disturbed the child and that he could not live with either one of them any longer. The mother was equally angry at her husband. According to her, he had in effect abandoned the family and paid no attention to any of their problems. She admitted that she tried to keep things from her husband because she felt everything would upset him and that their marriage "was fast going on the rocks." She tended to blame the child for the marital difficulties saying that up until a few years ago when Jack was about twelve or thirteen their marriage had been relatively happy. However, in a subsequent interview she broke down in tears and admitted their marriage had been unhappy before Jack's birth.

The mother also said that Jack had always been a "difficult child to deal with"; he was resistant from the moment he was born; he was difficult to toilet train, and she did not succeed until he was almost four; he wet the bed until he was about twelve; she could never get him to do what she wanted; and she was always at a loss. She felt that his father had never done anything to discipline him but was always preoccupied with his own activities. She said that Jack's behavior had really only grown worse over the years.

After the initial interview, Jack did talk more about his family. He was extremely bitter about his father, repeating some of his mother's accusations. He complained that his father left early in the morning for work and did not return until early in the evening. He also complained that dinner was never on the table until almost 8 o'clock at night at which time "I'm starved." On weekends, his father was either tinkering with his sports car, or in his garden, or in his shop in the garage. He also spent a great deal of time playing golf with his fellow engineers and other people at the firm where he was a minor executive. The father also frequently went on business trips across the country and around the world, conducting engineering surveys. When Jack was 12 his father spent nine months in Saudi Arabia; his mother refused to accompany him although it would have been financially possible. Jack felt that his father paid no attention to him except when his mother demanded that his father discipline him. Except for this discipline, Jack said that there would be no difficulty with his father. Yet he complained that his father would become outraged over what Jack regarded as petty matters such as carrying out the trash. His mother, in fact, frequently carried out the trash in order to avoid a hassle between father and son. About his mother, she is "constantly on my back." If he spilled a little milk when he got his afternoon snack, she would be after him immediately to have it mopped up. He could not stand her constant nagging and her depression. He said that he knew very well that his mother and father were in constant disagreement over every little thing. Like his father he called his mother a "neurotic." By this Jack meant that his mother seemed always to be in tears, to be quite irritable, and to just "give up." Jack admitted that he did fight with his sister, but he was also worried about her. He said his sister also spent a considerable amount of time in her room. She tried to be a very good girl but got no rewards for it. Jack said with a smile, "I get more attention by being bad."

Although the delinquent behavior had been the main source of difficulty, it soon appeared that Jack was having many problems at school. He attended school very irregularly, but the parents had not responded to the school's complaints until Jack was finally expelled approximately a week after he came to the clinic. The father again was furious, but he paid little attention to the fact that Jack might be having problems at school. He complained again about expense and cited as an example that Jack had lost a costly leather jacket that the father had bought only a few weeks ago when school began. Jack's response had nothing to do with what his father was talking about. He seemed to defend himself by saying that he had difficulty in getting to school which was about four miles from home. It was all his mother's fault. She didn't awaken him in time for the bus. Then she refused to drive him so he had to hitchhike to school and was frequently late. She did not fix breakfast, and he had no lunch money. He then would be held over after school by the school authorities. He had missed so much school over the last several years that he was quite behind in his work. Jack felt very stupid and inadequate declaring, that he never could understand what the teachers wanted. However, the school reports from his elementary school years showed that he had made B's and C's and a few A's, and his academic skills as measured by tests were within the normal to above-normal range.

During his junior high school years Jack often felt very isolated and had few friends. He had begun to associate with a group of youngsters who were "into the drug scene." By using drugs, Jack was tolerated by this group. He placated them by obtaining marijuana and other drugs. Jack had first tried marijuana when he was about 12 years old, before most of his friends had their first drug experience. Thus he came into the group as an oldtimer in use of drugs. Within a year he had tried both the amphetamines and LSD. The first time he was arrested, Jack and his friends were gathered in a public park in the evening where they had been smoking "grass" and someone had passed him some "acid." When the police investigated this group everyone fled. Jack was so "stoned" that he was unable to plan any escape and ran at random, dashing after the other youngsters. He tried to climb into a car in which the youngsters were driving off but fell backwards, and his foot was run over. He was dragged to the city jail by the police, in considerable pain. He did not mention to the police that his foot had been crushed because he did not really want to give his name or other identification. Many hours passed before the police were finally able to convince him that his parents were needed before he could receive any kind of medical treatment. When his parents did arrive they were so upset over his arrest that initially they did not realize he was injured. Several hours passed before his broken foot was attended to. Jack never forgot this incident and used it over and over again to cite how little his parents cared for him and what "criminals" the police really were.

Despite his adventuresome drug use, Jack really was not on the "in" of the group of teenagers he associated with. Although there were several homes he visited quite frequently, especially if he had been kept after school and didn't want to answer any questions from his parents, he admitted that there was no one he could count on as a "real" friend. Thus, when he hung around the home of one or two other youths who were in the same general crowd, he often sat off in the corner unable to enter the conversation. He felt left out but made no move of his own to join in the laughter and teasing and "horsing around." He admitted he felt ugly and stupid and unwanted by the others. Frequently he was the butt of jokes and would become so angry that he would strike out; then he would be thrown out bodily and not allowed back for days. By the time he was in the ninth grade, many of his friends had girl friends and a few were having heterosexual experiences. Jack was very shy and felt no girl would be attracted to him. He was very envious of his friends who boasted of their sexual exploits and tried to pretend that he too had "made out" with various girls; when faced with the truth, however, he would be laughed out of the crowd.

Jack's worst memory was of his friends reporting that they knew that his father had a girlfriend. He pretended that he knew about this all along, but he was actually very embarrassed to learn it from his friends rather than knowing about it directly. Jack found himself more and more preoccupied with sexual fantasies and obsessively masturbated, particularly when he was unable to find friends to be with for the evening. The second time he was arrested was when his father smelled the marijuana he was smoking in his room and called the police. Jack was furious because he considered his father more of a criminal for being unfaithful to his mother than any crime he was committing by using drugs. However, he was far too embarrassed to say anything about the knowledge of his father's behavior.

After Jack had been arrested twice he was well known to the police. He had been put on probation twice and was thus under surveillance. He no longer spent much time in anyone's home but became more and more a lone wolf. He would go miles from home, down to the beach, up in the hills, with nothing to do but rage at the whole world. Several times he thought of suicide but had not made up his mind how he would go about it. His trespass arrest came when he thought he was spotted by the police who were cruising the neighborhood where he was walking alone. He ran off into the bushes and tried to sit quietly, but the owner of the home thought he was a peeping-tom and called in the police who again captured him. Each time his father bailed him out with dire threats of letting him go on to jail. Each time the probation officer explained to the court that Jack was emotionally disturbed and needed treatment, but the parents did not follow upon the court's recommendation. The probation officer reported the situation to the court but so far no action was taken.

Family Background. Although there was almost enough information about the distresses in the current family situation to explain a great deal of Jack's behavior, the psychologist who was assigned to work with Jack believed that it would be necessary also to work with the parents and thus decided to explore further some of their background in order to understand the whole family problem.

THE FATHER: Jack's father had been given the name Tremont when he was born but was so teased by his classmates that he initiated the nickname Ted. Ted, the youngest of 12 children, came from a very poor family in the Appalachian hills of West Virginia. His father was both a farmer and a minister. Ted remembered receiving harsh discipline and little affection from both his parents. He completed high school with high honors, but no one appreciated his achievement. He was a slight built youngster who was never very successful at sports and thus received no special acclaim from his classmates. He was almost glad when he was drafted into the Army in the Korean conflict for it meant a chance to get away from his home. While in training in the Army, he met his current wife, Dorothy, at a dance and subsequently had his first sexual experience with her. He felt so very guilty about this that he insisted that they be married before he went overseas. Dorothy agreed to this marriage, but they had to be married secretly since her family objected considerably. Her family were well-to-do "pillars of the community" who considered her affair with this soldier to be at best a lark; they were dreadfully shocked when they found that the youngsters had married.

Ted then went to Korea where he was in the front lines. He was advanced with the American troops to the Yalu River where the Americans were subsequently defeated and driven back. During the retreat in the snow, he froze one foot and lost his toes. He was awarded medals for his valor and conduct but was embittered by this experience since, he later said, he never understood why the Americans were in Korea in the first place. He continued to have a slight limp and always felt that the military had really done him an injustice. Upon discharge from the military he immediately went to college, and for the first time he and Dorothy set up housekeeping. Dorothy, disowned by her family, went to work to support them while Ted went through college. Her salary and his pension allowed them to get by. However, they agreed they would have no children while Ted was in college. Even after he got his engineering degree and found a good job Dorothy decided to continue to work until they got established. Dorothy had been used to a fine home and cars and luxurious living, and Ted was determined to give these to her. Thus some six to eight years went by before Jack was born. In the meantime Ted had obtained a high paying engineering position and was able to make a down payment on a large and expensive home and to buy both himself and Dorothy expensive cars. However, he was deeply in debt by the time Jack was born and continued to pile up debt after debt during the next 16 years. It seemed to Ted that nothing ever really got paid for. By the time he had purchased the equipment needed for their house, the various appliances needed repair or replacement. Periodically he needed a better looking, more sporty and expensive car in order to compete with his fellow executives. The day before Jack's last arrest they told him at the garage that his sports car needed a complete overhaul which cost $500. Ted was quite depressed and worried as to how he could possibly meet this expense on top of his mounting monthly bills.

THE MOTHER: Dorothy was the only daughter of a well-to-do merchant in a small city in Georgia. She was pampered and petted as a child by her parents as well as her two brothers who were quite a bit older than she. She was called "the little princess." She was a beautiful child, and pictures of her throughout her childhood hung in the family home. She had never known deprivation of any kind. At the same time it was almost silently understood that she would conform to the mores of upper-class southern country life. She had many friends and enjoyed her teenage years. Yet she disliked most of the boys she had met, particularly because her brothers continually reminded her that none of them were good enough for her. She had avoided any sexual adventures, although many of her male companions pressured her continuously. She found it very difficult to explain how it was that she became engaged in this sexual adventure with a man who was really a stranger, who was a young soldier from a nearby camp. "Maybe there was more rebel in me than I thought," she sighed as she related her life history to the psychologist. At first she did not want to marry Ted hoping that the whole adventure could be forgotten. Yet she was very much attracted to him. She thought his country ways quite strange but enchanting. He was more easy going and less socially conscious than most of her friends and family, and she felt she could relax with him. After the runaway marriage she returned home to introduce Ted to her father who rejected the whole idea of the marriage. Before the couple could decide what to do about it, Ted was transferred overseas. Dorothy returned to live with her family who tried to ignore the whole situation. Once Dorothy's father attempted to get the marriage annulled, but Dorothy was too proud to "admit I made a mistake" and rejected the idea of the annullment. "I really didn't feel trapped into the marriage but I must admit I might not have taken up with Ted again had I not been too proud to kneel to my father's dictates," Dorothy reported. At first Dorothy enjoyed the whole change of life style, of being the poor student's wife who went to work. All the time she really had the feeling that this was an adventure rather than a necessity. It really had never occurred to her that if she did not work she would not be taken care of. After Ted completed school and started working she really wanted to have a child but realized that they were not quite ready financially. However, Ted encouraged her to quit work, and soon afterward Jack was born.

Dorothy never knew much about Ted's finances as he kept his books to himself. She bought everything on credit, and although at times Ted seemed quite upset when the bills came in, he never really complained to her. Initially she enjoyed caring for her baby but really didn't know much about child care and housekeeping. Ted insisted that she have household help, and so she often found herself idle and wondering what to do. The F.'s had moved to a suburb of a large city where Ted worked. Most of the other people knew one another and she was not really a member of the in-group in the community in which they lived. She found it difficult to make new friends. She occasionally joined her husband in social events connected with his work, but she did not really know how to entertain. She finally made one or two friends among the wives of Ted's fellow workers and spent time shopping or just coffeeing with these women, but mostly she was quite alone and lonely. The birth of her daughter four years after they moved to the suburbs seemed to give her a second lease on life. She really identified with this little girl. Dorothy felt at ease doing feminine things with the daughter, and the two of them spent many hours together.

Dorothy had felt particularly helpless trying to raise a boy. Even when Jack was very young it seemed that he was always in mischief or causing some kind of trouble. She wished that she had more help from her husband, but Ted always seemed too busy to pay much attention to the children. As Ted grew more busy and was away from home more hours, Dorothy experienced increasing loneliness and became very angry at him. Very often when the two of them were together they drank quite heavily, and their quarrels increased. Dorothy also found her drinking was increasing during the daytime. Although she was never really drunk, she often went around the house with a glass in her hand or would join her friends in the afternoon at some bar where she would drink. To add to Dorothy's unhappiness, her father, whom she had not seen for years, had died approximately two years ago. Dorothy went to the funeral where she was upbraided by her mother for being the cause of her father's death. She thus feared that her father had died of a broken heart because she had rejected him.

Course of Treatment. Initially the psychologist brought the family together hoping to center on the family interactions that were creating the immediate stress for Jack. However, Jack was unable to say a word to either of his parents who continued to point accusing fingers at him and list his "crimes" for the week. His father grew more and more angry when Jack would not respond and declared that it seemed hopeless for everyone to be there. He insisted that the psychologist see Jack separately rather than in family sessions. The mother at times tried to intervene between Jack and the father whereupon the father then would turn upon her accusing her of coddling the boy and making too many excuses for him. In each succeeding family session the parents fell to quarreling between themselves, exchanging vituperative accusations. Initially Jack's thirteen-year-old sister was invited to join these family sessions, but she soon refused to enter the room. Finally the psychologist insisted the whole family be present. Both parents continued to contrast Cindy's success and good behavior against Jack's constant troubles. Cindy said almost nothing and crouched in the corner of the couch up against her father. When the parents began to quarrel Cindy would dash from the room and refuse to return. Dorothy explained that Cindy had a nervous stomach, and tension made her vomit. The family had always considered Cindy to be quite frail and had protected her a great deal. She had been ill from time to time throughout her childhood but no clearcut diagnosis was ever made of her illnesses. Like her mother and Jack, she had few friends and often spent hours propped up in bed ill, reading or watching television.

The psychologist did yield to the family's insistance that Jack be seen separately, particularly since Jack also requested this. However, the psychologist tried to get the family to continue the family sessions as well. Several times the father was out of town and missed the sessions. The others in the family said it was useless to come unless the father was there since he did most of the talking. They seemed unable to initiate any conversation without him present. The psychologist remarked that this seemed strange since all of them quarreled with the father. Several times no one appeared for the family sessions except Jack who then pointed out to the psychologist how useless it was to do anything about his family. Finally one evening the family gathered, and Jack did not appear. The father then announced he was not going to return to the sessions unless Jack cooperated. When his wife pointed out to him that he had missed several sessions, Ted was furious with her saying that she had no idea how hard he worked to support her and the children and that she was a spoiled rich woman who was becoming a drunk. Dorothy began to weep; Cindy rushed from the room, and Ted also left. Jack continued to appear for several individual sessions over the next four or five weeks. Thereafter he frequently canceled or merely did not appear. After Jack had missed several sessions in a row the psychologist called the home and was advised curtly by Dorothy that Jack and his father had moved out of the home and she hoped she never saw them again.

Approximately a year and a half later the psychologist received a call from Ted who then came in for an appointment. He looked very depressed, and said that now he really felt he needed some help. He did not seem nearly as angry or as skeptical about the possibility of getting some help from the psychologist. Instead he explained that he himself had become depressed and upset, that he had moved out of his home that he had treasured so much to a small apartment where Jack soon followed him. He had hoped by separating from Dorothy that he could live more peacefully. He admitted that he had been carrying on an affair with the ex-wife of one of his associates but that he was not really interested in this woman either. He had hoped to become closer to Jack, but this proved to no avail. When he returned home in the evenings, Jack had either already disappeared or would soon leave. Jack did not help him at all with the care of the apartment, and Ted found himself being housemaid to Jack. He realized that he did not know whether or not Jack was going to school. Moreover, he was more and more aware that Jack was using drugs quite heavily. He hoped the psychologist would see Jack again and apologized for his behavior in the family sessions previously.

Soon afterward Jack did call the psychologist for an appointment. He seemed quite depressed and more willing to talk about his troubles. He did not seem nearly as angry with his father, but he was furious with his mother. He had tried several times to visit her, but she would not even let him in the house. He had become more aware of his father's financial problems and more sympathetic with him. Yet he found it extremely difficult to make any day-to-day living arrangements with his father. He agreed that he probably should help more around the apartment. However, he came in constant conflict with his father whenever they were home together and thus was not motivated at all to pay attention to his father's demands. Ted in turn became increasingly angry that Jack would leave the house in such a mess and continued to call the psychologist, tattling on Jack. Jack's greatest concern at this time was his new-found girl friend, Debbie. He seemed deeply in love with Debbie and spent every moment he could with her. Her parents were becoming very upset with his infatuation over their daughter and tried to insist that Debbie not allow him to monopolize her. Finally Debbie's parents would not permit him to come to their home or for her to leave the home in the evening except on weekends. Jack spent hours sitting in the street across from Debbie's home or trying to telephone her. He attended school only because he could see her there, but he paid no attention to any of his lessons. Debbie highly disapproved of Jack's use of drugs and alcohol and up until the time that he was not allowed to go to her house he had stopped using drugs. Now he was more frequently drunk and often got into fights with other teenagers. The school several times had tried to contact Ted because of Jack's low school achievement, but Ted had not responded to their messages. Finally, after a bloody fight in the schoolyard, Jack was expelled from school. Jack's jaw was broken and he almost blinded another youngster. Again Jack was furious at his father because his father was more concerned about his poor school record and was unsympathetic about the pain that Jack was experiencing. Jack's contacts with the psychologist at this time lasted approximately four months. Jack turned 18 and declared that he was not returning to treatment any longer since he was no longer on probation and no longer under his father's authority.

Approximately a year later Ted again called the psychologist. Jack had tried living on his own by moving in with various other teenagers but never found sufficient employment to pay his own way. Several times he had moved back in with his father, but this had not worked either. Now Jack seemed quite ill and depressed and was spending all day and all night in his room in his father's apartment. The father said this was intolerable since he was now remarried and did not want his new home disturbed by Jack. The previous night Jack had tried to beat his way into his mother's home, and his mother had called the police. Thereafter Jack was discovered in the park comotose and taken to the emergency room. He had evidently consumed large amounts of unknown drugs and was barely alive. In the subsequent days his life seemed to hang in the balance and finally he began to recover. Ted was really reluctant to pay for anymore psychotherapy, but felt very guilty about Jack's condition and agreed to finance any further therapy that the psychologist thought Jack could use. Jack made an appointment with the psychologist but never kept it. Four days later Jack was dead on arrival at the hospital from an overdose of drugs.

Questions for Jack F.

1. What do you feel were the basic conflicts in Jack F.'s life?

  a. What needs or drives appear to have been frustrated and associated with anxiety?

  b. What appear to be the stimuli in Jack's environment which were eliciting these emotions or drives?

  c. What psychological defenses had Jack developed to reduce this anxiety level? Why did these defenses fail?

2. Depression during adolescence is often characterized by extreme swings in mood (i.e., restlessness and boredom) which manifest themselves in acting-out behavior.

  a. What acting-out behavior did Jack employ?

  b. What other evidence would suggest that Jack was suffering from depression? (Review the clinical characteristics of adolescent depression.)

  c. What specific events contributed to this disorder?

3. What was Jack trying to express during the years he continued to wet the bed? What do you feel was the reason that Jack stopped wetting the bed at age 12?

4. Compare Jack's sex-dating patterns with those of his peers at the time Jack entered the clinic. In what ways were Jack's sexual needs expressed and gratified? How were they frustrated?

5. Discuss the implications of Jack's heterosexual relationship with Debbie and the effect this had on his subsequent behavior.

6. Quite often a pattern of psychopathology can be understood through a matrix of interpersonal relationships in which it exists. Discuss the following:

  a. Jack's relationship with his mother

  b. Jack's relationship with his father

  c. Jack's feelings about his sister

  d. Jack's feelings about each parent individually

  e. Ted's feelings about Jack

  f. Dorothy's feelings about Jack.

7. In order to obtain a clearer understanding of the present family situation, it was necessary to investigate the background of each parent.

  a. What effect did the attitudes and values of Ted's parents ultimately have on his role as a husband and father?

    b. Discuss the circumstances that surrounded Ted's marriage to Dorothy. Take the following into account: (1) Ted's sexual conflict and the effect this eventually had on Jack's sexual growth (2) the social background of each parent.

    c. Consider the following: Dorothy's loneliness during her marriage; her inability to make friends; her indulgence in alcohol; Ted's trip abroad for nine months; the final separation between Ted and Dorothy. What effect did these ultimately have upon Jack?

8. After reviewing the background of Jack's parents, can you understand why they were inadequate in performing their parental roles? How was Jack affected by this? With whom did he identify?

9. According to your text, what are the criteria for classifying a drug abuser? What drives or emotions seemed to be operating around the time Jack began taking drugs?

10. What are some possible underlying reasons for attempting suicide? Support the thesis that Jack's death was an example of suicide rather than merely an "accidental" or "unintentional" overdose.

11. Consider the circumstances under which Jack sought treatment. If the court had decided to send Jack to "camp," do you feel the outcome of this case might have been different? Can you suggest a course of treatment which might have ultimately prevented Jack's death?

12. From the information presented in this case, what problems will Jack's sister eventually experience? What current forces seem to be operating that would lend support to your prediction?

References

ADLER, P. T., & LOTECA, L. Drug use among high school students: patterns and correlates. *International Journal of the Addictions*, 1973, **8**: 537–548.

BURKS, H. L., & HARRISON, S. I. Aggressive behavior as a means of avoiding depression. *American Journal of Psychiatry*, 1962, **32**: 416–422.

CHWAST, J. Depressive reactions as manifested among adolescent delinquents. *American Journal of Psychotherapy*, 1967, **21**: 575–584.

GLASER, K. Masked depression in children and adolescents. *American Journal of Psychotherapy*, 1967, **21**: 565–574.

HETHERINGTON, E. M., & MARTIN, B. Family interaction and psychopathology in children. In QUAY, H. O. & WERRY, J. S. (Eds.), *Psychopathological disorders of childhood*. New York: Wiley, 1972, Pp. 30–82.

HORMAN, R. E. Alienation and student drug abuse. *International Journal of the Addictions*, 1973, 8: 325–331.

LITMAN, R. E. Suicide as acting-out. In SHNEIDMAN, E. S., FARBEROW, N. L. & LITMAN, R. E. (Eds.) *The psychology of suicide*. New York: Science House, 1970, Pp. 293–304.

PAPANEK, E. Management of the acting-out adolescent. *American Journal of Psychotherapy*, 1964, 18: 418–434.

ROSENBAUM, M., & RICHMAN, J. Suicide: the role of hostility and death wishes from the family and significant others. *American Journal of Psychiatry*, 1970, 126: 128.

TEICHER, J. D. A solution to the chronic problem of living: adolescent attempted suicide. In SCHOOLER, J. C. (Ed.) *Current Issues in Adolescent Psychiatry*, New York: Brunner/Maxel, 1973, P. 146.

VOGEL, E. F., & BELL, N. F. The emotionally disturbed child as a family scapegoat. *Psychoanalysis and the Psychoanalytic Review*, 1960, 47: 21–52.

WEINER, I. B. *Psychological Disturbance in Adolescence*. New York: Wiley-Interscience, 1970, Pp. 157–202.

THE CASE OF MARYANNE H.

What It Means To Be a Woman

Mrs. H., who had been in treatment in the clinic for about a year for her depression and insomnia, asked her doctor if someone in the clinic could examine her daughter, Maryanne, age 16. She was not sure that Maryanne really needed any special therapy, but had noticed that over the past several months, she had not seemed her usual exuberant self, but had been listless and dispirited. She was most troubled by Maryanne's complaint that she believed that one of her legs was longer than the other. Maryanne even complained of slight pain and began to limp. However, physical examination revealed no abnormality of her leg. An appointment was made for Maryanne to see another staff member.

While Mrs. H. herself was a rather pretty woman, she dressed in a rather dowdy fashion. Maryanne, in contrast, looked like a model who posed for a magazine cover. She had long blonde hair and was dressed in an old shirt and cutoff trousers. She stood, walked, and sat with a natural seductiveness of a 16-year-old girl. Every male turned his head as she walked by; every woman exclaimed over her with envy. She appeared unconscious of the immediate attention people gave her physical beauty. Her naturalness and unaffected manner and her flashing smile only added to her attractiveness.

She entered the psychologist's room and sat slumped slightly in the chair, her arms over her breasts—almost as if to hide them. She seemed rather anxious, mentioning that she was not quite sure why she needed to come to see the psychologist at all. When she was asked about her physical complaint, she said that she knew that many people had one arm or one leg slightly longer than the other, and she had studied her physique and was quite sure that she had a mild dysplasia. She seemed familiar with medical terms and went on to say that she was not quite sure how one leg had grown longer than the other, but that she was aware of it and at times it gave her a slight pain. She could not say what in particular brought on the pain but that it seemed a bit irregular and sometimes she even had headaches and nausea accompanying this pain. She could not explain why the physician's measurements had not revealed any differences in the length of her legs. At times she wondered if her mild pain sensations were "psycho," but they were very real to her and she was concerned about her condition. Her physical development had been quite normal as far as she knew. She could not remember having any significant illnesses or injuries and had always been very physically active and agile. She was a medal winner in swimming and was becoming an expert in tennis; she suffered no pain when engaged in either of these athletics. She loved to play softball and she admitted, blushing, that she often played touch-football. Recently her father had prohibited her from entering this activity on the streets and in the parks.

When she mentioned her father her face grew grim and angry, and she said that perhaps the real reason she needed to see a psychologist was her current "war" with her father. She said that ever since she entered high school a year ago, her father had become exceedingly restrictive of all of her activities. He questioned her every move, especially when she left the house. He demanded that she set a time to return, wanted to meet every companion, both boys and girls, and was constantly suspicious of her activities. "I think he feels that every boy is going to ball me and that I will be pregnant next week." "I think *he's* the dirty old man." She denied that she had had any sexual experience, "not even making out." She was also angry at her older half-brother who also intimated that she was sexually promiscuous and who also tried to stand guard over her. Maryanne was almost in tears as she discussed this topic, vouching that she was "a good Christian" who went to church every Sunday and to prayer meeting every Wednesday night and who sang in the choir. "I will never let a boy touch me until I get married." Yet she was also angry because she had overheard some of the women in the church discussing her and intimating that they thought she might be sexually active. "Everybody thinks I'm a whore." "The truth is my little sister, Lisa, who is only 14 is playing around with the boys far more than I would dare to." The entire previous day her father had not spoken to her after an intense quarrel the night before. She explained that she had gotten ready for bed and decided to come down and give him a kiss. She had not put her robe on and was dressed only in a nightgown. He lept to his feet and cursed her for "going around the house with no clothes on" and ordered her immediately to bed. She had wept half the night wondering how she had offended him.

Maryanne's responses to the psychological tests showed her to be an intellectually brilliant youngster (IQ 141) who was also very emotionally sensitive and spontaneous. She had a creative mind and a social awareness far beyond her years. She had usually made A's in all her classes from first grade to her current time in her junior year in high school. Her fantasies were like those of many young girls: quite romantic, with the usual daydreams about courtship and marriage. For example, to Card 11 of the TAT (the picture of a snake-like creature coming from a cliff), she told a story about the ancient dragon who guarded the beautiful princess and was able to dispose of unwanted lovers one by one. But when the princess saw the lover that she desired, she distracted the dragon, and the hero was able to carry away the princess. On a projective test in which a person is asked to draw a picture of a house, a tree, and a person, she drew a large house in which there were a couple and many children and decorated it with many flowers and plants. Her tree contained a hole just before the branches separated from the trunk in which she drew a bird's nest. Her drawing of a person was of an idealized surfer with broad shoulders and a hairy chest. She was a fair artist and everything was drawn in detail. None of her test responses suggested any gross emotional disturbance, although a few of her stories and associations did indicate that she had depressive moments.

As far as Maryanne could remember, her life had always been very happy. Her father made an excellent living as an insurance salesman. "He sold over a million dollars' worth," she boasted. The family lived in a large, nice home, with three cars and a swimming pool. Besides Maryanne, there were her parents, Debbie age 14, Scott age 10, and her half-brother Phil, who had only lived with them the past year while going to college, having lived with his own mother during his childhood years. Maryanne could not remember anything that had been unhappy previously in her childhood. She and Debbie did quarrel occasionally, but they were really very close and shared the same room and the same secrets. Scotty was a pesty little brother, but she often took care of him when he was little, and he called her his "second mother." She said that as he was getting older he was "a disgusting male" but she could not explain what she meant by this and blushed. She could not remember exactly when her father's restrictiveness began, but she believed that it occurred when she entered high school. She could not remember any particular incident during her junior high school that was at all comparable to the way he was behaving to her currently. When asked directly about her own physical development, she blushed again but readily explained that she had her menarche when she was about 12 and that her figure had developed since. She then admitted that she was quite uncomfortable at the way that many men and boys looked at her. "You'd think that all a girl had was sex by the way they look at you," she said. She admitted that she, of course, was interested in boys and there were several boys that she considered to be boyfriends, but that her father prohibited her from seeing them except at school, or home, or well-chaperoned parties. She admitted that some boys had made very open sexual propositions to her, and that even at the church parties "the boys seemed to be all hands." Just the previous week she had slapped a boy so hard she almost knocked him to the ground because he had put his hand on her breast. "I don't really do anything to make them do that, Doctor, honestly, I don't." The psychologist then asked her if she had looked in the mirror. She flushed and said, "I can't help it, no matter what I do or how I dress people are going to think the worse of me." She and her mother had purposely picked out a modest ankle length gown to wear to church, but the women at church still remarked on the way that she stood and walked. She wore unattractive clothes, but they even made her look more sexy. As she described the constant attention she received she was near tears.

Family Background. No particular effort was made originally with Maryanne to obtain a history of her family background, since this did not seem particularly appropriate to the problem she was having. Of course, such a history had been given by the mother for the purposes of her treatment. The psychologist noted, although Mrs. H. looked like she was in her mid-forties, she was actually only 31 years old, which revealed that she was only 15 when Maryanne was born.

Further on in the history Mrs. H. revealed that she had become pregnant in a romance with a young high school teacher who was already married. Her father threatened a criminal prosecution if the teacher did not leave his wife and marry her. The couple were married under this threat, although as far as Mrs. H. knew her husband was very much in love with her. Maryanne was the result of this pregnancy. There was no indication in Mrs. H.'s report as to whether Maryanne was herself aware of the conditions surrounding her birth. However, in a subsequent interview when Maryanne mentioned her half-brother, she was questioned a little further about what she knew of her father's previous marriage, and Maryanne readily revealed that she was quite aware of how her mother had become pregnant while in high school by her own school teacher. In fact Maryanne laughed about this and said that she considered her father to be a hypocrite since he had gotten a high school girl pregnant himself. "On the other hand," she said seriously, "that's probably why he is so scared that I might get knocked up."

Although Maryanne continued to be concerned about her father's reaction to her teenage companions, she began to spend more and more time in the interviews talking about her social activities. She was quite concerned that her best girlfriend was pregnant and unmarried and anxiously asked for advice as to where her girlfriend might go to get some help with this problem. She revealed that she was ignoring her father's dictums about staying out past the hour that he set, or going to places she had been told to avoid. It was now the summertime and she was free both day and night and went where she pleased without ever reporting to him. He was becoming more and more angry and frightened and complained constantly to her mother. However, she revealed that her mother seemed relatively unconcerned since she was often ill in bed and made no inquiry as to Maryanne's comings and goings.

During this vacation Maryanne was spending most of the time at the lakeshore at the edge of town, usually with other girlfriends and their families, since her father was too busy to take a cabin on the lake and her mother too ill to accompany her. Maryanne often talked excitedly about the very handsome boys whom she "adored" but seemed to have no one young man whom she really thought of as a steady boyfriend. She again mentioned that almost every day and evening she had to avoid the continued sexual approaches that most of the young men were making to her. She was even more upset to find that over half of her girlfriends were engaging in sexual intercourse almost daily. She sighed and said, "I guess I'm the only real virgin left." She enjoyed the sports, the music, and the social chit-chat and seemed to be forgetting any other problems. Yet at times she would say, "but I lay awake all night"; or there would be times when she would return from the lakeside and stay home all evening by herself.

Maryanne also had many intellectual interests. She was reading almost a novel a week, including many classics. She kept up with the news and seemed to be well informed about the political matters of the world. She complained that when her boyfriends discussed things she felt left out. One boy that she liked very much was very interested in cars and racing; in order to keep up with him she read a book about cars. However, it turned out that Maryanne knew more about cars and more about races than the young man in question. Sometimes she would find boys telling her to shut up and get out. She was very angry at the way these young males treated her when she tried to have any intellectual intercourse with them. She resented her father and her half-brother for kidding her whenever she tried to discuss politics with them.

As might be expected, scarcely a month of summer passed before Maryanne fell in love. Dick, who accompanied her to the clinic on every visit thereafter, was tall and handsome and as physically attractive as Maryanne. Maryanne readily confessed that she spent every possible hour with Dick, and when she could not get out of the house she was on the telephone talking to him. Her father had taken a dislike to him and would not permit him to come in the house because "he did not dress properly." He always wore the same cutoff jeans and a white shirt with shirt tails out and unbuttoned completely down the front. Maryanne was furious with her father and was openly defying him and disobeying him. He threatened to send her to her grandmother at the other end of the country, and she threatened to run away from home with Dick. She admitted that she was very sexually attracted to Dick and often wondered what it would be like to have intercourse with him, but unlike other boys he had not immediately pressed for sex and seemed content with petting almost to the point of orgasm. Maryanne boasted of his control over himself sexually, and declared this to be the most beauti-

ful love affair possible. She admitted quite readily that she was
quite tempted at times to complete the sexual act with him, but she
was proud of herself that she resisted. She was also proud that Dick
did not use marijuana, or alcohol, or other drugs as did the majority
of her teenage companions. Although they did not have the same religion, which disturbed her parents, he did come to her church with
her and even attended the prayer meeting. However, her delirious
happiness lasted scarcely six weeks when she began to complain
that he paid attention to other girls at the parties or on the beach at
the lake. She was particularly furious at one of her closest girlfriends
who she felt was making an obvious play to take Dick away from
her. She complained bitterly that Eileen was throwing herself sexually into Dick's lap, but she had hoped that Dick could resist her.
Later that summer Dick went off with Eileen, and Maryanne believed Eileen to be pregnant by Dick. The rest of the summer she
spent mostly at home alone, moping and disconsolate. Despite the
fact that she was not going out, her relationship with her father remained at sword's point. Everything he said she regarded as an in-
sult or as a restriction. Everything she did seemed to upset him. Because of her mother's neurotic illnesses, the family did not take a
vacation away from home, but her father spent two weeks around
the house. Maryanne was sullen and defiant and picked at every
word he said. He called the psychologist to complain of his despair
and difficulties in relating to her. The psychologist proposed that she
have a joint session with her father, but she rejected the whole idea.

Finally her father, in an angry outburst, told her that she could go
ahead and go where she pleased and with whom and that he really
didn't care what happened to her any longer. Several of the boys
whom she had rejected continued making sexual demands on her,
and finally she admitted she was having intercourse with one or the
other of them almost every day. When the therapist expressed concern about the possibility that she might become pregnant, she became angry and declared that the therapist was treating her just like
her father did. However, she admitted that she knew she was in
some danger and wondered if she might be able to convince her
mother to let her "have the pill." Her mother had told her father
about this and the family were really horrified when she admitted
her behavior to them. Finally, her mother convinced her father that
if Maryanne were going to behave in this direction, it was wise to

give her some kind of contraceptive. However, once Maryanne got the contraceptive, she became much less sexually active. However, she began to engage in other forbidden adolescent activities such as alcohol and marijuana but did not seem to be attracted to the use of any more dangerous drugs.

By the time school started, she seemed to be over her summer fling and devoted herself to her school work. In her therapy she also began to think more seriously about herself and her own feelings and impulses. She said that she realized that the danger to her was not altogether what the boys wanted to do sexually with her but what she herself sexually desired. It was pointed out to her that she had found that she could handle her own sexual impulses in a realistic fashion, and her parents had in effect accepted this part of her growing up. During this, her senior year, she was taking many courses in science and making excellent grades. She ran for student body office and was easily elected, "although I think they voted for my body," she said with some despair. She also was on the debating team and had particular relish in debating against Dick, her boyfriend of the summer, and winning the debate. However, she was very angry about his remarks that she was "a smart-ass girl who thinks she knows everything." Although she went to an occasional party and had several flirtatious adventures with one or two boys, by and large she seemed to be avoiding any intense heterosexual relationships and during most of the fall and winter seemed to be closest to a childhood girlfriend whom she had not seen for many years previously. She was very protective of this girl who had had two abortions and seemed to be in tragic situation with her own family. In fact, at one time the girl had run away from home and spent most of the time in Maryanne's home without the complete knowledge of Maryanne's parents that the girl was really living there. Finally the girl's parents discovered her and brought her home, and she was sent away to an institution for delinquent girls. Maryanne was heartsick and disconsolate and seemed to be entering into an even more depressed period. She flung herself entirely into her schoolwork and had almost no social relationships. This was even more marked since she was in her senior year and many of the social activities surrounding graduation were being planned and her advice was sought as a student body officer. She had applied and was admitted for the fall semester at several of the major universities, including Berkeley and Harvard, but her father discouraged her a great deal in leaving home and insisted that she attend the local college. Her father was most adamant that she did not join her half-brother in Berkeley where the free-speech movement was then in full swing. Finally he revealed to her that he had made all the arrangements for her to enter a small religious college in the midwest which was quite conservative. Maryanne rebelled entirely at this idea and announced that she might not go to college at all but instead would move away from home. This declaration threatened her father a great deal, and he finally permitted her to go to the University of Hawaii. In some way, the fact that her father permitted her to leave home made it possible for Maryanne to begin a reconciliation with him. He took Maryanne and her sister for an Easter vacation to Hawaii to look over the campus and to make preliminary application for admission. On this trip he admitted to her that he had been very afraid that she would become pregnant because he knew that so many boys were physically attracted to her, and he even told her that he was proud of her that she had been able to take care of herself sexually. He, in effect, said that he trusted her to go away from home and be on her own.

Follow-up Visits. Approximately two years later, Maryanne returned to the clinic looking very depressed and asked if it might be possible for her to see the same therapist. She was quite upset as she had just gone through an abortion and moreover had broken up with the boyfriend who had impregnated her and with whom she had been living for the past year. She had not been able to tell her parents about this adventure, although she really had needed to confide in someone. She felt very sad that she had betrayed the trust of her parents.

Although she had been enjoying the easy life of the Islands, she felt that the university did not really offer the courses in science that she wished to take, and, moreover, she really did not want to return to the scene of her unhappiness. She convinced her father to permit her to go to Berkeley as she hoped to prepare to enter medicine. Her father asked no questions about her affair in Hawaii, although he seemed to be quite aware that she had had some kind of unhappy love affair. Nor did he disagree with her decision to change universities. During the following summer, a year later, she went to the clinic for several more sessions with her therapist. She had become very active in the political activities of the day, particularly the anti-war movement. She had had a brief affair with a black student but "he was as much of a pompous male ego as the rest of them, I guess it doesn't matter whether they are black or white." The psychologist noted that Maryanne seemed to be gaining considerable weight and when he remarked on this, she excused herself saying that she had not been able to keep up with her athletics as she had in previous years and she knew she should be on a diet.

The psychologist did not see Maryanne for another five years. He then met her at a scientific meeting, but did not recognize her as she weighed nearly 300 pounds. She was very proud that she had received her medical degree and was engaged in biological research. She was very proud of her work and explained it to the psychologist in considerable detail, mentioning the size of an enormous grant which she had been given to carry out this project. She said nothing about her extreme obesity but finally remarked, "I guess you do want to know about my love life. Now just sit down and I'll tell you about it." She revealed that she had had one more love affair and one more abortion and finally had decided that there was no way she could ever relate to men; thus for the past year she had been living an almost exclusively homosexual life.

Questions for Maryanne H.

1. When Maryanne entered the clinic, she complained that one leg was longer than the other even though the physician's measurements revealed no difference.
   a. What was Maryanne trying to express by her complaints?
   b. Discuss the relationship between Maryanne's physical appearance and the form of her complaint.
   c. What methods of coping with anxiety do Maryanne's symptoms suggest?
2. An adolescent's level of physical maturity subjects him/her to a social and psychological environment that can greatly influence the personality development.
   a. Discuss how Maryanne's physical attractiveness affected her interpersonal relationships—with peers, adults, therapist.
   b. What social processes account for this?

3. In what ways did Maryanne cope with the normal sexual and achievement drives of adolescence? Discuss the life problems in terms of goals that Maryanne was faced with because she was female.

4. How would you explain Maryanne's ambivalent behavior toward her growing sexual awareness and needs? Identify and discuss the defense mechanisms that were operating at this time. Why were they effective? Under what conditions did they fail?

5. What type of relationship existed between Maryanne and her father? Take into account the circumstances surrounding her birth. Review the events which occurred around the time Maryanne began to openly defy her father. How would you explain her behavior?

6. What problems of role identification were evident in this case?
   a. from a psychological point of view
   b. in light of social change.

7. How would you describe Mrs. H. and the effect of her relationship with Maryanne? If Mrs. H. had been a "career" woman, what changes (if any) might have been evident?

8. Maryanne's intellectual pursuits were never affected by her tragic romantic encounters. How would you account for this?

9. Can you see any patterns in Maryanne's early life which would indicate a tendency toward lesbianism? Take into account her hobbies as well as the nature of her relationships with men and women. (Review the etiology of female homosexuality.)

10. Maryanne's early history was void of any tendency toward overeating and obesity. What hypotheses can you raise which might provide an explanation for Maryanne's enormous weight gain?

11. What is your analysis of Maryanne's abandonment of heterosexual relationships? Does it appear to be a sign of maladjustment or psychopathology? Does it reflect adaptive coping?

12. Why was Maryanne unable to utilize her physical attractiveness in a more positive manner? What barriers existed within her and in her social environment which prevented her from integrating a self-concept of a sexy and highly intellectual woman?

13. To what extent was Maryanne a victim of women's ambivalent role in modern day society? How would ardent women's libbers interpret her dilemma and her ultimate reaction to it? How would a male chauvinist interpret the same facts? Which interpretation makes best sense for you?

References

BAYLEY, N., & TUDDENHAM, R. Adolescent changes in body fluid. *43rd Yearbook, National Society for the Study of Education,* 1944, Pp. 33–55.

BROVERMAN, I. K., VOGEL, S. R., BROVERMAN, D. M., CLARKSON, F. E., & ROSENKRANTZ, P. S. Sex-role stereotypes: a current appraisal. *Journal of Social Issues,* 1972, 28: 59–78.

BULLOUGH, V. L. *The subordinate sex: a history of attitudes toward women.* Urbana: University of Illinois Press, 1973.

CARLSON, R. Understanding women: implications for personality theory and research. *Journal of Social Issues,* 1972, 28: 17–32.

CARTWRIGHT, L. K. Conscious factors entering into decisions of women to study medicine. *Journal of Social Issues,* 1972, 28: 201–216.

HOFFMAN, L. W. Early childhood experiences and woman's achievement motives. *Journal of Social Issues,* 1972, 28: 129–156.

HORNER, M. S. Toward an understanding of achievement–related conflicts in women. *Journal of Social Issues,* 1972, 28: 157–176.

HORNER, M. S. Femininity and successful achievement: a basic inconsistency. In BARDWICK, J., DOUVAN, E. M., HORNER, M. S., & GUTMANN, D. (Eds.) *Feminine personality and conflict.* Belmont, California: Brooks-Cole, 1970.

JANEWAY, E. On "female sexuality" (A response to Sigmund Freud's 1931 essay of that title). In STROUSE, J. (Ed.) *Woman and analysis.* New York: Grossman, 1974.

KUNDSIN, R. B. *Successful women in the sciences: an analysis of determinants.* New York: New York Academy of Sciences, 1973.

MEDNICK, M. S., & TANGRI, S. S. New social psychological perspectives on woman. *Journal of Social Issues,* 1972, 28: 1–16.

REISS, B. New viewpoints on the female homosexual. In FRANKS, V., & BURTLE, V. (Eds.) *Women in therapy,* New York: Brunner/Mazel, 1974.

SIMON, W., & GAGNON, J. H. The lesbians: a preliminary overview. In GAGNON, J. H., & SIMON, W. (Eds.) *Sexual deviance.* New York: Harper and Row, 1967, Pp. 247–282.

THOMPSON, C. The role of women in this culture. *Psychiatry,* 1941, 4: 1–8. Reprinted in STROUSE, J. (Ed.) *Women and Analysis.* New York: Grossman, 1974.

WALSTOR, E., ARONSON, V., ABRAHAMS, D., & ROTTMAN, L. Importance of physical attractiveness in dating behavior. *Journal of Personality and Social Psychology,* 1966, 4: 508–516.

THE CASE OF THE R. FAMILY

What It Means To Be a Man

About my backaches senor, I think I find it hard to tell you, though my wife here knows too. You see it is like this, I am going down the street, my two little children want a piece of candy, but I do not have ten cents, I feel sick. I decide I will go home and lie down, my back aches. My back aches very bad and yet I would like to get up. I do not feel much of a man. I know my son will come home. He will not respect me. He will say "you are an old man with a bad back. You do not work, you do not take care of your family, I cannot respect you." And again I will not feel much of a man. How can I get my son to respect me? He too will not be a man, he will be a bum. He will not get to school. He walks around like a proud cock all the time. He does no work. He takes to drugs. He does not go to school. He will not be a man either.

The speaker, Mr. R., was a 50-year-old illiterate Mexican laborer. He had come with his wife to the psychiatric clinic on a referral from a juvenile probation officer regarding their second oldest son, Ramon, age 15. It was obvious that Mr. R. was extremely concerned about Ramon and Ramon's adjustment as well as the welfare of the rest of his family. He and his wife had to travel a long way across the city, out of the area where they lived and worked, to talk to people who did not speak Spanish. Furthermore, Mr. R. was a proud man who normally did not ask for help from anyone regarding his family.

Actually, the social difficulties that Ramon was encountering were not nearly as severe as those experienced by other Chicanos growing up in the Barrios or even, for that matter, many Anglos in better economic conditions in other parts of the city during the late 1960's. At that time many teenagers were using a variety of very strong drugs, many were dropping out of high school or making little use at all of any educational opportunities, some were in open defiance of the law, parents, and other authorities. The R. family lived in an area of the city which was known by the police and others to be "a high delinquency area." Ramon had committed no crime whatsoever; he had been referred to the courts mainly because he had stayed out all night after having had a violent quarrel with his father. Such quarrels had become increasingly frequent over the past year, and Ramon often would storm out of the house to spend the night with some friend. However, from time to time he would wander the streets late at night and would be picked up by the police. This time he was found to be in possession of a small amount of marijuana. However, no charges were made against him in court, and the case was turned over to the juvenile probation authorities for "further investigation." The probation officer discovered that Ramon did not belong to any of the street gangs, had no previous arrests, and was not reported to be truant from school. However, the school did report that Ramon was considered a "disciplinary problem" in that he frequently had a "sneering attitude" toward the teachers. He seldom completed his school work, although the school psychologist reported that he was of above average intelligence and his previous work prior to entering junior high school had been satisfactory. The school further noted that Ramon seemed to be spending most of his time "trying to make an impression on the girls." They compared him very unfavorably with his older brother, Salvador, and his older sister, Olivia, both of whom had been top students. Yet when questioned further, the boys' vice-principal could not think of any particular incident for which he had had to punish Ramon. The school checked the attendance record and it showed that Ramon had rarely been absent. Even when Ramon had been away from home all night, he would go to school the next morning, sometimes without returning home in the interim.

Family Background. Jesus R., who preferred to be called Jack, his wife, Marguerita, known at Rita, and their eight children lived in a two-bedroom home in a section of Los Angeles inhabited mostly by people of mainly Mexican or Latin American descent. The adolescents voiced the opinion that the crowded conditions of their home and the lack of privacy created conflicts between them and the rest of the family. The parents shared one bedroom, the four youngest children the other bedroom. The dining room was curtained off for Olivia, age 19, and her younger sister Marta, age 12. Ramon and Salvador slept on a screened-in porch that had been added to the back of the house. The living room was usually taken over by the four smaller children and Jack, who commandeered the television. Thus, there was no space for teenage activities of any kind.

Salvador, who was finishing high school and was very busy in school government and school activities, often spent many evening hours away from home either with his extracurricular activities or with a steady girl-friend whom he planned to marry that summer. Olivia was attending junior college and worked every evening as a sales clerk in the local department store. Thus the two older children could escape from the home. Marta was her mother's main assistant, spending many hours in the kitchen cooking, disciplining, or caring for the smaller children.

There was a great deal of rivalry between Ramon and his brothers and sisters. Ramon felt that he was given many more chores to do around the garden and home since Salvador was excused from household chores on the grounds that he had special jobs to do at school. It was evident that Jack was extremely proud of his oldest son and often made invidious comparisons with Ramon. Ramon often was at daggers points with Marta, who was praised for carrying out many tasks without complaint or hesitation. Ramon hated to have to care for the yard or run errands for his mother and was always ducking out or had to be ordered three or four times before he complied. Moreover, Marta was the one member of the family who resembled her father very much, having the high forehead and peak nose of his predominantly Indian ancestry. In fact Jack referred to Marta as "my little Indian." On the other hand, Ramon was quite fair-skinned, and resembled his mother much more so than the other children in the family. Sal and Olivia teased him and called him "pretty boy" which usually infuriated him. One of the most recent family quarrels occurred when 10-year-old George observed Ramon priming his new moustache in the mirror and yelled "pretty boy" at him; Ramon swung and knocked George into the wall bloodying his forehead whereupon Jack grabbed Ramon by the collar, and Ramon swung at him also. Before Rita could intervene Ramon had run out of the house.

The family conflicts were heightened by their constant severe financial problems. No one in the family worked full-time. Jack had been unemployed for almost two years and only a few months ago had been enrolled in a special governmental program to retrain unskilled and poverty-stricken men. He was to learn simple mechanics and how to read and write English. In addition to his schooling he received an allotment of $125 for the period of the course, which, as Jack pointed out, would not keep a single man alive and was less than any of his children earned working half-time. Jack was embarrassed not only by the fact that his contribution to the family income was so small but even more by the fact that his younger children could read and write better than he and that he had to ask Marta's help sometimes in his lessons. A major part of the family income came from Rita's part-time employment in a bakery where she worked from midnight to 6 a.m. four nights a week and earned $2.00 an hour. She was often very tired in the morning, but Marta and Olivia cooked breakfast for the family and saw all the little ones off to school. Olivia contributed over half of her earnings to the family coffers and used the rest of it to buy her own clothes and school books. Sal had a weekend job at the local service station where he earned enough for his clothes and for gas for an old car he had purchased. Marta earned some money baby-sitting. Ramon had no job and no money in his pockets. His mother would slip him a dollar, or his sisters would take pity on him and give him extra money to buy something to eat at the local hotdog stand. At one time Salvador, referring to the conflict between Ramon and Jack said, "I don't know what they are fighting about, neither one of them have a cent in their pockets."

As may be obvious from the above, the clinic almost immediately viewed Ramon's problems as part of the family situation and invited not only the parents and Ramon but the other teenagers into general family discussion almost from the start. In fact, George and Maria, age 8, were soon included in these sessions and at other times, especially when no neighbor was available for baby-sitting, Juan age 5 and Cecile age 2 came along. The older children focused on what they called the "generation gap" claiming that their parents were too old-fashioned and too determined to "preserve the old ways," and thus failed to understand the problems of today's adolescents. The parents, especially Jack, were equally adamant that the children did not appreciate the parents' efforts to protect them from a dangerous environment which might lead them astray morally and to make sure that they stayed in school and benefited from an education so they could rise above the illiteracy and poverty which Jack had experienced. Jack insisted that it was necessary for the children to respect their parents if they were ever to grow up and respect themselves and be respectable people. Ramon's teenage siblings did support Jack in that they felt Ramon was particularly disrespectful to his father, yet they gently but firmly began to insist that Jack lost his rights to respect when he would lose his temper and attempt to order them around like "a dictator" or to physically beat on them. Jack admitted that a great deal of the problem might stem from the fact that it was difficult for children to respect a father who was not earning a living, who was at times ill from a chronic back problem, who was illiterate and could not always understand what was going on in the world outside of his own home. The background of the parents thus became one of the main points of discussion in the ensuing family meetings.

THE FATHER: Jack, then age 51, was a tall lean man with a leathery complexion and streaks of gray in his black hair. He limped slightly as he walked due to the shrapnel which had never been extracted from his hip bone after he had been wounded in World War II. He was bent over slightly when walking or sitting due to a back injury which he had incurred some three years ago when a tractor he was driving turned over on top of him. Nevertheless he gave the appearance of being a physically powerful man. During the discussions he scarcely ever smiled, with the exceptions of the moments when the younger children climbed upon his lap. Most of the time he wore a scowl or frown. His rather fierce appearance was accentuated by an old burn scar on his left cheek, a result of an accident when he was a small baby.

Jack was the oldest son of a tenant farmer in a rural region of Texas just across the Rio Grande from Mexico. His parents had immigrated from Mexico only a few years before his birth. They and a group of other young couples rented land from a large ranch owner in a joint community venture. Jack remembered his father as being extremely strict and ultra-religious. The grandfather had to work very hard to make the venture be somewhat successful, and as soon as each child was old enough to work in the fields, he or she joined his or her parents in full-time labor with the crops and the farm animals. Thus Jack had attended only a few months of school each year for four years and eventually was not permitted to return to school. He said he got very little out of this schooling since, at that time, he spoke only Spanish and the school teacher spoke only English. However, Jack did recall that despite the severity of their life his father had encouraged him in his one enjoyment in life: baseball. His father permitted him to play baseball on Sunday afternoon and, in fact, encouraged him in the local team's competition with teams from other villages. For several years in a row Jack was the champion pitcher of the local amateur league. He attracted the attention of professional baseball scouts. "The proudest moment of my life was when I was invited to try out and then spend spring practice with a minor league team from a big city in southern Texas. However, disappointment came soon. The newspapers told everyone that a Mexican was going to play baseball. This was before Jackie Robinson had played, and no Mexican or Puerto Rican had played on any baseball team in the United States. "The first time we played the crowds all yelled and screamed and threw things at me. The manager then fired me and sent me home. I did not even get back the $300 my father had given me to buy my uniform." Despite this ignominious and discriminatory rejection Jack never lost his love of baseball and continued to play amateur baseball nearly every weekend of his life. However, he could never get Sal or Ramon interested in playing ball. Moreover, Rita never accepted Jack's ball playing and accused him of being more interested in his own sport than in his sons. None of the children were aware of this baseball incident, and Ramon, in particular, seemed to be most impressed and angry that his father had been discriminated against in such a fashion. "Why would they not let you play?" Ramon exclaimed. "You were a man like the rest of them." "But they did not think I was a man," said Jack sadly.

Shortly thereafter another incident occurred in Jack's life of which the children, until these discussions, were not aware. A young woman his age whom he knew only slightly complained to his father that she was pregnant by Jack. Jack's father immediately ordered him to marry this girl, even though Jack had no means to support her and was not in any way inclined to marry her or anyone else at that time. He did not even really believe that the child this woman was carrying was his own. Nevertheless he obeyed his father, and his bride moved into his parents' home. Jack was very angry at her; not only had she forced him to marry her but she contributed nothing in the way of work to the family and instead expected Jack's mother to wait on her as if the mother were a servant. Hearing this incident Olivia volunteered that she understood now why her father was so very strict regarding her boyfriends, why he was so very worried about Salvador and his girlfriend and getting married, and why the report from the school that Ramon was "fooling around with the girls" upset Jack so very much. Jack was very embarrassed upon revealing this fact about his life and would not have told it had not Rita insisted. Rita had pushed Jack to tell about this incident in his life by threatening to tell it herself since she felt that the children needed to understand some of the reasons that Jack was so very disturbed by their adolescent sexual interest and behavior.

Soon after Jack's first marriage World War II began, and he was drafted into the American military. He was sent, almost immediately, to North Africa as a foot soldier and was in battle almost continually for over two years. He was in the 8th Army and was first wounded in the landings in the invasion of Italy but was sent back to duty. He then spent the winter in the valley below Mt. Casino in the worst battle in the Italian campaign. Jack was wounded twice more and ended up in the hospital with the shrapnel in his hip. As soon as he was physically able he was sent home where he spent another several months in a military hospital before he was discharged.

At the time of his discharge he still was quite disabled, but was ignorant of the methods for applying for further medical care through the Veterans Administration or for obtaining any kind of compensation for his disability. Thus, he had never received any pension nor any further medical treatment through the Veterans Administration. At one time he did apply through a Veterans organization, but his case was never carried through, and Jack was aware that there were no Mexican members in this Veterans organization.

Again his children were quite impressed when they heard of their father's war record. World War II to these children was a matter of history; only the previous week Ramon had been reading of the battle of Mt. Casino, completely unaware that his father had suffered through that particular horror. What amazed Ramon most was that Jack did not see himself as any kind of a hero. Rather he was trying to tell his children the misery of war and to explain to them why he had to work so very hard and what he had suffered. The fact that he had fought very bravely and was unrewarded by his country had not really occurred to Jack as it had to his children. Furthermore, Jack again felt that he was "not much of a man" because he was now unable to continue in agricultural labor because of his war injuries.

His self-image was further denegrated by the fact that his wife and child had moved across the border to Mexico where she was living with another man. With his father's help he had the marriage legally annulled. Jack then decided he should leave the rural life, and he moved to Los Angeles where he hoped to find work which was not as physically demanding. When he arrived in Los Angeles he stayed with friends who were relatives of Rita's father. In fact, his first job was in the same factory where Rita's father worked and thus he saw quite a bit of Rita and her sisters over the following year. During this year his war wounds healed considerably. He learned to operate heavy construction earth-moving machinery, a job which paid considerably more than most unskilled labor. He now felt far more able to support a wife and family, and he married Rita. For at least a few years the family was relatively prosperous. With Rita's father's savings they were able to make a down payment on the little house they now reside in. Jack was particularly proud of being a home owner, even though, he sadly admitted, he had never been able to pay his father-in-law back the original loan for the down payment, and he often worried whether he could make the monthly mortgage payments.

Despite the fact that Jack was earning more money than he could on most any other job, he realized that since he and the other Mexican workers did not belong to the union, they were paid far below union scale. With the encouragement of some of his friends Jack approached the union and asked to have some help in having him and his friends join and having a union shop where they worked. Given encouragement by the union, he and the other Mexicans gathered together and formed a local union and went on strike demanding union conditions. Backed by the union headquarters in Los Angeles the Mexican workers under Jack's leadership were able to force the employer to recognize them as union members and to give them conditions held by other union workers in Los Angeles. However, at this time the union officials no longer gave Jack any personal support, and he was fired. Jack was advised by friends that the union felt that he was acquiring far too much political power because he had led the workers in this particular company to organize. There were no Mexican officials in this union at that time nor have there been since. Jack thereafter found it very difficult to find any job in construction because most of them were under union contract, and he found it difficult to get back into the union.

Jack went to work for the local county government for a number of years. It was while working for the county that he injured his back. He spent several months in the hospital and was given some compensation during the next several years while he was invalid and was unable to carry out some of the heavy duties of construction. Jack went back to work full-time about a year later and received no further compensation. Again, because of his illiteracy and lack of familiarity of the laws governing Workman's Compensation, it was very likely that he lost out on many of his rights.

Then all the county jobs were put under Civil Service. Jack, being illiterate, was unable to pass the written Civil Service examination, even though he was considered by his immediate supervisors to be an excellent and experienced construction worker. Shortly after he had been let out of this job, his immediate supervisor appealed to the Civil Service Board, and he was told that he might be able to return to the job without taking the examination but merely by filling in a form. He brought the form home and Rita filled it in for him and he signed his own name. However, later some official discovered that he had not personally filled out the form, which then made him ineligible for further county work in any place because this was declared a fraud.

For the past year-and-a-half Jack had worked at various odd jobs wherever he could find employment. Up until the time he started his present school he had worked mostly as an assistant to a friend who was a gardener, but the dampness and the particular type of shoveling required by this job, made Jack's back ache and the weakness in his thigh even worse. "Sometimes I feel as if I were no good to my family and certainly no good to my wife, I cannot earn a living and I cannot even be a lover to her."

Again his children seemed to be astounded. They were unaware that their father had ever been any kind of a community leader, that he had actively fought prejudice and discrimination, and that he had worked very hard against so many odds for them. Most of all, they had not previously understood his despair. Again it was Ramon who seemed to identify most with his father and to be most indignant over the injustices which he saw his father having to endure.

The children had accused Jack of being far too stern and of not understanding them. He wished to be understood as well as to justify some of his ideas regarding their behavior and their need for discipline. He also was in disagreement with his wife who accused him of being too strict and who often went out of her way to protect the children from him by not informing him of what was going on or by letting the children off the hook when he had restricted them or otherwise punished them.

THE MOTHER: Rita, who was approximately five years younger than Jack, was a rather pretty, plump woman, who looked more like 30 than 45. Despite the fact that there was little money for clothes, Rita and her children always came dressed very neat and clean, and Jack and the boys always wore a freshly ironed shirt. Once when the psychologist remarked how nice they all looked, Ramon responded, "Yes, mother makes us dress up more than if we were going to church."

Because the children had few or no complaints against their mother, she was not at first pressured to reveal anything about herself. However, Ramon was quick to point out that his father would have been unaware of any of his difficulties at school if his mother had not reported them to Jack. It was she, far more than Jack, who was worried that he might get into trouble outside the home. Although Jack and Ramon were often at swords points about work about the house, or about Ramon's lack of respect to his father, it was really Rita who was most concerned that Ramon would be in trouble with girls or drugs. When Ramon pointed this out, his brothers and sisters also began to realize that it was mother who had been concerned about their behavior, who had queried them when they had come home at night or the next morning, and who had reported her feelings and suspicions to their father. In fact, a constant source of conflict in the house was the fact that Jack permitted Sal and Ramon to drink a bottle of beer with him, much against Rita's complaints. It was Rita was supported continued religious observance and who carried the family problems to the priest. Thus it was when the children began to complain that Rita had little understanding of their social and sexual needs, that Rita began to talk about her background.

Rita was born and reared in the same village where Jack's family lived, but she was really unaware of Jack until he married his first wife who was her cousin. Her father had been a member of the same group as Jack's father which had left Mexico to form the tenants' commune; however, her father had not been quite as successful in running his small farm. Rather than having sons, he had three daughters, and shortly after the birth of Rita's younger sister, their mother died. Grief stricken, Rita's father decided to give up the farm and left his three daughters in the care of his older sister in Mexico. He then took up itinerant agricultural work, moving across the country as the different crops ripened, returning in late winter to visit his children. However, as the restrictions were put on immigration of Mexican agricultural laborers entering the United States, Rita's father began to fear that he might not be able to return to the United States to work each year. Moreover, his sister and brother-in-law had children of their own and were unable to care further for his three little girls. For the next several years Rita and her sisters lived with their father, moving from agriculture camp to agriculture camp throughout the southwestern United States and California. They had little or no schooling, although by this time Rita had learned to read and write Spanish. They lived in the hovels provided by the ranch owners or in open tents. Rita, approximately 10 years old, and her two younger sisters attempted to care for their father, to do his cooking and washing and housekeeping.

Rita remembered particularly that there often was absolutely no privacy for her and her sisters. They would carefully curtain off the father's bed, separate from theirs. Sometimes there would be other adult male laborers sleeping in the same tent. Rita remembered with horror once when she awoke to find her father in a knife fight with another man because the father felt that the other man might attack or sexually molest the three little girls. Another time Rita and her sisters had to flee from a young man who did attempt to molest them sexually. As Rita told about these incidents in her life she explained to her children that this was why she was so afraid of what might happen to them if they left the protection of her nest. When Rita was 13 her father was able to find a convent which would accept her and her two sisters, and she remained there until her father found emloyment in the city, a year before her marriage. At the convent Rita was able to obtain considerable more education and became literate in English as well as Spanish. Rita's experience in the convent also, of course, heightened her devotion to her religion as well as what Rita called her "fear of sexuality."

As might be true in any family, it was difficult for this old-fashion Catholic family to discuss sex with their teenage children. It was equally difficult for the youngsters to even let their parents give a hint that they, the parents, had sexual desires and pressures. Yet this family could be more open and direct about things, even about sexual aspects of their lives than many middle-class Anglo families who came to this clinic. The children tried to convince their mother that sexuality was not something to be necessarily feared. At the same time the two oldest children were pointing out that Ramon's need to sexually establish himself with a girl was only natural and even quite necessary "if he were to be a man." "Yes," replied the mother, "this is his machismo." She explained that this Spanish term referred to a particular high value placed, in most Latin American cultures as well as in Spain, upon masculine prowess and virility as proof of one's manhood. Olivia echoed this saying that the reason that she did not have a steady boyfriend was that she rejected the sexual demands of most of the young men she knew, even those whom she liked, because she regarded their demands not so much as a sign of their affection for her, but as a further need to prove their manhood. As this discussion ensued, Rita became more and more bitter and finally lashed out at her husband saying that this was the major difficulty in their marriage, that he continually had to prove that he was sexually adequate. Jack was acutely embarrassed by his wife's revelation of his sexual demands on her, particularly in front of the children and the doctor. At this point the older children wanted to know why their parents had had so many children in the first place, why Rita had not resisted her husband's demands, and why she had not used any kind of contraceptives? Rita said she had been taught that she must yield entirely to her husband's wishes and contracep-

tives were prohibited by their religion. They had succeeded in having no children in the past four years only because Rita had been
working nights and Jack had gone to bed with an aching back.
Again it seemed obvious that one of the sources of Jack's own lack
of self-respect was the fact that he could no longer prove himself in
his sexual relationships with his wife. This in turn heightened his
need for respect from his children, particularly from his sons.

Progress in Treatment. The family discussions continued every week
for approximately eight months. At this time the family was much
more open with one another, and there was much less quarreling in
the house. When Jack finished his schooling he was promptly hired
by the same agency which had trained him, to teach the use and main-
tenance of large construction machinery to younger men. Although
the pay was not very high, at least it was a full-time job, and Jack
felt he gained considerable amount of respect from these students.
Sal finished high school and was promptly drafted into the military.
His girlfriend was pregnant, and he married her the week before he
went into the Army. Thus both "repeated history," according to his
father. Ramon was still at lose ends but succeeded in completing the
school year without further incidence. He took his brother's job
when his brother went into the military and thus had some money
and felt a bit more secure. However, over the following year or so
the family continued to suffer tragedies. The next fall Ramon was
again arrested for possession of marijuana and was sent to prison
for six months. The money for the agency where the father worked
gave out, and he was again unemployed within a year. The worst
tragedy was Sal's death in Viet Nam. At this point the mother returned to the clinic for several visits, quite grief-stricken. Jack joined
her and was able to reveal his intense grief. He was quite embarrassed to be unemployed again, but in this matter he did not feel his
outlook was exceedingly grim.

Questions for the R. Family

Despite the many tragic aspects of this case, there is a great deal to
be learned from it concerning the dynamics of family functioning

and how they are affected by events within and outside of the family.

1. Discuss the following:
    a. Ramon's view of himself
    b. Jack's view of himself
    c. Rita's view of herself
at the time that the family first sought help from the clinic.

2. Relate how aspects of previous life experience of each individual could have shaped these self-views.

3. Discuss how each of the following family members might have viewed the others at the time of the initial clinic contact.

    a. How Ramon was seen by: Jack
                               Rita
    b. How Jack was seen by: Rita
                               Ramon
    c. How Rita was seen by: Jack
                               Roman

4. What conflicts exist between the self-views which you outlined in Question 1 and the other views summarized in Question 3. How might they account for Ramon's "behavior problem?"

5. Given your analysis in Question 4, why was the treatment of the whole R. family group preferred rather than the alternative of individual psychotherapy for Ramon?

6. a. What transpired in the family therapy to alter the self-perceptions of Ramon, Jack, and Rita?
    b. What also happened to the way they might have been perceived by each other as a result of their self-revelations?
    c. How might this process have facilitated productive relationships within the family?

7. Some people feel that families such as the R. family are so embroiled in overwhelming social problems that psychotherapy of any sort is futile. What are your reactions to this issue?

8. The classic view of neurosis is that of the internal conflict, i.e., the person is in conflict within himself. This case presents many external stresses. To what extent can you include both sets of factors to your view of neurosis? Cite evidence from this case.

9. What aspects of the R. family's problems represent:
    a. general emotional problems associated with poverty.
    b. general emotional problems associated with ethnic minority group status in the United States

c. general emotional problems arising specifically from Chicano ethnic status in the United States.

10. To what extent are the pressures and problems associated with masculinity and femininity unique to the culture from which these people come? To what extent is the problem "maschismo" a universal one?

References

DWORKIN, A. G. Stereotypes and self-images held by native-born and foreign-born Mexican-Americans. *Sociology and Social Research*, 1965, 49: 214–224.

FABREGA, H., & WALLACE, C. A. Value identification and psychiatric disability: An analysis involving Americans of Mexican descent. *Behavioral Science*, 1968, 13: 362–371.

GOULD, R. E. Strange lass: or how I stopped worrying about the theory and began treating the blue-collar worker. *American Journal of Orthopsychiatry*, 1967, 37: 78–86.

GRELBER, L., MOORE, J. W., & GUZMAN, R. C. *The Mexican American people*. New York: The Free Press, 1970.

KARNO, M., & EDGERTON, R. B. Perception of mental illness in a Mexican-American community. *Archives of General Psychiatry*, 1969, 20: 233–238.

MORALES, A. The impact of class discrimination and white racism on the mental health of Mexican Americans. In WAGNER, N. N., & HAUG, M. J. (Eds.) *Chicanos: social and psychological perspectives*. St. Louis: C. U. Mosby, 1971.

MURILLO, N. The Mexican American family. In WAGNER, N. N., & HAUG, M. J. (Eds.) *Chicanos: social and psychological perspectives*, St. Louis: C. U. Mosby, 1971.

THE CASE OF THE G. FAMILY

"Feed Me!"

Nancy G. sat between her parents in the hospital clinic office. Her mother and father had removed their coats, but Nancy remained wrapped in a heavy jacket, her hands thrust deep into the pockets. An extremely straight part divided Nancy's long black hair. Her skin was sallow, and she had dark circles under her eyes. Nancy was 14 years old, 62 inches tall, and weighed 68 pounds. She was starving to death.

Nancy's father wore a look of deep concern. He was a professional man, a dentist, but he did not appear professional or even competent as he sat beside his emaciated daughter. He struggled to hold back tears as he realized how close she was to death at this moment. Once he reached over to take her hand, but she abruptly pulled away from his touch. After that he sat motionless, leaning away from her. When the physician joined them, Dr. G. rose to greet him and then resumed his seat in silence. His wife was the family spokesman.

Mrs. G. was as worried as her husband, but her manner was tense and alert rather than depressed. Fluently, and in great detail, she described the series of events that had brought them to the hospital.

Last fall Nancy enrolled in a ninth-grade course in nutrition. She quickly became engrossed in the subject. She spent her allowance on calorie charts and health food books. She began helping her mother in the kitchen and enjoyed experimenting with novel recipes. Finally, she began to nag her mother about the opulent meals she was serving her family (all of whom were overweight) and begged to be allowed to help plan their menus.

Initially, Mrs. G. was delighted with her daughter's interest. The two of them enjoyed planning and preparing tasty, low calorie meals together. Nancy's participation turned out to be helpful as well. Mrs. G. was a woman who did her own housework and liked having her home meticulously clean and orderly. Nancy's assistance in the kitchen was truly appreciated. Neither of her older children had been cooperative or helpful in doing any chores around the home.

Dr. G. also was pleased at first by Nancy's new activities. He liked seeing her play a domestic role at his wife's side. It reminded him of his home as a child, where his mother and sisters seemed always to be busy together in the kitchen. Furthermore, he knew he could profit from watching his own weight. His cardiologist had advised him to reduce long ago. However, he had learned that enterprises started by any of his teen-age children were likely to be short-lived, and he expected Nancy's new venture to be little more than a passing fancy. Meanwhile he kept his thoughts to himself and went along with the culinary regime proffered by his wife and daughter.

Nancy's older sister, Sarah, routinely deprecated everything her "baby sister" said and did and generally dismissed her as a spoiled brat. Already following a weight-loss diet of her own devising, Sarah refused to participate in Nancy's plans for the family to diet together. Stormy encounters between the two sisters were commonplace, and now they centered on the subject of food.

Chuck, two years older than Nancy, knew little and cared less about nutrition. He offered Nancy neither criticism nor encouragement. His attitude was one of indifference no matter how she teased for his attention or tried to win his approval. But Nancy was discouraged by neither Sarah's nor Chuck's attitude. Her involvement with dieting grew.

It was not until the Christmas holidays that either of her parents took note of Nancy's excessive loss of weight. In three months she had lost 25 pounds. Both of them admonished her to quit dieting and, for a while, they reasoned patiently with her. Mrs. G. resumed cooking dishes that had enticed Nancy in the past and began monitoring her daughter's food intake. In spite of parental efforts, however, Nancy continued to lose weight. By her fourteenth birthday in January, Nancy's weight had decreased another 10 pounds. All efforts to make her eat were met first with argument and then with tears.

As Nancy's weight decreased there were increasing manifestations of emotional disturbance and personality change. She began to isolate herself from everyone in the family, particularly her brother and sister. In fact, she became quite agitated whenever she was in the same room with either of her siblings. Nancy had always been a fussy, perfectionistic child, but now her need for order and routine became an obsession. Her performance in school continued to be superior, but she worried endlessly about every assignment. In spite of her fragile physique, she continued to engage actively in sports, which she had always enjoyed. At school she played basketball vigorously. After school, when she wasn't studying or working in the kitchen, she was riding her bicycle or running with her dog.

What particularly disturbed her parents was that Nancy would frequently scrutinize her figure in the mirror and say things like, "How fat I am! Look at this disgusting stomach and these fat thighs." To her parents, this view Nancy had of herself was bizarre. Nancy reminded them of a concentration camp victim, emaciated and wasting away. They were also concerned because the girl's menstrual periods, which had started when she was 12, stopped completely soon after she began dieting.

Dr. and Mrs. G. consulted with Nancy's pediatrician, and he advised them to seek psychiatric consultation. In February Nancy was taken to a psychiatrist for evaluation. She continued to see him in weekly visits for three months. She also continued to lose weight. Frustrated by the futility of their own efforts to get Nancy to eat and impatient with the doctor's apparent inability to effect a change in her eating habits, her parents took her to a second psychiatrist. After meeting with Nancy a few times, this physician advised her parents to seek hospitalization for her. Now, nine months after first becoming interested in dieting, and weighing 45 pounds less, Nancy was being brought to the university medical center. Her parents' concern for her was clear. They wanted someone to save their daughter's life.

Nancy's concerns, however, had nothing to do with food. Alone with the doctor, she complained about being afraid of losing control of herself. She spoke of "habits" that she required to maintain control. She talked readily about these "habits," which were actually a variety of repetitive thoughts and behavioral rituals that she had experienced for many years. Now they centered around her dread of growing fat. Some of these ruminations were bizarre in nature. For example, she worried about the possibility of becoming obese just by being in the same room with another obese person like her sister. At times she longed to yield to her appetite for food; in fact, she was constantly afraid that she might "lose control" and do just that.

During her interview with the physician, Nancy was tearful and visibly anxious. She found it difficult to sit quietly in her chair. In a whining voice she complained bitterly about every member of her family: her father was a brutal tyrant; her mother didn't try to understand her; her sister was hateful to her; her brother had quit loving her completely. She complained also about the doctors she had seen. One minute she would plead with the psychiatrist for help; the next minute she would deny that there was anything anyone could do for her.

Nancy was hospitalized promptly. The diagnosis entered by the admitting physician was *anorexia nervosa*.

Family Background. Charles and Dorothy G. were caught up in the tragedy of their daughter's illness, but Nancy's anorexia was not their only concern. The other children and their relationship to one another were additional sources of conflict. Until a few years ago, their family life had seemed no more turbulent than the lives of their friends and neighbors. But as the children began to grow out of childhood and into adolescence, crises became the rule rather than the exception.

SARAH: Nancy's older sister, Sarah, had begun to lose interest in her studies as soon as she entered high school. After finishing the eleventh grade Sarah refused to continue her education. Her father was shocked by this attitude. Nothing he said could persuade her that she should appreciate the opportunity she had to get an education. Seeing school as a waste of time, Sarah complained that the courses bored her, the teachers were incompetent, and the school administrators treated the students like prisoners. Sarah dismissed her father's evaluation of education as a hopeless hang-up of his own—one that carried no weight with her. Charles' initial shock soon turned to outrage as Sarah refused to be moved by his arguments. He countered that she was lazy, indifferent, and too immature to judge either the educational system or what was good for her. During one of their heated arguments, Charles lost his temper and slapped Sarah across the face. The arguments abruptly ceased and so did most other exchanges between them. For almost a year, now, father and daughter have lived under the same roof without speaking more than a few words to each other.

Dorothy, too, was distressed by Sarah's abandonment of school, but she was furious with Charles for his authoritarian way of handling the situation. Dorothy's approach to her daughter was to plead with her to return to school for self-serving reasons such as personal fulfillment and the chance to be trained to support herself so that she need never be helplessly dependent upon a husband. Sarah relished having her mother as an ally against her father, but she remained adamant about not pursuing a formal education. She dismissed her mother's persuasions as also stemming from a personal hang-up. Her favorite rebuttal was, "If being on your own is so important, why don't you go back to school and get a job and leave Dad?"

Sarah finally found a job that provided her with enough money for clothes and incidentals, but not enough to support herself living apart from her parents. After dinner, whenever her father was in the house, she would lock herself in her room. She spent her weekends away from home with friends whom her parents did not know, in activities about which she volunteered no information even to her mother. Her parents tried to control Sarah's behavior by restricting her use of the family car, but the friends provided transportation. Thoroughly frustrated in their attempts to deal with Sarah, Charles and Dorothy attacked each other. Charles cited Dorothy's sympathetic support of Sarah as one more example of the way she continually undermined his authority as a father. Dorothy cited his rigidity and temper as proof that he was unworthy of respect either from his children or from her.

CHUCK: Chuck, Nancy's older brother, presented his parents with a different sort of problem. As a child he had been quiet and delightfully easy-going, but these attributes became less attractive to his parents as he became an adolescent. Nothing captured his interest enough to spur him to enthusiastic activity. He attended school during the day, watched television in the evening, worked a few hours at a service station on Saturdays, dated one girl occasionally, and strummed listlessly on his guitar from time to time. Charles observed his son's lassitude and struggled not to express the impatience he felt. He tried to engage the boy's interest in sports, in reading, in dating other girls, in anything! But every conversation he initiated with Chuck turned into a paternal monologue. Eventually Charles stopped making any effort even to talk with his son.

Dorothy's relationship with Chuck was more satisfying in some respects. She often stayed up reading after her husband had gone to bed, and she discovered that when no one else was around Chuck sometimes would talk with her about himself. What she learned now from him was not cheering, however.

Chuck was perceptive enough to realize that his father hoped he would follow in his footsteps and pursue a professional career, but Chuck felt no such interest or ambition within himself. He wanted to please his father, but he knew no way of doing so other than to pretend enthusiasm about something he found boring and distasteful, and this he could not bring himself to do. Caught in this dilemma, Chuck felt helpless and depressed. For over a year he had found relief from these feelings only by smoking marijuana. He knew that smoking pot contributed to his lack of involvement in other activities, but it provided him with his only pleasure in an otherwise joyless existence.

Dorothy received her son's news with mixed feelings. She was relieved that he could confide in her, but her new knowledge was a burden that she had to bear alone, for Chuck extracted from her a promise that she would not reveal it to his father. She worried about physical harm that the drug might induce. She was angry with his girlfriend, who was the source of his supply. But most of all, she was frightened by the possibility of his getting into trouble with the law, and her fear was realistic. A few weeks later, Chuck was apprehended by the police for possessing marijuana.

Charles' reaction to his son's arrest was not what either his son or wife expected. Instead of expressing fury, Charles acted as though he were stunned. He was barely able to go to his office and attend to his patients. In the evenings he retired from his family to his study, where he sat for hours holding a book open on his lap but unable to read. Chuck would have preferred having his father punish him, however violently, to having him sink into such profound despondency. The boy's experience of guilt over causing his father's depression became so intense that he contemplated running away or killing himself. Dorothy felt panic at the idea that her son would even contemplate either of these, and she was enraged by her husband's behavior. Whatever sympathy she felt for him at first was soon washed away in a flood of resentment over the responsibilities that fell on her shoulders, for it was she who had to deal with lawyers and courtroom procedures if they were to be dealt with effectively. She was caught between her husband's depression and her son's despair, and there was no one with whom she could share her own burden of anxiety. Dorothy felt utterly alone and without support.

The entire summer passed before Chuck's case was resolved by the court. As a minor charged with a first offense, he was treated leniently. The judge reprimanded him and placed him on probation. Unfortunately, the court could take no action that would reduce his internal conflict with comparable benevolence. He began eleventh grade the following week more ravaged by anxiety than he had ever been before. The same day, Nancy enrolled in her nutrition course.

THE FATHER: Charles G. was born and raised in Baltimore. His parents were German-born immigrants who came to the United States shortly after they were married. Charles' father was a baker who worked long hours to provide a comfortable living for his large family. His role was that of patriarch in his home, caring well for those dependent upon him and exacting from them in return strict adherence to the standards of behavior that he set. Charles' mother was a nurturing woman, content with her life in the home and proud of her husband and children, whom she served without complaint. Charles could not recall ever hearing his parents argue. The few disagreements they had were over the disposition of family funds, and his mother always yielded quickly to her husband's position. She rarely was stern with her children, but she did insist that they obey their father's rules and abide by his wishes.

The neighborhood in which they lived included very few other German-American families. Occasionally, they would attend a nearby Lutheran church, more for the social contact it provided than out of commitment to religion. For the most part, however, family members found the companionship and entertainment they needed within their home. Charles vividly remembered evenings when his father led the family in singing, after which his mother and older sister would surprise them all with some delicious pastry that they had baked. On these occasions, Charles' father would always announce that since his wife was such a splendid pastry cook, he was going to hire her to work for him at his bakery, and the children would shout in unison that he couldn't do that since she had to stay home and cook for them. Before Charles was old enough to understand his family joke, he felt frightened by the idea that his mother might consider leaving home to take a job somewhere else.

Tragedy in the form of illness and death struck Charles' family again and again. Of seven children, only three survived to be adults, and each of these, including Charles, was seriously ill at some time. Charles was deeply moved by the grief his parents suffered as their sons and daughters fell ill and died. Before he was ten years old he decided to become a doctor himself and devote his life to fighting disease. His ambition was reasonable, for Charles was a good student. He was also a disciplined young man, accustomed to working hard and foregoing frivolities.

Circumstances altered Charles' plans. Shortly before he was graduated from college, the United States entered World War II. He was qualified to enter medical school immediately and continue his training without interruption, but other factors had to be considered. Anti-German sentiment ran high in the neighborhood where his parents lived, and the few German-American families who remained in that community felt pressed to demonstrate their patriotism. Charles' older brother was married with two small children; he could not be expected to volunteer for military duty. It was up to Charles to testify to the loyalty of his family by enlisting in the army.

It was while Charles was stationed in the middle-west for his basic training that he met Dorothy, fell in love with her, and married her. One of the things that attracted him to her was her wholesomeness. She was someone he felt he could trust. He could talk easily with her because she didn't put on silly airs or act hard-to-get like the few girls he had dated in the past. And he was charmed by Dorothy's vivacity and warmth. He could relax with her and begin to discover things about life that he had never before even noticed. She was a pretty girl, too. Just chubby enough to be especially attractive to him. Falling in love with Dorothy made him realize how lonely he was and how little fun he had ever allowed himself in the past. They were married seven weeks before he was sent overseas.

His decision to marry led Charles to still another critical decision upon his return to civilian life. To enter medical school he would have to wait a year and a half, but he could enter dental college much sooner. He chose dentistry and found the choice surprisingly easy. He could be content as a dentist. His parents didn't see much difference between the two professions. And Dorothy was pleased because there would be less delay before they could settle down in a life of their own. Delay was the critical factor for Charles, too. He had a wife, but he wanted a home of his own and children, both as soon as possible.

They lived with Charles' family while he went to school. Dorothy seemed to delight in pleasing his parents and his sister, Ellen, and they readily grew to love her. Charles was relieved that they all got along so well. His brother's wife had never been interested in a close relationship with her in-laws, and Charles hated the kind of tension that this introduced into the family. Besides, he was grateful. Living with his parents and sharing expenses with them made it possible for Charles and Dorothy to live easily on the money he received from the GI bill.

Dorothy worked while he went to school. She was a secretary to a prominent lawyer in the community and earned a good salary. Charles disliked the idea of his wife working, but her earnings all went to build up the savings that would help them buy their own home when he finished training.

The middle-west was where Charles wanted to settle. He had visited the small communities in the vicinity of his army base, and it was in such a small town that he wanted to live, work, and raise his children, not in a teeming urban ghetto like the one in which he had grown up.

Charles decided on a small town south of Chicago, not far from where Dorothy's parents lived. It was predominantly a German community. This made Charles feel very much at home until he learned that most of the families were Catholic rather than Lutheran like the neighbors he had known in Baltimore. It was important for Charles to be accepted and not feel "different," so he worked especially hard and conscientiously to win the respect of his professional colleagues and the patronage of potential patients.

Within a year of their move, Charles' father died of heart disease. Dorothy was so close to delivering their first child that he couldn't permit her to travel with him to the funeral. In fact, Sarah was born the day after he returned from Baltimore.

Charles grieved for his father, but only briefly; he was caught up in a life that demanded his attention and met his every conscious need. He enjoyed his work, in which he took pride and performed well. He adored his baby daughter and devoted himself to her whenever he was home. Dorothy pleased him in every way—in her new role as mother, in her willingness to help with the business details of his office, and in her eagerness to represent him well in the community. He rarely voiced his pleasure to her, but, surely, that was not necessary. He spoke his love for her through his actions as a good provider.

Only one thing troubled him: Dorothy's relationship with her mother. He could see for himself, during Mr. and Mrs. M.'s frequent visits, that Mrs. M. was constantly critical of Dorothy. But, somehow, Dorothy brought the criticism on herself, because she was always her worst—childish and inept—when her mother was in the house. He tried reasoning with Dorothy, but to no avail. He soon found it easier to accept in silence her outbursts of tears and bad humor that followed each of her mother's visits.

After Charles Junior was born, when Sarah was two, the animosity between Dorothy and her mother intensified. It focused primarily on Dorothy's way of handling Sarah's jealousy of her new baby brother. Her mother judged Dorothy to be too permissive with the little girl, and Dorothy angrily defended both herself and her daughter. On this issue, Charles found it hard to be sympathetic with his wife, because he, too, felt she was much too casual about Sarah's temper tantrums. He was concerned that his daughter's outbursts might seriously threaten little Chuck's safety. He felt it wiser, however, to keep his thoughts to himself than to express them. His wife had a sharp tongue, and he always lost in an argument with her.

Mr. and Mrs. M. visited one weekend when Dorothy was pregnant with her third child. While the two women were busy in the kitchen, Charles and his father-in-law talked quietly in the back yard. Mr. M. was a gentle, quiet man whose company Charles enjoyed. When dinner was ready, they entered the house, savoring the delicious fragrance that filled the room. As soon as they sat down, Mrs. M. began to fill her husband's plate with food. Charles saw Dorothy pale and clutch the edge of her chair. A few moments later she fled from the table and locked herself in their bedroom. It was not until after her parents departed the next morning that Dorothy left her sanctuary. She emerged to announce to Charles that she couldn't put up with her mother another day without getting psychiatric help. When Charles tried to reassure her, she flew into a rage with him. His patronizing manner and refusal to see how miserable she was only made matters worse. Nothing he could say dissuaded her. Painful as it was to face up to Dorothy's demands, Charles had no alternative but to consult with one of the local doctors for referral to a Chicago psychiatrist.

Dorothy's treatment began. To others Charles could explain her absences as shopping trips to the city or visits to her parents. But he couldn't explain to himself her need for psychiatric treatment. What could she possibly want that she didn't have? His sister, Ellen, unmarried and living alone since their mother had died, visited them briefly during this period. When he compared the two women, he found it difficult to understand how Dorothy could possibly be so upset, fulfilled as she was as a wife and mother?

Then Nancy was born. She was a beautiful child who grew more lovely every year. Charles acknowledged, but only to himself, that she was his favorite child. She was his "baby." Even as a little girl she seemed to want to please him, and everything about her pleased him well. Little else was genuinely pleasant for him at home any more.

Dorothy terminated her therapy when Nancy was one year old, but the relationship between her and Charles remained strained. She continued to manage the house with superb efficiency. She was still charming to their friends and affectionate with their children. But with him she was now aloof and distant. Most of the time they were together she was silent.

As the children grew, so did the family's problems. Dorothy refused to make the children adhere to even the basic amenities of courtesy and respect toward Charles. Sarah would scream hateful things at him whenever she lost her temper. Chuck would slink away from him whenever he was reprimanded. And Dorothy stood as their advocate against him on one issue after another. He felt undermined as a father and bereft of the important loving relationship he had had with his children when they were little. The detente with his wife resembled an armed truce more than it did a marriage.

Charles tried to make sense of his family's complaints. They all chided him for being more involved with his work than with them. Perhaps this was true. He had become more absorbed in his profession, since it was one of his few sources of pleasure. His wife and two older children wanted to move away from middle America, which they found physically and politically oppressive. Perhaps they were right. He found nothing about the middle-west life oppressive, except his family, but perhaps he was near-sighted. Even Nancy agreed. "Please, Daddy! Let's move where you can spend more time with us!" His family wanted to move to the west coast, and it was important to him to see that his family was happy. He sold his practice, and they moved to southern California.

Charles associated himself with a group of dentists practicing in Long Beach. The transition wasn't easy for him, but his professional skill was welcomed by his colleagues, and he found the shorter hours a relief. He waited in vain, however, for the salubrious results that this move was supposed to provide for him and his family. His wife and children liked their attractive new home and adapted readily to their new style of living, but they continued to shut him out of their lives. Even Nancy, now twelve years old, found excuses for no longer being close to her father. She would wriggle away from him whenever he tried to hug her or hold her on his lap, and she would pout and whine whenever he called her his "baby."

It was Sarah's decision to quit school that made him realize just how alienated he had become from his wife and children. Her behavior had challenged him as a father, and he had failed to meet the challenge adequately. His wife openly opposed him, and Chuck and Nancy reproachfully indicated that their sympathies lay with Sarah.

He was perplexed by Sarah. This was the first born child, the little girl who had at one time been such a delight to him. He tried to blame the decadent culture of southern California for what had happened to her. In spite of his efforts to excuse her, however, he found himself looking at her slothfulness and obesity with disgust and responding to her with anger because she had rendered him so utterly ineffectual.

When Chuck became involved with a disreputable girl and, through her, the local illicit drug scene, Charles was stunned. He fell into a profound depression over which he had no control. He found himself ruminating about the grief that his own father had experienced with each child that died. It frightened him to find that sometimes he envied his father. How much easier it would be if both Sarah and Chuck were dead! Alive, they testified to his personal failure as a father.

Nancy's illness was almost more than Charles could bear. His wife had found her a difficult child to raise, but for him, at least, she had remained one source of joy. Now she was starving herself to death.

THE MOTHER: Dorothy grew up in a small semi-rural community in northwestern Illinois. Her father owned one of the town's two dry-goods stores. Mr. M. was an easy-going man who found it difficult to refuse credit to his customers. This made him well-liked as a person by the townspeople, but it did not earn him much respect as a businessman.

Dorothy's mother was the practical individual in the family. She managed her home, her husband, and her children with force and efficiency. Furthermore, she worked as representative of a Chicago cosmetic firm, a job which required her to spend hours away from home soliciting customers and delivering her wares. Mrs. M.'s persistence made her an effective saleswoman. In contrast to her husband, she was easy to admire but difficult to like.

Dorothy and her brother, Steve, only a year her junior, learned early in life to conform to their mother's expectations of them and to seek neither sympathy nor indulgence from her. For support and affection they turned to their father. Mr. M. occasionally served as their advocate with his wife and succeeded, at times, in obtaining special dispensations for them. One such triumph was persuading her to let them have pets. Mrs. M. reluctantly agreed, but only on the condition that they be wholly responsible for whatever animals they kept.

The two children soon acquired a large menagerie and caring for the animals served as the basis for a close relationship between sister and brother. They day-dreamed together about becoming veterinarians, talk that was dismissed by their parents as childish fantasy. However, Dorothy's interest in going to veterinary school increased rather than diminished as she grew older.

At sixteen Dorothy was shocked to learn that her parents had absolutely no intention of providing her with any education beyond high school. It was then that she learned how bad her father's business had been and how dependent the entire family was upon her mother's earnings. Mrs. M. saw no reason for money to be wasted on sending her daughter to college. Dorothy could take commercial courses in high school and be employable as soon as she graduated. It was for Steve's college education that Mrs. M. had been saving her hard-earned money through the years, and it was on Steve's education that the money would be spent.

Dorothy was furious with both of her parents, with her mother for considering her unworthy of an education, and with her father for being powerless to act in her behalf. She had no alternative but to submit, however. Her anger toward her father gradually diminished, diluted by remembered affection and new-found pity. But nothing lessened the resentment she felt toward her mother. She would feel overwhelmed with rage whenever she overheard her mother describe herself as a woman who "served her children first, her husband next, and herself last." To Dorothy it seemed quite the reverse.

By the time Dorothy graduated from high school the United States was at war. She easily found a job in Chicago, where she lived with a widowed aunt. At first she returned home each weekend, but after a few months she began to stay in the city and devote her weekends to volunteer work. She also began to think about enlisting in the army. Being a WAC would permit her to play a more active roll in the war effort, something she wanted very much to do. And it would also devastate her mother, who was outspoken against the very idea of women being in uniform. It was at this time that she met Charles at a USO center.

Dorothy had dated frequently during her high school years, but she had never found herself truly enamored of any of her boy friends. Her relationship with Charles was a new and different experience. She was attracted primarily by his maturity and his determination to become a doctor. She was flattered by his attentiveness

and excited by her own capacity to please and interest him. She felt
certain that he would be a successful man and a generous husband.
The affection Dorothy felt for Charles was genuine. She only partially admitted to herself that marrying him was also an attractive
way of putting distance between herself and her parents and of
securing her own future.

She continued her job in Chicago while Charles was overseas.
Somehow just being married made her feel less resentful of her
mother, and her visits home became less tense for everyone. Mrs. M.
actually approved of Dorothy's marriage and felt relieved that her
daughter need no longer be her concern. Other worries preoccupied
her now. Steve was in college and was dating a girl of whom she did
not in the least approve. Dorothy enjoyed having her mother's critical attention directed toward someone other than herself.

When Charles was discharged from the service Dorothy met him
in New York City and they journeyed together to his parent's home
in Baltimore. She felt some apprehension because she desperately
wanted his family to like and accept her. They, in turn, were eager
to welcome Charles' wife into their home, and the relationship between them was successful from the start. In fact, Dorothy and
Ellen quickly became close friends.

Dorothy worked while Charles went to dental college. When she
came home from work, she devoted herself to helping around the
house far more than was expected of her. Whenever she felt impatient or irritable, as she occasionally did, she bit her tongue and
dusted the living room a second time, reminding herself that living
with Charles' family made it possible for them to save all of her
salary and accumulate the funds they would need for their future
home.

She was relieved, however, when it came time for them to move
back to the middle-west and into a house of their own. She was not
the least dismayed when Charles selected a small town within two
hours' driving distance from where her parents lived. During the four
years she had lived with Charles and his family, Dorothy had matured a great deal and she felt secure and self-confident. Besides,
she was far too excited about furnishing their new home and preparing for the birth of their first child to worry about her relationship
with her parents.

The relationship became a problem, nevertheless. The first time her parents visited them Dorothy was appalled by what she observed. Her father had totally capitulated. His wife made every decision for him: what he could wear, what he could eat, what he should say. Dorothy felt utter disgust toward him for the passive way he submitted to her mother. There was no remnant of the affection or even of the pity she had felt before. She was thankful that she was married to a man whom she could respect, someone who would never allow himself to be so humiliated.

She also had to listen to her mother complain bitterly about her brother. Steve had married Lisa, the girl Mrs. M. had so keenly disapproved of, and he had left college to go to work. Mrs. M. refused to acknowledge Lisa as her daughter-in-law or receive her in her house. Now Steve and Lisa were strangers to the rest of the family. Mrs. M. didn't even know where they were living. Dorothy remembered the warmth with which she had been accepted in Charles' home and looked at her mother with cold contempt. How determined she was never to be anything like her! She would never drive any of her children away through such stubborn tyranny.

After Sarah was born, Dorothy's problems with her mother intensified. Mrs. M. never ceased criticizing Dorothy's role as a mother. Every time her mother entered her house, Dorothy felt anger and anxiety well up within her. Her parents' visits became agony for her. It didn't relieve her tensions, either, to hear her mother extravagantly commend Charles for everything he did. Nor did it comfort her when Charles would prevail upon her to be more charitable and patient with the older woman.

One way Dorothy tried to handle her feelings was to plunge herself into activity. She busied herself with things that would win Charles' approval and help her feel good about herself. She kept her home immaculate. She prepared meals that she knew Charles enjoyed. She donated her evenings and her experience as a secretary to help Charles with the business details of his growing practice. She found time to be active in medical auxiliaries and community action groups. But no matter how hard she tried, she never felt that she was doing enough. Whatever she did certainly was not sufficient to elicit praise from Charles nor protect her from denegration by her mother.

By the time she was pregnant with Nancy, Dorothy had reached the end of her rope. Seated at the dinner table during one of her parents' visits, Dorothy sat watching her mother select food to put on her father's plate and dictating to her children what they should put on theirs. There sat her father, looking as if he actually enjoyed his wife's attention instead of being man enough to tell her to leave him alone. And there sat Charles, smiling at both of her parents and thanking her mother for the meal that she, Dorothy, had prepared. She fought off the impulse to scream. Instead she fled to their bedroom, locked the door behind her, and wept. She didn't know how to cope any longer. In fact, she felt sure she would go out of her mind if she didn't get some kind of help immediately. The next day she grimly informed Charles that she had to see a psychiatrist.

Dorothy's treatment sessions were helpful. Her doctor paid attention to what she said. He never considered her feelings to be foolish. Above all, he didn't criticize her like her mother or try to reason with her like Charles. She continued in therapy until Nancy was almost a year old. By then she understood many reasons why her mother was able to upset her so and she felt able to master the situation. Indeed, she was now capable of handling her mother patiently, much to Charles' relief as well as her own.

Her relationship with Charles worsened, however. She particularly resented everything he took for granted about her, even though she expected all of these things of herself: being an attentive mother, a superb housekeeper, an excellent cook, a help to him in his office, an asset to him as a hostess, and a tireless worker for charitable causes.

She tried hard not to express her resentment, for she recognized that it was an irrational sort of feeling. But she knew it colored everything she did and that Charles was perplexed and troubled by her aloofness. She shrugged off his concern. He was smart enough to figure out what was wrong. He obviously just didn't care enough to do anything about it.

As the children grew, Dorothy found herself saddled with more of the responsibility for them. Charles had been a great help with them when they were babies or small children, but now he handled them poorly and constantly provoked them into disobedience. He disliked seeing Sarah get so chubby, but he should have sense enough to realize that girls often gain weight temporarily at puberty and that it only made matters worse to fuss at Sarah about her overeating. He should know better than to keep pestering Chuck to play baseball when the boy obviously hated the sport. He should stop lecturing all three children about cleaning their rooms and finishing their projects, because it only made the older two sulk and Nancy cry.

Dorothy watched her husband's ineffectual attempts to deal with his children and felt a grim kind of satisfaction. He didn't fool either them or her. He tried to conceal his preference for Nancy by always making his pompous speeches about self-improvement to all three of the children together, but it was clear that his criticism was directed toward the older two. Nancy could do no wrong in his eyes.

Nancy was far from the little angel her father thought her to be. She was much more difficult for Dorothy to cope with than either Sarah or Chuck. Nancy was neat, to the point of fussiness. She whined constantly. She clung to her mother and made endless demands for attention and reassurance. Charles saw very little of this, of course, for when he was around Nancy was always at his side. She behaved herself then because he indulged her every whim. Dorothy had pointed out to him that he favored Nancy over her sister and brother, but he refused to acknowledge the fact. Dorothy certainly couldn't blame Sarah and Chuck when they demonstrated their jealousy by teasing Nancy, sometimes mercilessly.

Dorothy began to find her days more tiresome and her activities less diverting. For years she had fancied the idea of living in California, and now she decided that moving was what she and the family needed. She argued that life would be more interesting for all of them if they lived on the west coast. She pointed out that in a larger city Charles could join a group of dentists and by doing so would not have to work such long hours and could spend more time with his family. She enlisted the children in support of her cause, and they joined her in a campaign to persuade Charles to move.

Dorothy felt triumphant when he finally yielded. She had convinced herself that the change would truly be best for everyone in the family. At first it seemed as though she had judged correctly. As a family they explored the beaches and mountain areas near their new home and rediscovered pleasure in family outings. But soon the children developed different interests and preferred being with their friends to taking weekend trips with their parents. Without the children along, Charles and Dorothy didn't risk many outings.

To be alone with each other was uncomfortable for both of them.

Charles would lapse into silence and assume either a watchful expression or a hurt one. If she started a conversation, he would respond in monosyllables. If she tried to consult with him about some practical matter, he would put off giving her advice or making a decision. He had become boring and indecisive, and she could hardly bear to be around him. Along with irritation, Dorothy felt guilt. Charles had moved to California at her insistence. He was the generous provider she had known he would be. Compared to many women, Dorothy was fortunate and she knew it. Knowing it didn't lessen her annoyance with him however. It just made her feel ashamed of herself every time she lashed out at him or she turned away from his overtures of affection.

Their crises with Sarah and Chuck, and now with Nancy, had only made matters worse between them. She and Charles were totally estranged. She wasn't so unfair as to blame her husband for everything that had happened, but she was sure that if he had ever treated any of them as persons in their own right with lives of their own to lead, things would have been better. Now that his precious Nancy was sick, maybe Charles would face up to what was really going on in the family. Dorothy knew that *anorexia nervosa* was an emotional disorder. Charles was simply going to have to accept the fact that his children, and his wife, had feelings.

Course of Treatment. Nancy was admitted to the hospital's psychiatric inpatient service for adolescents. The unit provided a comprehensive program of care that included schooling, occupational therapy, group and individual therapy, exercise, and recreation. Several times a week the patients met together with various members of the staff, sometimes to discuss individual problems, sometimes to deal with issues of unit management and interpersonal relationships.

The mealtime regime for anorectic patients like Nancy was handled in a very matter-of-fact way. Each girl (adolescent anorectic patients are almost always female) was given the opportunity to select what she wanted to eat from the food offered to everyone. The portions she took were measured. If she did not voluntarily consume her minimum quota of calories, she was given a portion of nutritious liquid equivalent to what she still required. If she drank all of it, fine. If not, it was fed to her by stomach tube. The girls rarely had to be fed by force.

As long as an anorectic girl's weight remained dangerously low, she was observed carefully after each meal to make certain that the food remained in her stomach. After she attained a weight at which her life was no longer threatened, observation was discontinued. When she weighed as much as was normal for her size and age, her caloric intake was no longer measured.

The staff adhered strictly to these mealtime procedures, but this was the only aspect of the ward's treatment regimen for anorectics that focused on their symptom. Experience had demonstrated to the staff that an anorectic patient benefited little from having them share her preoccupation with body weight. Instead, they directed their attention to other facets of her troubled life.

Nancy met with her psychiatrist four times a week in individual psychotherapy. At first she talked with him only about her unspecified fears and her assortment of "habits," and for weeks she maintained the conviction that nothing about her was physically deviant. Eventually, she could recognize not only how much she resented being dependent but also how frightened she was by the idea of taking responsibility for herself. She felt unable to exert any mastery over anything that happened to her. Gradually Nancy came to realize that taking control of what she ate had been a way of demonstrating to herself that she was not helpless.

Nancy had to be hospitalized for two years, and during that time the course of her recovery was very uneven. She remained under post-mealtime observation much longer than usual, because she proved to be particularly clever at finding ways to conceal the food she vomited. She was one of the few anorectic patients who had to be tube-fed. Finally Nancy began to make genuine progress. Her fears lessened, and she learned to recognize what sorts of experiences gave her personal pleasure. As she gained understanding, she was able to gain weight as well.

Family therapy was included in the hospital's treatment regimen. Everyone participated willingly because, by now, they recognized that Nancy was not the only troubled person in the family. At the outset, Dorothy led in a litany of complaints against Charles. As the extent and intensity of her resentment toward him unfolded, Charles became even more depressed, but, supported by the therapists, he eventually risked voicing some of his own hurts and disappointments. Gradually, Sarah and Charles contributed information about what troubled them as well. Nancy, working in individual therapy at the same time, began to recognize some of the feelings that lay buried beneath her symptoms and was able to share these feelings with the others.

The family began to learn something about itself. No one ever directly asked for what he wanted from someone else. Each person knew what he longed for from the others, what would help him feel better about himself or make him more capable of fulfilling his needs, but to ask for what one wanted was to risk being refused, and refusal was what each of them always expected. It was safer to wait for the other person to divine what was needed and take the responsibility for meeting that need. But although waiting was safe, it was never satisfying. It only provided time during which anger could grow over rejections that never actually took place but which were constantly anticipated. And each person, of course, felt far too personally impoverished to be able to nourish anyone else.

Family therapy continued for 18 months. During that time, the children learned that they were capable of separating themselves from the conflict that permeated their parents' marriage and could take more responsibility for themselves. Sarah was able to tell her father how much she had wanted the affection he always showered on Nancy but, even more important, she was able to take his hand in hers and tell him she loved him. Subsequently, Sarah went east to continue her education and seek psychiatric therapy for her own problems.

Chuck spoke little during all those months of therapy, but he listened well. He learned that his responsibility was to make something of his own life rather than to meet what he thought were his father's expectations of him. He sought individual career counseling and discovered that he had both an interest in and aptitude for graphic arts. Free of anxiety about how to please his father, Chuck discovered that it felt good to be himself.

It was another six months before Nancy was discharged from the hospital. Occasionally, she joined her parents for a session of family therapy, but her work continued mostly in individual therapy. During this time Charles and Dorothy met with the therapists to examine their relationship with each other. In her previous treatment experience, Dorothy had learned a great deal about how she felt toward her mother, but she had not comprehended the extent to which her relationship with both of her parents had diminished her capacity to have a healthy, mature marriage of her own. She was determined never to be anything like the aggressive, domineering self-centered woman her mother was. Yet, Dorothy was a competent person, capable of taking charge of things and of managing well. She had to reject these assets in herself, however, because they so closely resembled the attributes she rejected in her mother.

Dorothy was equally determined never to let her marriage resemble that of her parents. Charles had to be a strong, assertive husband who would protect her from having such a thing happen. Dorothy's need to have Charles be like his father rather than her own blinded her to the kind of man Charles, himself, really was—a passive, vulnerable, needful person in his own right. When Dorothy no longer could avoid seeing these qualities in him, she felt frightened and betrayed.

Charles had always known himself to be a needful person, but he saw his needs as weaknesses and was too ashamed to share them with anyone. In the course of therapy Charles realized that his silence concealed more problems than it solved. When he was able to put his concerns into words, he discovered that they were neither unreasonable nor uniquely his. As the dynamics underlying Dorothy's dilemma unfolded, Charles no longer needed to accept all the responsibility for their troubled marriage, and some of his guilt diminished.

Neither Dorothy nor Charles solved all of their problems in the six months that Nancy remained in the hospital. They did come to recognize the extent to which their children's problems had helped keep the two of them together as well as alienate them, however, and were able to explore healthier reasons for staying married and alternative ways of functioning as parents. They were even able to discuss divorce, which neither of them really wanted, and their discussion helped them rediscover positive reasons for remaining married. By the time Nancy was discharged, they could work together constructively to help their daughter readjust to life outside the hospital. They could at least recognize her ambivalence about growing up and could lend support to her struggle to be responsible for herself.

Questions for the G. Family

1. Summarize Nancy's behavior and attitudes regarding food during the one year prior to her hospitalization.

2. List other symptoms or behavior which were obvious at the same time (e.g., perfectionism, hyperactivity, body-image distortion).

3. What relationships do you see between the behaviors which you listed in response to Question 1 and those listed in response to Question 2? Consider such factors as

    a. desire for control over herself and others

    b. attitudes toward her body and her biological needs.

4. Symptoms such as Nancy's almost always appear in early adolescence around the time of puberty. What are the normal developmental problems faced by a young girl at this time, and what earlier conflicts might be reactivated?

5. What aspects of Nancy's family situation might have made these normal conflicts extremely difficult to handle? Specifically, why should signs of growing up and womanhood threaten her so?

6. Symptoms of psychopathology can be seen as *expressions of conflict* or as *defenses* being used to ward off painful thoughts or feelings. Which aspects of Nancy's behavior (which you outlined in Questions 1 and 2 above) appear to be

    a. expressions of conflict

    b. defenses or mechanisms for coping with the conflict?

How can you account for the fact that Nancy could pursue a pattern of behavior which brought her perilously close to death in order to avoid deep-seated conflicts?

7. Problems such as Nancy's are often more clearly seen within a total system of family transactions. Considerable evidence has been presented concerning the background of Nancy's parents as well as her siblings. First let's look at her parents.

Family problems are often understood if one considers the unresolved problems that people bring from their family of origin to their marriage.

    a. What unresolved relationship problems did Charles bring to his marriage? Consider:

     i. problems of dependency and intimacy
     ii. problems of self-assertion
     iii. problems surrounding death and loss.

b. What unresolved relationship problems did Dorothy bring to her marriage? Consider:

     i. problems of dependency and autonomy in regard to her mother
     ii. her feelings about the mother-father relationship between her parents
     iii. her self-esteem and self-confidence.

c. In what ways did the unresolved problems that Charles and Dorothy brought to the marriage fit with one another, that is, in what ways did their needs support each other?

d. In what ways did their unresolved problems lead to conflicting needs which served as sources of tension within their marriage?

e. Consider what needs Dorothy brought to her marriage, based on her family problems, which Charles was unable to fill because of his family problems, and vice versa.

8. What dynamic changes occurred over the course of Charles' and Dorothy's marriage? Consider:

    a. role and leadership structure
    b. emotional climate
    c. hostility-tension levels which evolved in the family.

9. In what ways did Sarah and Chuck experience the same type of family environment as Nancy; in what ways was it different? How might these differences account for the different types of emotional problems that Sarah and Chuck manifested?

10. Sarah and Nancy both manifested focal problems around food, one obesity, and the other, anorexia. What aspects of their family life may have sensitized them to food as an anxiety-ridden area? To what extent were these food problems symbolic of deeper emotionally based needs that were frustrated in the family?

11. By virtue of the dynamic changes which occurred in the G. Family over time (see your answers to Question 8 above), what special role did Nancy play in the G. family? What frustrated parental and sibling needs did she fit into, and in what ways was she a focus of these needs?

12. How did this special role sensitize Nancy to

    a. subsequent problems regarding autonomy from parental figures

    b. sexual conflicts

    c. obsessive-compulsive methods for binding her anxiety?

References

BERLIN, I., BOATMAN, M., SHEIMO, S., & SZUREK, S. Adolescent alternation of anorexia and obesity. *American Journal of Orthopsychiatry*, 1951, **21**: 387–419.

BRUCH, H. *Eating disorders: obesity, anorexia nervosa and the person within.* New York: Basic Books, 1973.

BRUCH, H. Family transactions and eating disorders. *Comprehensive Psychiatry*, 1971, **12**: 238–248.

KAY, D., & SHAPIRO, K. The prognosis in anorexia nervosa. In MEYER, J., & FELDMAN, H. (Eds.) *Anorexia nervosa.* Stuttgart: Verlag, 1965.

SOURS, J. Anorexia nervosa: nosology, diagnosis, developmental patterns and power-control dynamics. In CAPLAN, G., & LEBOVICI, S. (Eds.) *Adolescence: psychosocial perspectives.* New York: Basic Books, 1969.

PART III NEUROTIC REACTIONS IN ADULTHOOD

THE CASE OF FRANCIS P.

The Divorce

As he contemplated his current situation, Francis recognized that he probably had been depressed for many years almost without realizing it. However, his feelings now were centered entirely around the threat of the divorce. Before this threat arose his life seemed happy, at least outwardly. He had been living in a beautiful home with his young, lovely wife and three children. They were in general good health, it seemed to him, although later he realized that both he and his wife had endured systemic dysfunctions which were actually a threat to their lives. If anyone had asked him four months previously about his marriage, he would have replied he could not have considered himself more happy. Thus it had been an acute and severe shock to him when his wife Carol had informed him that she was very much in love with another man and that she wanted him to move out of the house and get a divorce. His initial reaction was that this was unimaginable, and he could not even understand what she meant. Surely she was joking. When he realized that she was quite serious, his first reaction was to disbelieve that she was in love with anyone else but rather that he had done something which displeased her and which he could rectify. She responded that she no longer loved him and did not feel that there was any way she could really change. Still he pleaded with her that maybe they both needed to change, maybe they both should enter psychotherapy. He would try his best. He knew he hadn't been a perfect husband in many ways. At least for the sake of the children she should try to reconsider her situation and her feelings. Finally she agreed; yet she maintained that they should not see the same therapist but rather they should work out their problems separately. Moreover, she demanded that they temporarily separate and that he leave the home. He acceded to all of this with the hope that his marriage could be reconstituted.

Francis maintained he was not really jealous of his wife's lover. As far as he was aware, the immediate situation stemmed from Carol's illness of a year ago. She had suffered some infection of her sexual organs which was not easy to diagnose but which made intercourse quite painful and which left her enervated and weak. Her gynecologist was one of Francis's college classmates, and they had been social friends for many years. Only two years before her doctor and his wife had separated, the first of several marriages in their circle of friends to break up. They continued to see the doctor socially from time to time, and Francis was aware that Carol would have lunch with the doctor right after an appointment and sometimes at other times during the week, usually with other friends along. Francis was unable to join Carol and her friends for these luncheons, but he encouraged her to get out since he knew she had been restricted to the house for the past year with her illness and for the past three years before that during her pregnancies.

Initially Francis was much more prone to blame himself. Perhaps he had been a poor husband and father. Most of his lifetime he had had to fight being overweight and had frequently been on diets, often to no avail. During the six years of his marriage he had risen from 185 to almost 225 pounds, varying at times as he attempted to diet. He realized also that he probably over-used alcohol; usually he had a drink or so before dinner and two or three after dinner, whereupon he would sit dozing in front of the television. Quite frequently, when socializing with his friends on weekends, he and his male friends would become quite inebriated. Yet no one in his crowd thought of themselves as alcoholics, and their use of alcohol was socially well accepted.

As Francis reviewed his marriage, he realized that he probably was not a satisfactory sexual partner. He had no sexual experience prior to his marriage at age 23, and his sexual relationships with his young bride had really been amazingly few since they had agreed not to have intercourse while she was pregnant. Francis felt guilt-stricken about his masturbation from childhood on and found that he was "addicted" to masturbation after his marriage. In Francis's mind, it was this "sin" of masturbation which underlay the breakdown of his marriage. He refused to accept the possibility that the masturbation after his marriage might be the results of his need for sexual satisfaction because of the poor sexual relationship between him and his wife.

While Francis berated himself for being an inadequate husband, he was unable to accept his wife's suggestion that he was also a poor father. There was no doubt, as Francis spoke of his children, that he held them in great affection. He was proud of them and encouraged their development in every way. In his own mind he felt he spent a great deal of time with them. Although occasionally he did not get home until almost their bedtime, it was understood that they were not to be put to bed until he arrived. He read each one a separate story and tucked each one into bed every night. Most of his week-end hours were spent with the children. If he had errands to run, one or more of them went with him, and he often gave up his own activities to see that they had something enjoyable to do. He was particularly anxious that they have a good Catholic education, and the whole family went to services together. Francis never missed mass, even when his wife was ill, and he always took the children. He dutifully saw to it that the children spent some time with each of their grandmothers, although he could not stand his own mother and would not have visited her otherwise.

He felt more at home with his mother-in-law, at least up until the time that Carol decided to separate from him. He was embarrassed to find that Carol's mother took his side and even wanted him to move in with her which he refused. Carol's mother was then in the process of separating from her third husband. Francis felt that she was looking to him for sympathy, whereas Francis had really always felt more sympathetic toward his father-in-law. Moreover, almost from the time that he first met Carol, Francis considered that his mother-in-law acted very seductively toward him. Actually his mother-in-law was only 16 years older than his wife and 10 years older than Francis. Francis feared that if he did not watch his step he could easily be involved in an affair with her. He sheepishly admitted that some of his masturbatory fantasies included sexual relationships with his mother-in-law whom he saw as a "sexually liberated" woman. Such fantasies only increased his guilt feelings. It was only much later in therapy that Francis realized the parallels between Carol and her mother, i.e., that both had married as soon as they finished high school and both had had three children before they were 25, at which time their first marriages broke up. It had seemed unimaginable to Francis that Carol had any but the most strict Catholic morals.

As might be expected, Francis began contemplating how this mar-

riage ever came to be. He remembered that he was a very shy
adolescent who attended an all-boys Catholic high school. Partly because he was a very large youngster, he had considerable success in
football which made him very popular with his friends. However, he
seldom joined them in their dates and had no girl-friends of his own.
The few times that he did date in his senior year in high school, they
were arranged by his friends or his mother. Francis felt that one reason that he might have avoided girls at this time was that he was
very upset at his mother's remarriage. His father had been the domi-
nant figure in his life until he was 12. He died very suddenly of a
coronary, leaving Francis, his sister, and his mother grief-stricken.
Francis could thus not even imagine, let alone accept, his mother's
very sudden remarriage when he was 16. To Francis his mother's remarriage indicated that she was unfaithful to his father; such was
the infamy of all women.

Even during his college years, Francis dated infrequently. For a
while he considered going into the priesthood, but his grandfather
and mother insisted that he prepare for the business world in order
to take his father's place. Francis became convinced of the necessity
to do this when he realized that his stepfather might otherwise take
over the family business.

When a senior in college Francis fell in love with a most charming
girl, Rita, who led him a social whirl. Eventually, however, she rejected him and married one of his best friends. Carol was Rita's closest companion and at that time she too had had an unsuccessful love
affair. There seemed many reasons to Francis that he needed to
marry as he finished college. Carol was young and pretty and would
make up for the lost love affair with Rita. He liked Carol's family
who were much more relaxed and less formal than his own. He
wished to leave his mother's home, but saw no other suitable excuse.
His mother was encouraging him to marry declaring it would "mature him" and make him "more responsible" to conduct the family
business. He had a Naval ROTC commission and could avoid the
Viet Nam war, then in its early stages, only by marrying. Later he
remembered that his priest, a father confessor he had known for
many years, raised the question of how much an "arranged" marriage might seem to be a marriage of "convenience." Yet it was this
priest who presided at the large, elaborate, and expensive wedding.

Initially Francis said little about his work. In passing, he mentioned that he was no longer in the family firm but was employed as a stock broker in a competing and larger national brokerage. He seemed almost to avoid discussion of his finances until the therapist inquired more directly. Even then he seemed to regard it as relatively unimportant. It was only slowly through the therapy that Francis began to reveal the tangled web of his finances and financial difficulties. It became apparent that there was one other major motivation to his marriage as he finished college: his father's will provided that upon marriage he would receive his inheritance of almost a million dollars; at the same time he took his father's seat on the stock exchange. Yet he found that his mother did not actually relinquish control of the firm. He felt that she did not trust him and never let him make the ultimate decision in any case. He was surrounded by many of the employees that had worked for his father, and decisions always seemed to be made and sealed before he was aware of them. He found he had little to do at the firm and was considerably frustrated by his powerlessness there. It seemed to Francis that if he could successfully invest his own inheritance and make a large profit, he could prove to his mother and to the senior members of the firm that he was an upstanding and successful business man. He refused to ask the advice of anyone else in the firm and made his investments secretly. Within less than three and one-half years he had lost his entire inheritance and was a half a million dollars in debt. To cover his debts, he borrowed money from the trust fund his mother had set up for his children. His salary and allowances from the firm were actually quite small, and he hesitated to ask for any increases since there would then be questions raised as to what had happened to his inheritance and as to why he was not able to live upon the interest and profits from investments. He was barely able to make payments on the expensive estate home that he had felt obliged to purchase immediately after his marriage. Often he was behind in payments on his automobiles and in other debt.

He was too embarrassed to mention his financial problems to his wife who presumed that there was always plenty of money and spent money on herself, home, and children without restrictions. The month prior to his wife's threat of divorce she had discovered that the department stores and other establishments in town no longer respected his credit and was raising serious questions with him about money matters. Francis admitted had he not been Catholic he probably would have committed suicide even before she threatened divorce. He felt excessively guilty that he found himself even contemplating suicide.

For the next several months Francis remained depressed and defeated. He went to work each day but barely was able to carry out the daily activities at his place of employment and seemed to have little or no emotional investment in his work. He was criticized several times by his employer for "lack of initiative." During this time he kept hoping that there would be some way he could reunite with his wife and that everything would be "back to normal." He was overjoyed for a few weeks when he found that Carol and the doctor had broken up but was thrown into even deeper despair when he discovered that Carol had another boyfriend who had all but moved into "my house." During this time Francis returned to "my house" several times a week. He particularly enjoyed being there when Carol was not home. During these hours he would do gardening and house cleaning, even though Carol had kept the gardener and housekeeper. He found many excuses to be with his children; Carol did not seem to object to this although she made it plain that she did not want him in the house more than the few minutes it took to pick up the children and return them. He tried at various times to spend a few hours with her when he returned the children, but she gradually but firmly began to deny him the privilege of being with her even at these times.

As it became obvious to Francis that his wife was determined to end their marriage, he became more and more openly angry and bitter. He became openly critical of her, her lack of morals, her indolence and even believed that she was inadequate as a mother. He had murderous daydreams toward the doctor and the second boyfriend, who was a good 10 years younger than he. He became much more religious and went to mass every morning before breakfast. He viewed Carol as breaking her holy vows of matrimony and was determined to prove to himself and God that he was a faithful believer. At the same time Francis began to feel that God had let him down. He had prayed to God for help in reconstituting his marriage and felt that God had not listened to him. Gently but firmly, his priest advised him that one could only pray for one's own soul and one could make no specific demands on God. Francis's anger became more specific toward the Church. He was angry that the

Church only restricted Carol from participating in the mass while it restricted him from doing the same thing that Carol had done. She could "play around" but he must remain loyal to her no matter what she did.

As his anger mounted, he grew less depressed and more assertive. He was able to work out through his attorney a relatively fair division of the property and the custody arrangements of the children which gave him not only weekends but midweek visits and considerable vacation rights. Carol did not object to any of the settlements. Of course, as it turned out there was really little to divide as the property was going to be returned to the bank since Francis could not meet the mortgage payments. He barely could make adequate child payments, and Carol had to find a job to supplement what little he was able to pay. In fact, at one point Francis was in the embarrassing position of having his mother pay his apartment rent. Despite the fact that Francis already had experienced a considerable amount of grief and depression, followed by righteous anger, he was again quite depressed when the actual day of court hearing for the divorce, "D-Day," as he labeled it, was set. With some support from his therapist, he arranged to go on a religious retreat the day after the divorce. This three week isolation in quiet meditation provided the time he needed for the final healing of his wounds. He did continue at times to miss his wife and to feel very lonely. He regularly spent time with his children and seemed to enjoy them; and they filled many of his emotional needs.

Approximately a year after the divorce Francis decided to make some major changes in his life. He resigned his position at the stock broker firm and remained unemployed for several months. He took arts and crafts courses, such as copper engraving and pottery, but did not seem to find anything immediately to satisfy his needs. He was still very reluctant to form relationships with any other women, although he admitted that he often felt sexually attracted to some of the girls in the office. Moreover, it was soon gossip throughout the firm that he was single and available and he had many invitations from young women. At this time he met a friend of his father's who was a construction contractor in a rural area who invited him to join in the business. For the next year or so Francis worked very hard at physical labor constructing homes, barns, and other buildings. When he returned to town he looked up the psychotherapist whom he had seen before. The therapist almost didn't recognize him since Francis had lost some 40 pounds, was much browner complexioned, and almost completely gray-haired. He now formed a small contracting firm of his own which he worked at sporadically, just enough to help support his children. Shortly thereafter he met a woman some four or five years older than himself who was a good Catholic but had never married. They decided jointly not to ask for any dispensations of the Church and had only a civil wedding. He returned to visit his therapist, and he seemed quite happy and content without any further signs of depression.

Questions for Francis P.

1. When faced with life crises, people generally select active or passive means for dealing with the crises.
   a. List the various crises which Francis P. faced in his life
   b. next to each one indicate whether his response was active (e.g., an attempt to reorder his life situation by altering the environment) or passive (avoiding recognition of threat and backing into decisions). What pattern emerges?
2. Consider the factors in Francis's earlier life which may have disposed or shaped his particular style of coping. Consider in particular:
   a. his father's image and early death
   b. his mother's personality, relationship to him, and remarriage
   c. his attitude toward his religion.
3. Consider his marriage to Carol. What *short-run* difficulties did this solve? What *long-term* problems did it set up?
4. How do you reconcile Francis's total involvement with his children with his limited heterosexual involvement with Carol? How could it be that he was such a nurturing father and such an inadequate husband? What does this contradiction suggest about Francis's identity conflicts (particularly in the sex-role area).
5. Up until the time of his divorce, how did Francis attempt to resolve these sex-role conflicts?
6. Masters and Johnson suggest that "fear of inadequacy is the greatest known deterrent to effective sexual functioning, simply because it so completely distracts the fearful individual from his or her

natural responsivity by blocking reception of sexual stimuli" (1970, p. 12–13). They further suggest that such fears may grow out of (a) religious orthodoxy, (b) psychosexual trauma, (c) homosexual inclinations, (d) excessive intake of alcohol, and (e) socio-cultural factors. Which of these seems related to Fancis's sexual problems?

7. In the latter parts of the case, after divorce and extended psychotherapy, Francis made a number of changes in his life style. How may these be viewed as more adequate solutions to his identity conflicts? In what ways do we still see conflicts in this area?

8. What did it appear that psychotherapy succeeded in doing which permitted Francis to make these life changes? Consider:

   a. the supportive role of the therapist
   b. the encouragement of self-examination
   c. the reinforcement of autonomy strivings
   d. the alliance with Francis's religious value systems.

9. Many marriage counselors are ambivalent about the value of divorce as a solution for marital discord. What are your feelings about Francis's and Carol's divorce—was it a productive act for this couple, or should greater efforts have been made to keep this couple together? Describe the reasons for your feelings.

10. What role did Francis's commitment to his religion play in the resolution of his life difficulties?

References

EISENSTEIN, V. W. Neurotic interaction in marriage. New York: Basic Books, 1956.

FRIEDMAN, A. S. Hostility factors and clinical improvement in depressed patients. *Archives of General Psychiatry*, 1970, 23: 524–537.

KREITMAN, N., COLLINS, J., NELSON, B., & TROOP, J. Neurosis and marital interaction: I. Personality and symptoms. *British Journal of Psychiatry*, 1970, 117: 33–46.

MASTERS, W. H., & JOHNSON, V. E. Human sexual inadequacy. Boston: Little-Brown, 1970.

NELSON, B., COLLINS, J., KREITMAN, N., & TROOP, J. Neurosis and marital interaction: II. Time sharing and social activity. *British Journal of Psychiatry*, 1970, 117: 47–58.

PAYKEL, E. S., MYERS, J. K., DIENELT, M. N., KLERMAN, G. L., LINDENTHAL, J. J., & PEPPER, M. P. Life events and depression: a controlled study. *Archives of General Psychiatry*, 1969, 21: 753–760.

THE CASE OF SHIRLEY K.

Death in the Attic

Shirley K., a twenty-three-year-old housewife, came to the clinic with a complaint of frequent attacks of headaches and dizziness. During the preceding three months, she had been disturbed by recurring thoughts that she might harm her two-year-old son, Saul, either by stabbing or choking him. She constantly had to check to reassure herself that Saul was still alive; otherwise she became unbearably anxious. If she read a report in the daily paper of the murder of a child, she would become agitated, since this reinforced her fear that she too might act on her impulse. At one point, while relating her fears, Shirley turned to the interviewer and asked, with desperation, whether this meant that she was going crazy.

After describing these symptoms, Shirley added that she had other problems, mainly with her marriage. She had always considered herself sexually responsive to her husband, but lately, she had noticed a considerable decrease in her sexual drive; frequently she had not been able to achieve orgasm. Worse still, Shirley was beginning to find her husband's advances repugnant. Instead of finding satisfaction in their relations, Shirley was resorting to masturbation; during these times she achieved orgasm while fantasying violent sexual attack by men. Usually these were men of a physical type she had not before found attractive.

Shirley, a petite and attractive brunette, was dressed simply and in excellent taste. Her young and naturally pretty features were noticeably marred by her evident facial tension. She seemed visibly disturbed when she related her fears concerning her son. Yet her manner changed completely as she went on to her other problems. For instance, she appeared quite detached when she related the early events in her life; her tone was monotonous, and at times the interviewer had difficulty ascertaining if Shirley was discussing her own problems or those of a stranger, even when she recalled some particularly traumatic events.

As she became more comfortable in the interview situation, Shirley acted in numerous ways that indicated she was trying very hard to please the interviewer. She followed each statement with the phrase, "Is that right?"; when discussing future appointments she made it clear that she would come at any time convenient for the interviewer.

Current Life Situation. Shirley and her husband, Bill, had been married for almost two years. This was Shirley's second marriage and Bill's first. They had recently undergone some serious crises. Bill had just started his third job in four years, as a lawyer in a large manufacturing concern. He had lost his last job three months before because he was "overly ambitious." Shirley had been very upset when Bill was fired; she had started to wonder if he would ever straighten out and provide for the family. Shirley claimed that for once she would like to have a man who would take care of her. Although she had never been aware of wanting much in the way of material possessions, recently she had begun to have ambitions for a higher standard of living. For example, she wanted to move into a better neighborhood, where Saul could have "nicer friends." She found herself restricting Saul's playmates for various reasons, but this proved particularly upsetting since it repeated a pattern of her own childhood. Shirley found it virtually impossible to ask Bill for anything, and when she did bring herself to ask for anything, either for herself, Saul, or the house, she became so guilty that occasionally she ended up returning the item to the store. Shirley related that there were times, difficult to correlate with any external events, when her recurring thoughts concerning Saul subsided. During these periods, she enjoyed Saul immensely and derived much pleasure in taking care of him. These were the kind of "normal maternal feelings" which she felt she should be experiencing at all times.

Past History. Shirley grew up in a lower-class neighborhood of a medium-size city. She was an only child, and her parents were economically better off than their neighbors. Her father worked as a railroad engineer and made an adequate lower-middle-class income. Shirley's parents impressed upon her that they regarded themselves socially above the rest of the neighborhood, and they controlled her playmates very rigidly. Thus, Shirley spent many days in an enforced isolation while the other children played on the streets. She described her father as a "good guy" who spent a good deal of time with her. However, he was also quite strict and demanded a high standard of behavior from her. Shirley received an occasional spanking from her father, but on the whole he was passive, and he left the actual disciplining to his wife. Her mother attempted to control her by constantly screaming at her, which Shirley found intolerable. She recognized that her parents were concerned with her welfare although they found it difficult to be openly affectionate. Shirley's mother was preoccupied with illness; she would become "ill" whenever the pressures of family life became too great. These illnesses, largely hypochondriacal, brought support and sympathy from both Shirley and her father, and they were her mother's most effective means of controlling the family. During the periods of her mother's "illnesses" it became Shirley's duty to take over the responsibility of the home. Her mother supervised her very closely; from the vantage point of her bed she unabashedly criticized Shirley's performance. Although often very annoyed with her mother's illnesses, Shirley kept her irritation to herself, believing that there was no alternative to this state of affairs.

Shirley's early physical and social development was essentially normal. When the restrictiveness of her parents seriously limited her friendships, she made up fantasy playmates to while away the time. At the age of six Shirley started in a grade school which was composed of students from lower-class homes. Shirley regarded the other students as much rougher than herself, and she found much of their behavior difficult to reconcile with the standards of conduct set in her home. During her school days, Shirley's parents continued their policy of keeping her apart from the "bad" children of her neighborhood. Though frustrated and lonely, Shirley never felt that it was a matter which she could discuss with her parents.

As she approached puberty, Shirley's father in particular tended to restrict her contact with boys very vigorously. Initially, as she entered her teens, she was not permitted to associate with boys or to be away from home after dark. There were numerous indirect warnings about the dangers of sex, but she received little or no sex instruction. Shirley entered high school at fourteen and found herself at a loss in an essentially upper-middle-class school. Her clothes were inferior to those of the other children, and their poise and snobbish ways made her feel extremely uncomfortable. At this time, against her parents' wishes, she transferred to a vocational school, where she felt much more at ease. However, the expressed antisocial behavior of many of the children shocked her. Some of the boys already had police records and the girls were not ashamed of recounting their sexual adventures. It was at this time that Shirley began to date. Her father bitterly opposed this; it was only after a violent fight that permission was granted to be out until ten at night. During this period, Shirley met Don, who was her age. One evening, after a few dates, Don induced her into having sexual relations, using, as Shirley described it, "considerable force" to get his way. However, Shirley described the experience in rather bland terms, suggesting that she found the experience neither pleasurable nor unpleasurable. She also did not remember experiencing any guilt over this incident, but she did have a fear of social disapproval should the other kids find out. Shirley and Don continued to have sexual relations for the following two months, during which she submitted without pleasure to Don's demands. Then Don became interested in another girl and their relationship gradually dissolved. She remembers feeling relieved at the end of this affair. After the break-up with Don, Shirley continued to date boys, but she avoided intercourse. She was interested in kissing and petting, but was at a loss on how to communicate this to the boys in a respectable fashion. She finally hit on the solution of pretending to be asleep when alone with a boy. During these periods she would permit the boy to make advances, waking up when the advances went beyond what she desired.

Conflict and discord within the home remained intense during this period, and Shirley often had to fight with her father in order to obtain permission to go out on a date. Frequently she had to endure physical punishment from her father before he would relent and finally let her go. It was during this period that Shirley met Al, a man in his late twenties. Shirley was sixteen at the time and found Al quite attractive. After a brief courtship which involved some abortive sexual experiences, Al asked Shirley to marry him. Although aware that she was not completely in love with Al, Shirley found his proposal desirable as it would get her out of her oppressive home environment. They were married three months later with her parents' approval. Shirley described Al as a "nice guy'" who took care of her and was kind of fatherly toward her. At the beginning, she found sexual relations gratifying, but gradually she lost interest and became frigid. In many ways, Shirley's description of Al was very vague, and further questioning produced little additional information.

After a few months of marriage, Shirley found herself growing more distant from Al, and she began to look around for other interests. She signed up for a course in music appreciation given by a local musician of some repute. She found herself very much attracted to the teacher, James, and within a short time, they were involved in an affair. When she was eighteen Shirley divorced her husband and went to live with James. To help supplement the meager income James derived from his music appreciation courses, Shirley successfully operated a small record and sheet music store. She found James was a very bohemian type who cared little for material things and gradually left the financial support of the relationship up to Shirley. Shirley's relationship with James was a very tempestuous one. In addition to working infrequently, James conducted a number of affairs with other women, often flaunting them in front of Shirley. Shirley reported that she was jealous to a mild degree, but also, she felt more desirous of James and more interested in him because other women were. At times, Shirley threatened to leave James and he usually replied with an unconcerned "OK goodby." When this happened, Shirley became terribly upset and she would beg James to take her back. Throughout the affair, Shirley felt an intense sexual attraction for James and not once did she experience the loss of desire or the frigidity characteristic of the situation with her first husband. James constantly emphasized his inability to support her and his lack of desire to conform to society whenever Shirley raised the issue of marriage.

It was during the affair with James that Shirley's father became seriously ill. She received a telegram from a relative asking her to return to her home town; however, she did not want to go because she was having considerable difficulties with James at that time. Her father died shortly afterwards, and Shirley felt intense guilt because she failed to see her father before his death. Shortly after her father died, Shirley's mother became emotionally ill. She was going through the menopause and developed acute involutional symptoms. Shirley went back to her home town and found it necessary to have her mother committed to a state hospital for treatment. Again Shirley experienced intense guilt feelings about taking this action, particularly since she left her mother in the hospital shortly after commitment in order to return to James. Shirley's mother remained in the state hospital for one year at which time she was discharged as improved.

During the latter phase of her affair with James, Shirley tried several times to leave him, but eventually realized that it was impossible. She was amazed to see how intensely she was bound to James. At times, she felt that he could do anything to her, regardless of how cruel or humiliating, and she would endure it without complaint. At one point, James expressed a desire to have a child and shortly thereafter Shirley became pregnant. During this pregnancy, Shirley was often ill, suffering frequent bouts of nausea and headaches. James worked very little and Shirley continued to work parttime in the afternoons. She often longed to stay home in the mornings to rest, but James insisted that she should get away from the house. During the pregnancy Shirley found it possible to make some demands on James. One morning, Shirley and James had a particularly violent argument in which Shirley was annoyed that James wouldn't help her clean the house. She was particularly determined that James should clean the attic. Shortly after their argument, when Shirley got into the car to leave for work, James kissed her goodby and said, "Don't be angry at me." When Shirley returned home she found James dead, hanging from a rafter in an immaculately clean attic. Shirley was shocked, but recovered in a few hours without any visible disruption in her behavior. She called the police, and made arrangements for the funeral. Shirley was very surprised at her reaction to the whole affair. Although she had lived with James for three years, she believes that she must have been secretly relieved that the relationship came to an end. She found herself strangely unable to cry or to experience any emotion after James's death; however, at the funeral, she found it necessary to feign a grief reaction so that her friends would not think her peculiar. Shirley's behavior after James's death was so well controlled that her friends continuously praised her "for carrying on without going to pieces." Shortly after the funeral, Shirley left the city to return to her home town, where she moved in with her mother.

Six months later, Saul was born following a normal and easy delivery. Two months after Saul was born, Shirley went to work as a secretary at the large factory where she met her present husband. Their courtship was a stormy one but they decided to get married after six months of an on-again, off-again, engagement. Bill seemed to take to Saul very early in their relationship and was pleased with the idea of having a ready-made family. At the time treatment began the couple were trying to have a child of their own, but had not succeeded.

Course in Treatment. Shortly after an initial interview, Shirley K. entered intensive psychotherapy. Initially, she behaved in a deferent fashion to the therapist, obviously trying to please him at every turn. The ambiguity of therapy threatened her and she constantly asked the therapist to structure the situation for her. She claimed that she would talk about whatever the therapist indicated was of importance, but that she could not initiate lines of investigation. Gradually Shirley began to cautiously look into her relationship with James and into the meaning of his suicide to her. Shortly after this period, Shirley's disturbing thoughts and headaches disappeared. Her whole relationship with the therapist changed at this period. At this time, Shirley started reporting sexual fantasies about the therapist (a man), and spent hours expressing her frustration in not being able to have a more personal relationship with him. The therapist continually interpreted these feelings as representative of feelings from an earlier life period. Gradually and with much difficulty, Shirley became capable of exploring her feelings about her mother and father in detail. This phase of therapy lasted over two years at which time Shirley's level of discomfort was markedly reduced. Since her relationship with Bill and Saul had greatly improved, Shirley's therapy was terminated at this point.

Questions for Shirley K.

1. What events were going on at the time Shirley's obsessive symptoms first appeared?

2. What emotions or drives were most probably stimulated by these events?

3. What relationships may be seen between these emotions or drives and the type of symptoms Shirley developed?

4. What methods of coping with anxiety do Shirley's symptoms suggest?

5. Shirley's relationship with James was obviously very important to her. How would you characterize this relationship?

6. In particular, what emotions and what psychological mechanisms do we see operating in Shirley at the time of James's suicide?

7. How might Shirley's disturbing thoughts have been related to James's suicide?

8. Why did Saul become the object of Shirley's disturbing thoughts?

9. How would you characterize Shirley's relationships with men?

10. Do we see some evidence in Shirley's relationship with either of her parents which helps us to understand why she related to men as she did?

11. How would you characterize a relationship in which the partner suffers continual abuse from another, yet feels unable to break off the relationship?

12. What drives or motives appear to underly such behavior?

References

BERGLER, E. On pseudo-dependence. *Psychiatric Quarterly Supplement,* 1955, **29**: 239–247.

CHAPMAN, A. H. Obsessions of infanticide. *Archives of General Psychiatry,* 1959, **1**: 12–16.

LESSER, G. S. The relationship between overt and fantasy aggression as a function of maternal response to aggression. *Journal of Abnormal and Social Psychology,* 1957, **55**: 218–221.

REIK, T. *Masochism in Modern Man.* New York: Farrar and Rinehart, 1941.

WAHLER, H. J. Hostility and aversion for expression of hostility in neurotics and controls. *Journal of Abnormal and Social Psychology,* 1959, **59**: 193–198.

THE CASE OF VERONICA F.

The Invisible Net

For several months prior to her application for treatment Mrs. F. had been unable to leave her home without generalized feelings of panic, which she could not explain. "It is as if something dreadful would happen to me if I did not immediately go home." Even after she would return to the house, she would feel shaken inside and unable to speak to anyone or do anything for an hour or so. However, as long as she remained in her own home or garden, she was able to carry on her routine life without much problem. Otherwise she suffered no emotional or physical disturbance. Because of this agoraphobia, she had been unable to return to her position as a mathematics teacher in the local high school after the summer vacation.

In appearance, Mrs. F. was a tall, slim woman, neatly and conservatively dressed in a gray tweed suit. She wore little make-up, no nail polish, and her dark hair was bound neatly in a bun at the nape of her neck. Her expression suggested considerable depression; her face was taut with tension, her lips pursed, and her forehead had a perpetual frown. She spoke in a low voice which at times was almost inaudible, and she seemed to be constantly clearing her throat.

Mrs. F. stated that she had always been a somewhat shy person who generally preferred keeping to herself, but that up until approximately a year ago she had always been able to go to her job, shop, or go to church without any particular feelings of dread or uneasiness. It was difficult for her to recall the first time that she experienced this panic when in public, but it seemed to her that the first major experience was approximately a year before when she and her mother had been Christmas shopping. They were standing in the middle of a crowded department store when she suddenly felt the impulse to flee. She left her mother without explanation and drove home as fast as she could. Her mother was extremely angry, and she

162

was unable to explain to her what had happened. She admitted that shopping with her mother was a trial, as her mother was a loud-voiced person who would badger store clerks and often "create a scene" if she did not get the immediate and complete service she demanded. Veronica said that she "just knew" that sooner or later her mother would embarrass her on this shopping tour. However, Veronica felt that this incident in itself did not explain her phobia, since it continued to occur whether or not her mother was present. She could not remember when it first might have occurred, but believed that this was not really the first time. Over the next several weeks, during the Christmas vacation, she had several similar attacks; at a church party, at a friend's house, on the way to the dentist, and even just going to the grocery store. After the Christmas vacation she seemed to recover for a while and was at least able to return to her classroom duties without any ill effect. During the ensuing several months she had several similar experiences, usually when she was off duty; but by late spring these fears were just as likely to occur in the classroom. Sometimes she would excuse herself and lie down in the teachers' room, but by the end of the spring semester, her panic states occurred almost once a week and made it necessary to return home. In thinking further about the occurrence of her phobia, it seemed to Veronica that there was actually no particular stress which might account for her fear. Often it seemed to come over her when she was momentarily relaxed, although always she was in public. For example, it might come over her while she was standing in the classroom watching her pupils during an examination, or, as in the initial experience, when she was standing in the middle of the ladies' dresses section of the store waiting for her mother to return from the restroom. She had no memory initially as to what she was thinking or feeling at the time the fear came over her.

At the end of the spring semester Veronica had hoped that her fears might disappear during the summer. She had stayed at home, rarely leaving the house during the entire summer vacation, and her symptoms seldom appeared. However, as soon as it was necessary for her to return to work, her phobia returned even more intensely; she realized that she must get help. She was rather ashamed to admit it to anyone and did not know where to turn. She had read about a woman with a similar condition in a newspaper article written by a

THE CASE OF VERONICA F.

man purporting to be a psychologist. She telephoned him and was given an appointment. At the end of the initial interview he told her confidently that he knew exactly what was wrong and would have her back to her normal state within a few weeks. She was encouraged by his confidence and requested a brief leave of absence from her school at the beginning of the semester for "health reasons." Her principal was reluctant to accede to her request, particularly because she would not state the nature of her illness, but because she was a highly respected and efficient teacher he agreed to this arrangement. She returned to see the newspaper columnist psychologist, who advised a regime in which she should leave the house for brief periods, going a short distance and telling herself that she had nothing to fear. He telephoned her each day, asking how she was progressing, and advising her to go a longer distance for a slightly longer period each day. She tried to follow his directions and, at first, suffered no ill effects. However, she still felt unable to return to her job at the end of several weeks, and when she tried to go to church, she re-experienced her phobia so intensely that she was unable to continue on the prescribed regime of the "psychologist" for the next several days. She went to see him and he scolded her for disobeying his orders. He then suggested that perhaps the whole problem was much deeper than he had originally estimated and suggested that she take a series of psychological tests, which would cost her $200. She had received a bill the day before from him for several hundred dollars, which he had explained covered not only the cost of her initial visit to see him but also his half a dozen phone calls. When she arrived the next day to take the tests, she discovered that the "psychologist" was out and the tests would be administered by his secretary. She became somewhat perturbed and rather angry, feeling that her case was being taken too casually. Nevertheless, with the encouragement of the secretary, she filled out a sheet with questions asking about her personal life and answered a series of true-false questions. A week later the "psychologist" telephoned to apologize for having been out of town and to ask that she come in to see him again. She was becoming more and more uneasy about seeing this man and asked what he had found out from the tests. He explained that he now realized that she had a serious sexual problem and that he felt that by exploring this he might help her. At this point she declined to see him further.

Later a fellow teacher called on her to see how she was, since she was missed at school. Although Veronica had not previously discussed her problem with anyone, she did confide in this friend, who advised her to check up on the alleged "psychologist" by calling the psychology department at the nearby university. She was advised that the man in question was not a member of any recognized professional group in either psychology or psychiatry and that his newspaper claims and his behavior, as Veronica and others had reported it, made it questionable that he was a qualified person. Veronica's friend visited the "psychologist's" office, pretending to seek help, and asked him about his qualifications. He pointed to his diploma on the wall, from a college of which neither Veronica nor her friend later could find any record. At that time there was no law in the state as to who could or could not hold himself to be a practicing psychologist. Veronica was considerably depressed by this experience and wondered where to turn next. She again telephoned the university and was given the names of three reputable psychologists in the community.

At this time Veronica was twenty-seven years old. She was living with her widowed mother at the same house in which she had spent most of her childhood years. Usually her schoolwork kept her fairly busy. Aside from her job she spent most of her time caring for her home and garden. She attended the local Protestant church fairly regularly, occasionally participating in some of the social events when requested to do so by a friend or the minister, although she was not a member of any of the church groups. She also enjoyed playing bridge with her friends each week, but had dropped even this social activity at the end of the summer.

Past History. Veronica's parents were in their early twenties when she was born. They had been married only a little over a year. Veronica knew well the story of her parents' wedding, for her mother had told it to her many times during Veronica's childhood. Furthermore, in her mother's bedroom, in a prominent place on the wall, was an enormous enlargement of her parents' wedding picture, which she had often studied in detail. Her mother was a very beautiful young woman, tall, blonde, and shapely. She had often wished that she had inherited her mother's looks. Even today, Veronica said, her mother is an attractive woman, who at fifty still had the complexion and figure of a much younger woman and who only recently stopped "touching up" her graying hair, to dye it a fashionable silver. Studying her father's features, and comparing herself in the mirror, Veronica long ago decided that she much more resembled her father. As far as she could ascertain, he was about the same height as her mother, slim, dark-complexioned, and boyish-looking. He had just finished his law degree and had started practice with a prominent firm, and was looking forward to a promising career. Both parents came from well-to-do families from whom they received many expensive presents at their elaborate wedding; their new home had been a gift from her father's family.

When Veronica was scarcely two years old, her father was called into the military service during World War I. Two years later, only a week before the end of the war in Europe, he was killed in action. One of Veronica's earliest memories was of the funeral (his body having been returned to the United States). She remembered being very puzzled by the collection of relatives who arrived solemnly at their home. She believed she did not know exactly what was going on but remembered crying in echo of her mother's tears. Her mother, who had previously been a fairly vivacious and sociable person, retreated into a prolonged mourning. She seldom went anywhere, continued to dress in black, and would break into tears at the sight of her husband's picture or mention of his name. At this time Veronica's maternal grandmother, who was also widowed, came to live with them.

Aside from her father's death and her mother's reaction to it, Veronica could not remember anything particularly unhappy or disturbing in her childhood. She remembered very little of her childhood prior to her father's death. As far as she knew, she and her mother had been very happy together, awaiting her father's return from service. Her mother had had many friends and was quite active in their church. They entertained frequently and their home was often full of friends. After her father's death, her mother invited no one in and seldom left the house. Veronica believed she had few or no playmates prior to attending school but rather spent all her playtime with her mother, who was fond of making up little games and entertaining her.

After Veronica's father died her mother seemed less inclined to spend so much time playing with her or amusing her. When she was not in school Veronica was at home with her mother and grandmother, but Veronica could remember little exchange among the three of them. Grandmother busied herself with the housework, mother seemed preoccupied with her own thoughts, and Veronica retired to her room with her collection of dolls. Although Veronica had schoolmates who lived in the neighborhood, she does not remember playing with them very much. By and large she was encouraged to stay at home and play. If other children came over either her mother would discourage them from staying, telling Veronica that the other children would bother grandmother, or grandmother would scurry them out on the excuse that Veronica's mother wasn't feeling well. In some way it became an accepted fact among the three of them that anyone else entering the house was an intruder who would upset things. Veronica herself would become annoyed if some child would enter her room and disturb her playthings. She had had many gifts over the years of dolls and stuffed animals, all of which she kept displayed in a set fashion across the shelves, dresser, and bed. Each of these dolls had a name and almost an identity. Her favorite fantasy was that she was the princess of the court in which she commanded these dolls, each of whom had some way of disobeying her which she had to correct. Her mother and grandmother commented on how strict a disciplinarian she was with her dolls. She spent many hours dressing and redressing them. Even as an adult, some of these dolls remained in her room.

In many ways Veronica's mother and grandmother appear to have had an overprotective attitude toward her. For many years, one or the other of them always walked with her to school and was there waiting to meet her to see that she got home safely. She was warned again and again about staying on her own side of the street and having some adult to guide her across the street when it was necessary for her to go anywhere. She was the only child in school who always had a raincoat whenever a cloud appeared in the sky. Moreover, it was a very special raincoat with large multicolored polka dots, which her mother thought was very pretty but which Veronica came to hate. Veronica loved animals but was not allowed to have pets because mother and grandmother said they would carry germs. However, at one time she was allowed to keep a kitten, which was killed soon afterwards by a truck. To console Veronica, her grandmother helped her conduct an elaborate play funeral with a cement block headstone for the grave in the garden. Later in treatment Veronica remembered having a repetitive dream in which the kitten seemed to be a monster of some kind which was attacking the polka dot raincoat and ripping it up. Veronica would awake disturbed and check in the closet to make sure the raincoat was all right. Although Veronica was concerned about discipline with her dolls, she could not remember ever having been disciplined by her mother or grandmother. "I always did what I was told without question; I have always been a good girl, I guess I still am," Veronica said, a little sadly.

Aside from the fancy raincoat, Veronica was usually dressed in very plain clothes. At the girls' school she attended she wore the middy blouse and skirt uniform of the day. For church she was dressed in dark clothes like her mother and grandmother, and even her play clothes were, in Veronica's memory, drab. Until her late adolescence, her hair was cut in a Dutch bob. She gained in height very rapidly, was always taller than most of the children in her class, and reached her present height of five feet, six inches by the time she was thirteen, when she was head and shoulders above all the girls and taller than many of the boys. From approximately age seven her mild astigmatism was corrected by glasses in steel frames much like her grandmother's spectacles. At about age nine she began the long orthodontic correction of her dental malocclusion with a series of braces which she wore for the next three or four years.

Her feeling that she was not like the other children in looks and behavior was further added to socially by the fact that, although she was a Protestant, she was sent to a Catholic girls' school. It was her mother's idea that this school would offer a more intensive education and "better discipline" than the public school. Her grandmother frequently "spoke her mind" on this topic, declaring that this was a mistake because of the difference in the religious background. At the grandmother's insistence, it was specified that Veronica need not attend the hours of religious training at the Catholic school. Each day while the other children were in the chapel, she sat alone in the classroom; she was thus in yet another way marked as apart from the other children. Her grandmother frequently queried her about what they taught at school, maintaining that it was necessary to "clear the child's mind of any funny ideas." When grandmother remarked that she did not understand how unmarried women like the nuns could possibly understand children, Veronica's mother became irritated and told her to be quiet. Veronica heard that the Sisters were considered "brides of the church"; she asked one of her teachers about this but did not remember the answer except that it seemed confusing to her. One of her teachers gave her a colored and detailed calendar picture of the crucifixion, which she kept in her room. She remembered regarding this figure of Christ in agony on the cross with a mixed feeling of attraction and horror. Although she attended Sunday school regularly, she remembers little of her training and does not believe that she ever felt very religious. In some way, however, this portrayal of the crucifixion stuck in her mind; she often wondered about it but felt prohibited from asking either her grandmother or the Sisters about it. Later, in adolescence, she was somewhat fascinated with the idea of death and violence, secretly reading mystery and murder stories and being particularly concerned with the manner of the death of the victim.

When Veronica was graduated from the eighth grade, the Catholic high school proved to be too distant, and her mother agreed with her grandmother's protest against continuing her in school where the religious training was not compatible with that at home. She was allowed to go to public high school, but there was considerable concern in her home about this move. Veronica had been allowed to go to school by herself for a number of years, but the idea that she might not be able to take care of herself out on the streets was renewed when she had to go almost a mile to high school. In this instance Veronica did protest her mother's overprotectiveness and was met with repeating warnings about "knowing how to take care of yourself." Exactly what her mother meant by this Veronica was not sure. Both her mother and grandmother repeated these warnings in various ways to indicate that they disapproved of children who attended public school, as if the children were of a different social class. Though Veronica was allowed to get some new clothes to start high school, she soon discovered that her mother's taste was much different from that of the girls at public school. She felt different from the other children, was socially shy, and felt very much the ugly duckling. Although she had been an above-average student in the Catholic girls' school, at public high school she was so embarrassed that she found it difficult even to recite in class, much less to take part in any extracurricular activities. Her grades fell off slightly although her achievement remained above average. She did absolutely no dating throughout high school and had very few girl friends.

In·her senior year she did form one very close friendship with another girl, Eloise, who also was a social isolate, heavy-set, and aggressive, and in manner quite opposite from Veronica. Her friend was much more likely to tell others off, to say what she thought, and to use vulgar language to which Veronica had not been exposed. Veronica's mother and grandmother made it clear that they thoroughly disapproved of Veronica's friend, but Veronica secretly defied them by spending as much time with this girl at school or at the girl's home as she could without causing too much disruption with her elders.

Prior to meeting Eloise, Veronica does not remember having any knowledge whatever of sex or even any curiosity about it. She had had her first menstrual period at age thirteen, for which she was entirely unprepared. She remembered being puzzled and uneasy, but was somewhat reassured by the casual attitude of her mother and grandmother. Her mother actually said little about it, and her grandmother explained only that it was "the curse of all women" and gave her instructions in caring for herself hygienically. Eloise told Veronica the "facts of life" in vulgar terms, which both fascinated and upset Veronica. As her mother and grandmother never mentioned anything regarding sex, Veronica understood from their attitude that this was a prohibited topic and did not dare to ask them about it. Eloise further initiated Veronica into mutual masturbation which excited Veronica and which, for reasons she could not fathom, left her feeling guilty. Eloise moved away just before Veronica was graduated from high school. Veronica again felt lonely and depressed and left out of the rush of social affairs.

For the next two years Veronica attended the local two-year college. Her social habits changed little. Shortly before the end of this college training her grandmother died and her mother went into a second intense period of mourning. Veronica could not remember exactly how she felt about her grandmother's death. "I don't remember that I really felt sad, but my mother's mourning was depressing." Upon her grandmother's death Veronica was given a great deal more responsibility for their financial affairs. She discovered that both her paternal and maternal grandparents had been fairly well-to-do and that she and her mother were owners of a considerable amount of income property and other assets. Her mother loudly proclaimed that she knew nothing about business and felt very helpless. Veronica became involved in straightening out the financial affairs for herself and her mother and prided herself on being a good businesswoman. Her grandmother had specified in her will that part of the inheritance should be used for Veronica to continue her education. Veronica went on to the university where she completed her A.B. in mathematics and obtained a teaching credential in secondary education. Although it was unnecessary for her to work for a living, she wanted to go to work, if for no other reason than to get out of the house. She kept herself busy teaching school and tending to the many business affairs associated with the family property.

It was through one of the attorneys who helped her handle her business affairs that she met her husband. He was the son of another attorney, tall, slim, blond, and, like herself, shy and socially withdrawn. "The main thing we seemed to have in common was that we had no social interests," Veronica said sadly. She could not recall that there was really any courtship between them. She would see him in his office and would be invited to his home, or she would invite him to hers. Her mother encouraged their association and made it clear to Veronica that this was the type of man who would be a good son-in-law. Veronica was also aware that her future mother-in-law was very determined that she marry this man. The wedding was a social affair, planned by her husband's parents, which made the newlyweds quite uncomfortable, but since neither of them had ever made any protest against any plans of their parents they meekly submitted. She remembered that it was only the day before the wedding that she thought to ask her husband where they would live and found that he assumed that they would stay with his parents while she was assuming that they would live with her mother. It was she who made the suggestion they find an apartment of their own. The whole marriage seemed to Veronica to be artificial, as she looked back on it. She did not believe that either she or her husband were at all prepared to get married or were really interested in one another.

After their wedding she discovered that he was very difficult to communicate with, that he seldom volunteered any conversation, and that she herself did not know what to say to him or to do with him. Their sexual life was almost nil. He made no sexual advances toward her and the few times they had sexual relationships it was almost entirely on her initiative—which embarrassed and angered her. She tried pleasing him with cooking and housekeeping, but he seemed unaware of her efforts. Very often he would excuse himself in the evening and leave without explanation, to return late at night after she had gone to bed. At one time she angrily demanded an account of his behavior, but he shrugged it off and ignored her. She began to feel desperate. She did not want to confess her unhappiness to her mother, and she knew of no place to seek help. When she finally pressed the matter with her husband, he coldly told her that he felt it was useless to continue the pretense of their marriage. He informed her that furthermore he had made an homosexual adjustment before their marriage and he wished to maintain it. After she recovered from her initial shock, she was depressed and even ashamed, feeling that in some way she had been at fault for getting herself into such a situation. Her depression was partially relieved when her husband voluntarily left. She was thus able to file suit for divorce on grounds of desertion, so that no one knew the real reason for the break-up of their marriage.

Upon returning to live with her mother, Veronica tried to assume her previous life. Although she had stopped working during the year of her marriage, she was easily able to obtain another teaching position. Nevertheless, she began to feel extremely restless and dissatisfied at home. For the first time in her life she began to resist some of her mother's many petty demands to be waited on and cared for. "I felt as if my mother had an invisible net spread over me." She made plans for a trip abroad with a schoolteacher friend, but at the last minute cancelled them, as she felt that she could not leave her mother alone. "I don't really know why I felt that since my mother is still a young woman and is physically quite capable of caring for herself." Her mother had many friends in church and in the bridge club. When Veronica's phobia appeared and became worse, Veronica's mother was at first startled and then annoyed, but not at all sympathetic. She regarded Veronica's symptom as something which Veronica had "made up" and advised her to "snap out of it."

Course in Treatment. After her experience with the previous "psychologist," Veronica was apprehensive about further treatment. She admitted that she was not quite sure of what she did expect but felt that perhaps something more than "just talking" was the answer. She was able to leave the house and come to the therapist's office without difficulty, but sometimes experienced her panic attacks in the reception room. Veronica also felt shy and embarrassed when talking about herself, but soon found considerable relief in being able to express some of her feelings of frustration. In discussing her symptom further, she found that she did have the feeling that if she did not immediately return home, something awful would happen to her. It seemed connected with her feelings about death and her experiences of loss of various objects and people. Later she became conscious that her real fear was that something would happen to her mother. She began to discuss the restrictions which her mother had placed on her throughout her childhood and her mother's current demands on her. On a day following a treatment hour in which she had expressed considerable anger toward her mother, she was unable to come for her therapy session, and re-experienced her panic with a renewed intensity. Veronica also realized that she was very close to her mother and admitted that despite occasional hopes of living some kind of life of her own, she could not really bring herself to take any definite step to do so.

It was some time before Veronica could begin to discuss any of her feelings of a need for independence, and even longer before she could mention her sexual conflicts and desires. She admitted that she often felt inadequate as a woman, and wondered whether she really ever could make a successful marriage. "I've lived with women so much I don't think I know how to associate with men." She expressed a fear that her marriage to a homosexual might mean that she herself was in some way homosexual. It was with this thought in mind that she remembered her childhood association with Eloise.

After two years of psychotherapy Veronica was no longer experiencing her phobic attacks. She became softer in manner and more feminine in her dress and appearance. She remained socially shy and despaired of trying to make friends beyond her narrow circle of school and church. She did accompany one of her teacher friends to a dancing class and seemed to enjoy some of the men she met there.

During the summer two years after she began therapy, she took her long-planned trip abroad. She did not return to treatment, but shortly before that Christmas she telephoned her therapist to announce that she was getting married to a man she had met at the dancing class.

Questions for Veronica F.

1. Examine the circumstances surrounding Veronica's *first* anxiety attack in detail. List the events occurring at that time and the people present.
2. What impulses or feelings, which might have been considered dangerous by Veronica, could have been stimulated in that situation? Toward whom might these impulses have been directed?
3. After this initial episode, Veronica's anxiety attacks were elicited by a wider and wider variety of situations. What does this fact suggest about Veronica's ability to keep these impulses or feelings out of her awareness?
4. The danger that Veronica feared was evidently an internal one (the arousal of dangerous feelings or impulses in herself). However, her exclusive fear became one of leaving the house. What transformation in the object of her fear took place following the development of the phobia?
5. What psychological mechanism or mechanisms appear implicit in your answer to question 4?
6. What might have been the hidden or symbolic meaning of staying at home versus going out that made the former a means of reducing anxiety for Veronica?
7. Do we see any continuity over the course of Veronica's life in coping with conflict? Can you present any examples from Veronica's earlier history that suggest the operation of similar ways of coping with anxiety?
8. Although it is not always easy to specify an answer to this question, can you suggest some hypotheses about why Veronica was unable to handle her conflicts without resorting to a phobic reaction during the particular Christmas vacation when her symptoms first began?
9. How would you characterize the pattern of relationships which existed among Veronica, her mother, and her grandmother during most of her early life?

10. In view of your answer to question 9, can you now understand why Veronica would have difficulty in openly expressing certain feelings and impulses? *Explain your answer.*

11. All you know about Veronica's psychotherapy is that it was successful. Extrapolating from your answers to the above questions, what changes do you feel should have taken place in Veronica (aside from remission of her phobia) for the therapy to be labeled as successful? In particular, consider what changes in attitudes, feelings, and behavior Veronica might have shown which might act to insulate Veronica against a future neurotic breakdown.

References

FREUD, S. Analysis of a phobia in a five-year-old boy, *Collected Papers of Sigmund Freud,* Vol. 13, New York: Basic Books, 1959. Pp. 149–289.

KATAN, A. The role of displacement in agoraphobia. *International Journal of Psychoanalysis,* 1951, **32**: 41–50.

MURRAY, E. J., & BERKUN, M. M. Displacement as a function of conflict. *Journal of Abnormal and Social Psychology,* 1955, **51**: 47–56.

THE CASE OF GEORGE P.

The Flower Garden

George P., a single, white male, age fifty years, had requested re-admission to a Veterans' Administration general and surgical hospital, "Because my stomach had been acting up again." On admission, George had given a detailed description of his complaint, using many medical terms with which he had become familiar in his previous hospitalizations. At this time his disability had become so severe that he had been unable to work for the previous three months. Almost constantly during his waking hours he was aware of pains in his stomach, a steady "heartburn," and a generalized feeling of weakness and malaise. He was unable to eat any solid food comfortably without fear of vomiting. For the past several weeks he had lived chiefly on skimmed milk. During this time he had lost the fifteen-pound weight gain which he had assiduously accumulated over the year since his last hospitalization.

In appearance Mr. P. was a slight-built man, five feet, four inches tall, hollow-cheeked but bronzed in complexion. He walked jauntily around the hospital, sat relaxed in a chair as he talked, and seemed in general good spirits; in fact, at first glance, with the exception of his notable thinness of face, he appeared to be in the best of health. Indeed, although he said he was somewhat depressed by having to return to the hospital, he seemed most cheerful. He was quite friendly toward the examiner, although he admitted that he didn't see any connection between his physical illness and any possible "nervousness" and was merely being co-operative because his physician had recommended it. He himself felt sure that "nervousness" would be ruled out as a cause of his illness and that he would be continued on a regime of medication, with the possibility of surgery, as had been the case in his previous contacts with the hospital.

Usually wearing a hospital robe, even though not confined to bed, he was always neatly attired. His thinning, dark hair was plastered down against his skull and the nurses reported that he spent a great deal of time in his personal care and grooming. When not wearing his hospital robe he dressed in his working khakis and sported a bright-colored necktie and highly polished shoes.

This was the sixth admission to this hospital for George. He had first been admitted in 1947 shortly after his discharge from the military service, with the same complaint. He was admitted the second time ten years later and he had been readmitted annually since 1957 with the exception of one year. A stomach ulcer had been discovered on his second admission in 1957, and in 1958 he had a resection of the stomach wall. Since that time he had been treated by various medications but there had been no signs of an active ulcer in the last several hospital admissions.

One of the reasons George was referred for a psychological consultation was that his physician suspected in his current complaint signs of possible external emotional stress from which George might be seeking relief. At the time of this hospitalization George was living alone in a tiny one-room apartment near the hospital, as he had been since his mother's death in 1956. He had been employed steadily for the past three years as a serviceman for an automatic food machine company, refilling the coffee and other food machines in various business establishments and institutions in the local region. George went into detail in explaining his job and some of the difficulties involved. He had obtained the job through a friend who owned the company when it opened. He was the company's most experienced worker, having outlasted all other men who had worked for them. In his opinion, other men quit because the work was fairly demanding, keeping a person on his feet all day long and on the move, going from building to building. Not only was he responsible for seeing that the machines were stocked but also that they were in good repair; in addition he had to collect the receipts and make sure the machine was full of change. He had to answer the complaints of the customers vis-à-vis and was on call whenever a machine broke down. He was also charged with trying to sell the machine service to new firms throughout his area. His work was salaried, but he made extra commissions whenever he sold the service to a new firm. He found the work challenging, was proud of his service, and had made many friends by his cheerful and co-operative manner. He claimed that his customers were all very fond of him, called him by his first name, and looked forward to his visits. He boasted that he had expanded the firm's business in his area some ten times in his period of employment by the company. According to George his job occupied approximately ten hours a day, but he didn't mind because he had very little else to do and the job afforded him a great deal of social contact, which he lacked elsewhere. However, shortly after he joined the company his friend was stricken with a heart attack and a young relative of the friend took over the company. He felt that this new employer was letting the business deteriorate through disinterest and that George's own efforts to build up the business in his particular area were unappreciated. At times George felt that his new young employer actually did not want to see the business expanded and interfered with some of George's efforts to see new business built up. During George's previous periods of illness his employer had been most understanding and had not docked his pay although there was no definite sick leave provision on his job. However, during the past year George's employer was much less sympathetic with his occasional illness. George felt he had to struggle even harder to be there every day as there was not always a replacement for him and his customers were becoming dissatisfied. Thus he often went to work when he was really feeling quite ill and struggled through the day. He found the lifting of heavy boxes of supplies and the pushing around of large food-vending machines becoming almost impossible. He finally asked for a two-week vacation, which he had coming to him but which ordinarily he would have taken in midsummer rather than at this time, just after Christmas. His employer refused him the vacation, whereupon George suddenly resigned in a fit of anger. For the following six weeks' period he stayed at home, living at first on his severance pay and then on unemployment insurance. The week before his unemployment insurance ran out George applied for admission to the hospital.

Past History. George was the fourth of five children born in a small, Midwestern town to a veterinarian and his schoolteacher wife. His older brother and two sisters were respectively fifteen, twelve, and ten years older than himself, and his younger brother was one year his junior. George spoke in glowing terms of his father. He initially described him as a very kindly man whom everyone loved and admired. His extensive veterinarian practice left him little time for his family. As a mark of his father's prowess, George told how his father had been one of the first to utilize artificial insemination with cattle and was in George's words "the father of 5000 cows in southern Ohio." George claimed that "kindness and service to others" was the principle of his own life, which he had learned from his father in watching his father's work with animals. He described his father as a silent person who, in his firm and yet kindly manner, was able to subdue and win over the most recalcitrant or vicious animal. He remarked that his father probably regarded animals as more intelligent and as having more feeling than people, and indicated indirectly that his father was fairly impatient with human stupidity.

Another "virtue" which George claimed to have learned in his childhood was "hard work." From school age on he was responsible for many of the chores around their small farm, particularly as both his parents were employed and his older brothers and sisters were already grown and had left the family. George denied that he resented having to spend most of his after-school hours at these chores, saying he often wished he were back on the farm. He spoke with considerable nostalgia of his childhood years, particularly of the rewards of outdoor life and of "good, fresh farm food." He emphasized that although his mother taught school, she was always at home to take care of the house and to provide generous meals for the family and to entertain many friends. He spoke longingly of homemade butter, pork chops for breakfast, and his mother's baked goods. He learned to cook from his mother and enjoyed helping her around the kitchen. He volunteered that despite all of this good, rich food he never gained any weight and was always of slight build, and wiry. His lean build concerned his mother a great deal and she was always anxious to fatten him up. However, he said, he was built much like his father and up until the time of his illness had always been able to eat everything and anything without fear of becoming overweight.

George was a slightly above-average student throughout his primary-school years, when he was constantly coached by his mother. He admitted readily that this coaching by his schoolteacher-mother was a point of irritation to him, although he quickly added that this was the only thing he could think of about which he had actually been at odds with her. Apparently he was able to convince his mother when he began high school that he should be free of her teachings, but he was much less successful as a student in high school, where he was much more interested in sports. Despite his size he had been an active athlete, was always on the baseball team, and even played basketball until he reached an age when he did not have the required height. He had many companions and despite his home duties and extra studies he had plenty of time to play and to get into mischief. He admitted with a laugh that he often embarrassed his parents by his mischievous and somewhat destructive acts —which he thought all young boys did. Occasionally, his mischief brought him to the attention of the town constable, who took a special delight in hunting him down because he was the schoolteacher's son. His parents attempted to discipline him, chiefly by adding to his chores and attempting to restrict him to the confines of the family property. Occasionally his father administered the traditional corporal punishment in the woodshed. He described himself as being "a young rebel" during his teen-age years, who "gave the teachers a bad time at school." Approximately three months prior to the time he would have been graduated from high school he was called to the principal's office for infraction of one of the school rules, at which time in a peak of anger he threw his locker key on the principal's desk and demanded his twenty-five cents' deposit as an indication that he was quitting school. When he announced this decision later that evening to his parents, his father's response was that if he were old enough to make such a decision he was old enough to earn his own living and from there on his father would require room and board money from him.

George decided angrily to leave home. After a tearful scene with his mother he packed his bags and took the next freight train out of town. This was the first year of the depression of the 1930's and George found it difficult to find permanent employment anywhere. He roamed back and forth across the United States, often living in hobo jungles, picking up work where he could or living temporarily off of various kinds of relief from government agencies. Despite the many deprivations which he endured then, George talked about this period of his life as if it were actually enjoyable. When unemployed, he would go sightseeing, talk to people from every walk of life, and live a life of general freedom even though he no longer enjoyed the relative luxury he had been used to in his childhood. Some three years later, when he was approximately twenty-one, he returned home for a brief visit to find his father on the verge of death. His father had long suffered from an undiagnosed stomach problem. Some months before George's return home the elder Mr. P. had been told he had stomach cancer, whereupon he suddenly dropped his entire practice and sat around home in what must have been a deep depression. George was shocked to find his father so depressed and urged him to seek medical care, but the father adamantly refused, saying that he did not trust doctors. Finally the family almost forced the elder Mr. P. into the hospital, where over his protests he underwent surgery. Shortly thereafter George's father died from pneumonia.

After the death of his father, George attempted to operate the family farm for a short period. His older siblings were married and had families of their own and could not, at that point, contribute to his mother's support. His younger brother had gone on to college and was beginning a career in the theater in New York. After approximately a year, George convinced his mother to sell the family property. They then moved to Southern California, where George had spent some time during his travels around the country. Until World War II, George earned his living at various odd jobs, chiefly as a short-order cook and baker. He was drafted into the navy in 1942 and served for four years as a cook and baker. He was aboard ship a great deal of the time but saw no combat other than the constant strain of possible submarine warfare or occasional threat of air attack. He claims to have been deafened at one time by gunnery practice and was given a 10 per cent disability for hearing loss. After his discharge from the service in 1946, he returned again to live with his mother. Using some of his veterans' benefits, he borrowed money and went into the restaurant business. He operated two different restaurants and bars over the next five years, both of which failed. He explained that he had misfortune in the first such venture when the partner ran off with the funds. In the second venture, he foresaw the approaching depression of the mid-1950's and sold out because he was afraid of losing funds which he had borrowed from his mother. Although George never mentioned his inheritance directly, it appeared that his father's estate had been left under the control of his mother, who bought a home and was able to live on the income from investments whether or not George himself brought in any income.

George described his twenty years of living with his mother as almost idyllic. "She was my buddy." He spent all his spare time making sure she was comfortable, that she got where she wanted to go, and that she had all the comforts of home. He described in detail the flower and vegetable garden that he worked on year after year for her satisfaction. He was an avid fisherman and outdoor sportsman and he always took his mother along. He had a special "camper" built for her comfort and always brought back his fishing catch for her approval.

Despite his portrayal of himself as a good boy devoted to his mother, George gave many hints that his adult social adjustment was at times marginal. He admitted that he was in frequent trouble with the law because of his driving habits. He had numerous tickets for speeding, for driving under the influence of alcohol, and later, when his license was taken away, for driving without a license. He bemoaned the rising costs of fines for his illegal driving practices. Although he said that he had lost his business because of the depression, VA records indicated that he also had been in trouble for selling liquor to a minor. He later admitted that his business partner was a professional gambler and that he himself had tried to make money through gambling at various times.

When asked about his use of alcohol, George became tight-lipped and somewhat irritated, saying that he had better admit that he drank at least a six-pack of beer a day because this was already in his record. He explained that he had been in an altercation with a night nurse just the previous evening because she had suggested that he might go to an Alcoholics Anonymous meeting; he felt that it was unfair that he had any reputation as an alcoholic. On the other hand, in discussing his mother he admitted that the one thing she would never do was open a can of beer for him. He strongly denied that he drank anything stronger than beer, but then added with a smile that this was because he couldn't afford it.

In discussing his family, George repeatedly mentioned the successes of his younger brother, David. He described how his brother had become a major theatrical producer, with frequent plays on Broadway and productions in Los Angeles, and more recently in Las Vegas. He remarked how extremely proud his mother was of David and how David would send her theater tickets and a plane ticket to go to the opening nights of his new productions. George admitted that he himself had seen only one or two of David's plays. He admitted with a wink that when his mother was away from home he was able to get in a little extra fishing and drinking which she might not otherwise have approved of. He also described David's success as particularly amazing because, "frankly, David was a sniveling little brat" as a child, whom no one presumed would ever amount to anything. As he looked back on it, George remembered that when they were children David spent most of his time with his books instead of sharing the farm chores with George.

Asked why he had never married, George laughed and said he had always asked himself that question. He decided that he had been left with the responsibility for his mother and that life had been so easy and wonderful with her that he had just never gotten around to hunting for a wife. He went on to reflect that he had been so interested in sports as a youngster in high school that he did very little dating. He had had one girl he was very fond of, but always had to struggle with several other rivals. He recalled an incident in which he had lost his temper and beaten up a rival for this girl, and subsequently the girl's father had forbidden him to come around the house because of this. The girl married another man and many years later George heard that her husband had died. On hearing this, he made a trip back to his home town to visit her. He described her with considerable disgust, saying that she had grown obese and sloppy and "was wearing nothing but a thin dress." Asked more directly about his sexual adjustment, George shrugged and said he guessed he was about normal for a bachelor, explaining that he visited houses of prostitution once or twice a year "to get it out of my system."

George's mother died in 1956. Although he was able to discuss the details of her death and his feelings about it in the same garrulous fashion he had discussed other facets of his life, there was a noticeable lowering and depression in his voice and his eyes seemed near to tears once or twice. He overtly denied being depressed, saying that it was almost fortunate that she had lingered on for a long period because he had that way been able to get used to the idea that she was going to die. He explained that she had been an extremely active and independent person until the time of the accident which led to her death, even though she was approaching eighty. She had been shopping by herself, had slipped, fallen, and broken her hip. She was hospitalized for many months and returned home, where he had to nurse her. Shortly thereafter she suffered an embolism which left her paralyzed and necessitated putting her in a nursing home. His mother continued to "fight off death" for another six months while she lay paralyzed and almost unconscious. George had quit his job as a cook at the time of her injury and had stayed at home caring for her, living off the income of some of her investments. For the following year he continued to be unemployed. After his second hospitalization in 1957 for his stomach complaint, he went back to work as a baker. After his 1958 operation he obtained his present job.

Course in Hospital. The chief psychological problem with which the hospital was faced concerning George was the fact that his attitude toward medical care was becoming more and more resistant and demanding. Most of the staff physicians, nurses, and others knew George well but all were beginning to be despairing and even disgusted with him. His current physical examination and laboratory reports showed that he continued to have hyperacidity in his digestive system but that in general he was not in any gross physical danger nor suffering from any disabling disfunctions. The referring physician remarked that it was often difficult for the staff to understand the fact that the patient might suffer considerable subjective pain even when their examinations did not reveal gross pathology. He said that the nurses and other staff at times expressed open resentment that George required so much physical care from the Veterans' Administration so frequently. George made himself at home in the VA hospital and tended to order nurses and other staff around as if such care were his deserved right. George himself recited how he had previously been in altercations with the nurses over his rights in the hospital and had maneuvered a physician to be on his side to override the nurses' rulings. George's physician was very much interested in George because he felt that the management of such patients was a particular type of problem that needed to be solved.

Both the physician and the psychologist agreed that it was unlikely that George would accept any formal psychological treatment, but that perhaps some regime could be worked out where support by the physician would be of benefit to the patient. It was decided to recommend discharge from the hospital with outpatient medical care to be carried on by the interested physician. This outpatient care was to consist of both medication and supportive counseling. At the same time George was referred to the vocational rehabilitation section of the hospital, where the possibilities of physically lighter jobs were reviewed with him. Through a contact made partly by the vocational rehabilitation counselor and partly independently by George he found a position in a nearby sports repair shop, restringing tennis rackets. George, in his usual good humor, made the wisecrack, "It's a job I've got the guts for."

Questions for George P.

Note: In some instances, it is valuable to start an analysis of a case in the middle and attempt to work both forward and backward in your analysis. George P. is one such case in which this approach will be used in the questions.

1. Looking at George's life during the twenty-year period that he lived with his mother, what patterns of interaction do we see occurring between mother and son?

2. Which of George's needs appeared to have been met by these patterns of interaction listed in your answer to question 1?

3. What appeared to be George's reaction to his mother's death, both at the time of her death and in the years following?

4. In what way can we see George expressing the same needs in the years following his mother's death that were formerly gratified in his relationship with his mother?

5. Looking at George's earlier years, state what you see in regard to the following:

    a. Training in autonomy and independence.

    b. Indulgence of dependency needs by mother and/or father.

    c. The degree of contact between the parents and George.

6. Looking at your answer to question 5, what sort of emotional conflicts appeared likely to develop under these conditions?

7. Can you see any relationship between this conflict or conflicts and

George's physical symptom of stomach ulcer? Attempt to link up the conflict and the symptom on both a psychological and physiological level.

8. At various points in the case history, it is noted that George was happy, unconcerned about his illness, even pleased with his life situation.

    a. What defense mechanism do these attitudes appear to reflect?

    b. What emotions or drives did these attitudes appear designed to inhibit or avoid?

9. Consider the following points:

    a. George worked most of the time with food or in a food related industry.

    b. George tended to drink rather heavily.

    c. George had little to do with women sexually during his adult life.

In what way might these facts be related theoretically?

10. In what ways was George's behavior in the hospital consistent with his earlier personality?

11. Search in your textbook or in any other book on abnormal psychology for a theoretical discussion of the causes of stomach ulcers. Outline some of these theories. Which of them best fits George?

12. What suggestions can you offer as to how hospitals might better deal with patients who act like George while hospitalized?

References

KAPP, F. T., ROSCHBAUM, M., & ROMANO, J. Psychological factors in men with peptic ulcers. *American Journal of Psychiatry,* 1947, **103**: 700.

MAHL, G. F. Anxiety, HCl secretion and peptic ulcer etiology. *Psychosomatic Medicine,* 1950, **12**: 158.

WEINER, H., THALER, M., REISER, M. F., & MIRSKY, I. A. Etiology of duodenal ulcer: I. Relation of specific psychological characteristics to rate of gastric secretion (serum pepsinogen). *Psychosomatic Medicine,* 1957, **19**: Issue I.

THE CASE OF BARBARA Y.

Too Much To Remember

When Mrs. Y. was brought to the hospital by her husband, she was dazed, confused, and weeping. Apparently aware of her surroundings and able to answer brief questions in filling out the admitting form, she could not, at the time, discuss any of her problems with the admitting physician. Her husband reported that she had left their home two weeks previously while he was at work. All the efforts of her husband and the police to trace her had failed until approximately twenty-four hours prior to her admission to the hospital when Mr. Y. received a report that a woman of her description had been arrested in a nearby city. When he arrived and identified her, she did not at first recognize him, did not know her own name, and could not remember what had happened to her or anything about her past. The police informed Mr. Y. that she had been arrested for "resorting" after a motel owner had called the police to complain that several different men had visited the motel room she had rented three days before in the company of a sailor. Mrs. Y. seemed unable to remember any of these alleged events. Gradually she came to recognize her husband as he talked anxiously with her whereupon she began to weep and requested to be brought home. Their attorney was able to arrange a voluntary commitment to the hospital.

In appearance, Mrs. Y. was a short, buxom woman whose dress and demeanor gave the impression of a girl just out of high school rather than a woman of thirty-one. She wore her hair in a pony-tail and was dressed in a simple white blouse and dark skirt, bobby-sox, and low-heeled shoes. On admission to the hospital, her dress was disheveled and dirty, and she wore no make-up. Her face was flushed and her eyes were red from crying. Mr. Y. was a tall, heavy-set, gray-haired man who might be considered handsome. He was quite concerned about his wife's condition, and anxiously asked if the doctors thought she could be helped. He waved aside any questions about his possible concern over her arrest, saying that he cared only that she receive the best treatment possible.

Mrs. Y. was very fatigued, and for the next three days she slept a great deal of the time. When awake, she remained dazed, but responded if addressed by nurses or other patients. She ate very little at first, but then became quite hungry, requesting extra food between meals. Once she became severely nauseous and vomited several times but denied that she was at all ill and seemed very ashamed to have vomited. On the fourth day she became much more alert, joked with the other patients, watched TV, and joined in a card game. Her doctor attempted to interview her and she seemed eager to co-operate, but soon after entering the room she burst into tears and fled back to her bed. Her condition continued to improve, and two days later she was able to talk at length with her doctor about her marriage and her childhood, but remained amnesic about the events immediately preceding her hospitalization.

Only much later in treatment did the patient have any recollection at all of what had occurred during the previous two weeks and even then her memories were spotty. Pieced together with reports from her husband, it appeared that she had left the house with only enough money to purchase a bus ticket to the city where she had lived during most of her childhood. Much later the patient vaguely remembered spending much of one day walking the streets in the neighborhood where she had grown up, and standing several hours in front of the building where her father used to have his office. Further reports by the police indicated that she had taken a hotel room which was later paid for by an unidentified man. The patient believed that she had eaten very little during these two weeks and that she spent at least one night on a park bench along the beach. She had no memory of the man who allegedly paid her hotel bill, or of the other men later at the motel. She was very ashamed to hear of her behavior but did not express any disbelief or denial. She was very afraid at first that her husband would disown her because of these reports and was not relieved by his reassurance for many months.

Past History. Barbara's parents were in their mid-forties when she was born; as they had been childless, they were overjoyed at her arrival. From all of her accounts, they were very doting parents who lavished everything on her and made few demands. She knew nothing of the conditions of her birth, except that her mother was quite ill afterwards and remained in poor health during most of Barbara's childhood. Her mother would take to bed with malaise and headaches and remain there for several days, during which time Barbara was admonished to be quiet and was cared for chiefly by her father. However, she remembered these periods with fondness as her father was a very gentle and good-humored man who went out of his way to amuse her, take her places with him, and buy and cook special things for her. On the other hand, she remembered her mother as a rather fussy woman who always seemed to be afraid something might happen to Barbara, especially that she might become ill or have an accident. For example, her mother never permitted Barbara to play in front of the house because of the danger of being run over in the street. For the first several years after Barbara started school her mother would accompany her on the two-block walk to the grade school. As Barbara thought back, she could visualize her mother hovering over her with a sweater.

Barbara's health in general was fair throughout her childhood, except that she always vomited very easily. She would have brief periods of nausea frequently and vomit several times during an evening. Her mother took her to several different doctors who could find no physical cause for this. One pediatrician suggested that Barbara consciously induced the vomiting, and, although her mother overtly rejected the doctor's opinion, Barbara felt that perhaps she really did believe the doctor. When it was suggested during psychotherapy that perhaps this childhood vomiting might in some way have been associated with emotional disturbance, Barbara agreed that this might be true but could not immediately associate it with any particular disturbance. "If anything, I seemed to vomit more often after having a good time with my father." As far as she could remember the vomiting had gradually disappeared by the time she was twelve or thirteen.

She was a good student at school, made above average grades, and was a favorite of her teachers. The only trouble she remembers ever getting into was for whispering in class. "I was a great talker and Daddy used to tickle me, saying he was trying to find the button which would turn me off." She claimed she had many friends "and went to lots of parties" during her grade school and junior high school years. However, because of her mother's illnesses, she seldom could invite any playmates into the house, and because of her mother's fears she seldom was allowed to go to play in someone else's house. Her favorite game when playing by herself was "dressing up, usually in mother's old clothes." She loved to make up stories, "usually romantic stories," and act them out in front of the mirror. Later in junior high and high school she was quite active in amateur dramatics. She played the lead in the senior class play, "Mrs. Moonlight," a fantasy about a woman who never aged. She claimed that in her early years at high school she was very popular with the boys and was asked many times for dates. However, her father insisted on driving her and her date to and from the dance or movie, on the excuse that he did not trust teen-age driving. The boys seldom asked her a second time and gradually she had fewer and fewer dates. Asked if she resented her father's chaperoning, she laughed and agreed he was probably pretty old-fashioned but that she appreciated his protection and respected his advice. She said that she felt that her parents prevented her from becoming "real wild" like many of her high school peers, adding, "I probably would have gotten myself into some kind of a mess if it hadn't been for my father." She maintained that she had many good times despite the fact that she did not date much during her last year or so at high school, for she became quite active in the debutante auxiliary of her father's lodge. She was elected to several different offices including the presidency, and continued to be active in this debutante organization as "past matron" until her marriage a year ago.

Barbara claimed that the main reason for cutting down on dating activities was her "seizures." These "seizures" consisted of a feeling of vertigo and mild paralysis, but without loss of consciousness. "I would feel warm all over and then feel like I was about to faint and would crumple to the floor." The first of these seizures occurred just prior to her second menstrual period at age thirteen and seemed thereafter to be frequently, but not always, associated with her periods. She said that the relation between these seizures and her menstruation was difficult to ascertain because of the irregularity of her menses. Her menses were also accompanied by severe cramps and feelings of weakness. She remembered her initial seizure very clearly as it had occurred while her father was driving her to a very special teen-age party; he pulled to the curb and laid her out on the lawn where he administered artificial respiration. Throughout her adolescence and early twenties she was under the care of a local neurologist, who later was a consultant at the hospital where she was currently hospitalized. He reported that he had seen several of her seizures wherein she lay rather rigid on the floor, with her eyes rolled back, but that she had shown no clonic movements nor other indications of grand mal seizures. He was also puzzled by the fact that he found no abnormal neurological signs either in his examination or in the electroencephalographic record. Nevertheless for many years he considered her seizures and her childhood vomiting as "epileptic equivalents" and treated her with anti-convulsant medications. In later years he suspected that her seizures might have had some emotional etiology although he had no direct evidence for this hypothesis. However, on the basis of his guess, he told her that he had come across a new medicine which would completely eradicate her seizures if she took it faithfully every day for a month; he prescribed a placebo and she remained free of seizures from then on.

Barbara's mother died of lung cancer shortly after Barbara was graduated from high school. Barbara shrugged cynically as she mentioned her mother's death, saying, "Mother was a nervous chain-smoker and Daddy and I always told her that she would burn herself out." She took over the housekeeping duties at home after her mother died because "father would have just been lost without me." Soon afterwards she became her father's administrative assistant in his real estate business. Her father had always had a "weak heart" and after the death of his wife he suffered several coronary attacks. She assumed increasing responsibility in her father's business so that he could take afternoons off and rest. During this ten-year period "I was the man at the office and the mother at home."

Her father's death a little over two years ago was not entirely unexpected but was a very great shock to her. "I almost had a nervous breakdown then." She became very depressed, felt sick and weak, and thought she might die. She could not leave the house and for many days stayed home alone weeping. Her physician and friends advised her to take a long trip. She sold her father's interest in the business and used part of the money to take a tour of the Caribbean. Though she denied having any sexual experiences prior to this time, on the trip she had brief sexual affairs with three different men. The last of these affairs resulted in a pregnancy and abortion. In mentioning these episodes she said, "I guess I was just so upset by my father's death that I didn't care what I did or what happened to me." The abortion, which was done by a Cuban "doctor," left her with considerable pain and a serious infection which, when she returned home, required hospitalization for surgical repair and medical treatment.

This episode left Barbara depressed, but she was determined to break her depression and immediately sought employment in a real estate firm owned by her father's former partner. Soon afterwards she accepted an offer of marriage from this man, some seventeen years her senior. She had always admired her husband and had been secretly in love with him when she was a little girl and he a young man entering her father's business. At first she had many qualms about getting married, primarily because of her guilt feelings over the incidents on her Caribbean trip. Also she felt that she wanted eventually to have children and worried that the seizures which she had had previously might be an inherited epilepsy. However, her husband conducted an ardent courtship in a gracious manner, was quite affectionate, and aware of her every little need. As the wedding date approached she found herself more and more anxious and postponed it twice on flimsy excuses. On the night following her wedding she had her menstrual period one week prior to the time she expected it. She was very tearful and apologetic to her husband, but rejected his sexual advances. "He was so nice and understanding about it all." However, she discovered that she was completely unable to be sexually aroused by her husband; indeed, she felt disgusted by his sexual advances even though he was a much more gentle and undemanding lover than the men she had met on her Caribbean tour. She tried hard not to show her feelings about their sexual relations to her husband, and at first he made no complaint. It was obvious to her, however, that he was not really satisfied. One night he got her to drink rather heavily and became quite drunk himself. She permitted him to attempt intercourse but he was so inebriated and she so disgusted that it was a complete failure. He swore at her and compared her to a "rubber mat." She felt very guilty and tearful about this incident but did not remind him of it, and the next day he appeared not to remember it. The following week she disappeared.

Course in Treatment. During the ensuing two and half years Barbara was seen in outpatient psychotherapy interviews three times weekly. At first, she was quite loquacious, reciting much of the above history with many brief intellectual insights. She attributed much of her problem to the fact that she was "Daddy's little girl," saying that she had never really grown up. She began to dress in a more adult fashion, using more cosmetics and wearing revealing blouses or knit dresses that emphasized her shapely figure. Her walk and mannerisms became markedly seductive. She made many slips of speech, particularly referring to her father as her husband or vice versa. Once she slipped and said "daddy" instead of doctor in addressing her therapist. When these slips were called to her attention, and it was suggested that she confused her husband, father, and therapist, she would either smile sweetly and remain silent or attempt to make a joke of it, saying, "Oh you and your psychology!" After several months she reported that her sexual relations with her husband had improved markedly, "I'm so sexy every night that poor Bobby just can't keep up with me." She interpreted this change in her feelings to mean that her main problem had been resolved. She had about decided to stop treatment, but changed her mind saying, "I guess you've just become a habit with me." Shortly thereafter she became increasingly silent and obviously depressed. Whereas previously she had always been prompt for her appointments now she was frequently late and several times cancelled the appointment. It was suggested to her that her resistance might be the result of some feelings she might have regarding the therapist. She hotly denied this interpretation and became increasingly angry at the therapist, saying that she felt that he was pressuring her into something, to the extent that she felt as if she were being raped. Attempts to get her to explore these feelings further met with stormy silence. Finally, in tears, she admitted that she had recently had several dreams wherein she imagined the therapist making love to her. Following this revelation she had another brief amnesic period which lasted one day. She wandered the streets not remembering who she was, and finally found herself standing in front of the clinic. Thereafter, she was able to remember and relate several other sexual fantasies which had persisted from childhood. For example she had imagined that impregnation occurred orally and that the fetus developed in the abdomen. Her father had told her "the facts of life" soon after her first menstrual period, but did not say anything regarding the actual act of impregnation. Even after she learned about impregnation (in a physiology class), "it really never made sense to me."

Approximately two years later, she became pregnant, but failed to mention this fact to her therapist for several months, finally divulging it in a defiant, rebellious fashion. Her pregnancy proceeded without abnormal physiological difficulty, but she had several bouts of depression, even entertaining suicidal ideas, for which at first she could not account, though later associated with earlier guilt feelings regarding her love for the therapist and then for her father. She dropped out of treatment shortly before giving birth, returning for only three visits during the ensuing six months. She was wrapped up in the care of her baby boy, indeed, seemed a little too obsessed with the child and inclined to be overprotective. However, she declared she was happier than ever before in her life. She suffered no further symptoms. On the last contact with the hospital, she announced that she and her husband were planning a second child.

Questions for Barbara Y.

1. What is the technical term used for describing Barbara's condition during the two-week period after she left her husband?
2. What event or events were taking place in Barbara's life immediately prior to this two-week episode?
3. What events were occurring during Barbara's psychotherapy immediately prior to her brief amnesic episode at that time?
4. Taking into account your answer to 2 and 3 above, what feelings or impulses of a conflictual sort were most likely coming close to awareness immediately prior to both episodes?
5. If we view the amnesic state as a radical attempt to escape from an internal conflict, in what way did these episodes serve to help Barbara escape from awareness of her conflictual desires? Consider the following components of the amnesic episodes:
   a. the loss of the sense of identity.
   b. the amnesia for actions taken.
   c. the actions taken during the amnesic period.
6. Consider the following types of symptom patterns:
   a. a dissociated state.
   b. a blindness of psychogenic origin.

    c. a paralysis of psychogenic origin.

What common features can you discern in these three ways of handling intense psychological conflict?

7. Do you see other examples of reaction patterns illustrating this common feature or features, suggested in your answer to question 6, in Barbara's early life? List these other reaction patterns.

8. What conditions appeared to exist in Barbara's early home environment which reinforced her ways of reacting to conflict instead of some other ways (i.e. phobic reactions, obsessional symptoms, chronic anxiety states)?

9. What impulses and feelings appeared most conflictual for Barbara?

10. What conditions in Barbara's early home environment facilitated the development of these conflicts about her impulses? Consider, in your answer Barbara's relationship to both her mother and father and Barbara's early sex instruction.

11. Psychoanalysis, in particular, has focused upon the type of conflict which Barbara struggled with.

    a. What name does psychoanalysis give to this conflict?

    b. According to psychoanalytic theory, how does this conflict arise and grow?

    c. To what extent does Barbara's background fit the theory cited in your answer to *b*?

12. Is Barbara's selection of a mate consistent with your answer to question 11. In what way? Is it now clear why Barbara's conflicts were so intensified following this marriage?

13. Also, can you understand and explain, in light of your answer to question 11, Barbara's reaction

    a. prior to the delivery of her first child

    b. following the delivery of her first child?

References

ABSE, D. W. Hysteria. In ARIETI, S., *American Handbook of Psychiatry.* New York: Basic Books, 1959. Pp. 275–277, 283–288.

STENGEL, E. On the etiology of fugue states. *Journal of Mental Science,* 1941, 87: 572–599.

STENGEL, E. Further studies on pathological wanderings. *Journal of Mental Science,* 1943, 89: 224–241.

THE CASE OF CAL B.

Dribble, Drugs, and Death

It is somewhat difficult to relate Cal's story, since he was not able to tell us much about himself or his crime. However, his story can be pieced together from what he related, an interview with his mother, and some school records. There is also the court's testimony of the others who were tried for participating in the same bloody crime. This latter source, however, was not very reliable since the other participants in the crime also had very poor memories of it and were anxious to put the entire blame for the murders onto Cal.

Cal was born and lived most of his life in a small town in southwest Indiana. It was situated on a small rise above the Wabash River and consisted of large white houses with many trees and broad lawns. Cal and his parents and his younger brother lived in such a house (shown in a newspaper story on Cal). He attended the local schools and made fair grades. His father, the local undertaker, made an above average living so the family was in a comfortable financial position. Thus Cal had no economic deprivation. His family were well respected citizens of the town: at one time his father was on the City Council, and his mother was a leader in some of the town clubs.

The main activity that Cal and most of the other males of all ages were concerned about was basketball. Cal followed every team and every school in high school, collegiate amateurs, and professional basketball. However, the only time that Cal saw any of these games other than on television, was once or twice when he went to the Notre Dame game which was only 40 miles south of Terra Haute. Since his parents seldom left their small town, he had never been to Indianapolis and had been only once to Chicago when he was very small. Cal grew very quickly into a tall slim young man and became very adept at basketball. He made the varsity team when he entered high school and was one of their champion players. He also did fairly well in high school studies. The high school record showed that he made mostly B's, a few A's, and that his only low grades were in mathematics. He was very popular with the other youths since any champion basketball player was considered a hero. Cal did not seem to be quite as "girl-crazy" as his younger brother or the other boys in town, his mother reported. On the contrary, he was rather shy, and although one of the girls claimed him as a boyfriend throughout most of high school, he really did not go on dates but rather seemed to live by the athletic regime of early hours, no liquor, no drugs. Cal was also very active in church and taught Sunday School during his senior year at high school.

Since Cal was later involved in a bloody and senseless murder, one wondered whether there could possible be any connection with his interest in death and his father being an undertaker. Both Cal and his mother separately seemed surprised at this question. Both reported that Cal had never taken any open interest in his father's occupation and that his father kept his business quite separate from his family. Both Cal and his mother used the euphemism of "passing-away" rather than "dying" when referring to death. Cal reported that he had been curious at times about what happened at death and what his father did for dead people. But his father had told him that this was a very personal and private matter and that Cal was not to inquire into such personal matters. Other people's death was nobody's business other than their own and the mortician's. Cal rarely ever visited his father's place of business.

On completion of high school Cal applied to several of the local universities. However, since his scores on the College Entrance Exams were only average to below average in nearly all subjects and his high school was not rated as one of the top high schools from which graduates entered into the major universities of the central United States, his hopes of being accepted by Indiana or Illinois University and becoming a varsity member on a major basketball team were dashed. Instead he attended a small but respectable religious school known also for basketball. His parents were pleased that he was admitted to this college since they thought it might fan his interest and devotion to his religion. Exactly what happened to Cal's college career is not clear since Cal was later unable to remember much of his college years. The records show that he made C's and some B's in the first half of his freshman year, but at the end of the first half of his sophomore year he was failing miserably. He did not make the varsity team at college since the basketball competition was extremely stiff. As far as can be ascertained, it appeared that this sport's hero from a small town was no match for the competitors of other small towns in the area who also made better grades.

Cal was very lonely at school: he made only a few close friends, did not join a fraternity, and had not found any permanent girlfriend. However, he had met some other people who had at that time started using various drugs, chiefly marijuana and LSD. He felt very depressed at his relative failures at college and found some surcease from his depression through marijuana. His one or two experiences with LSD at this point were uneventful. Afraid to tell his parents that he was failing at school or even to admit it to himself, Cal came west to Los Angeles, partly to look up a girl that he had met at a drug party at the college. It was with this girl that he had his first sex experience. At the time he was also under the influence of marijuana.

On arriving in Los Angeles, he was able to locate this girl but found her living with two other young men. His arrival did not seem to disturb her and she invited him to join her menage. He found drugs to be very plentiful through this girl and her friends. He again enjoyed sexual experiences with her and with other girls that visited the apartment. Soon thereafter this entire group moved from the apartment to a ranch in the desert to join a much larger group of young men and women who called themselves "The Family."

This group was headed up by a slightly older man who seemed to have a great deal of influence over all the young people at this ranch. The press later described this leader as a "Svengali" who seemed to hypnotize those about him. Again there was an almost continuous use of a wide variety of drugs. During this year, Cal remembered he was continually "stoned" on something or other and had many sexual experiences with many girls. Cal still felt very guilty about his failure at college. He often thought of it when he was not drugged and worried about writing his parents. Cal remembered being involved in many "rap sessions" with the leader of this Family, where the leader seemed to preach a strange philosophy involved with death. Yet Cal was never very clear what this philosophy was about. He did

remember that most of the other young men quarreled with this
leader and left, so that just prior to the murders Cal, one other
young man, and five or six women were all that were left of the
Family.

At this time the leader seemed to be in a highly tense emotional
state, with which Cal identified. The leader kept talking about the
crowning event, the final thing, that would happen that would "release them all." Cal did remember that on the day before the murders, he had been drugged steadily. He awoke to get some supper
with the rest of the Family and was given more drugs. He remembered getting into the car with the girls and their being given knives
and a large pair of wire clippers. He did not remember where they
drove except that he was let out of the car and instructed to climb a
telephone pole and clip the wires. He could not account for the fact
that he was able to do this even though he was very drugged. He
barely had any visual memory of the murders. He remembers seeing
blood and hearing screams and thought that he was aware that one
of the victims was a pregnant girl. He accepted the account of other
witnesses that he had led the attack on several of the victims.
Sometimes he had nightmares, wherein he heard their screams and
awoke in horror, believing himself the murderer. Other witnesses at
the trial claimed that Cal did the driving on the return trip, but Cal
believes that he was so drugged that he would have been unable to
drive.

Despite Cal's near amnesia for this crime, it is likely that enough
of it remained in his memory eight months later to almost drive him
out of his mind. In any case, he was soon captured by the police along
with his companions and the leader and other members of the Family.
He was then unable to speak or even to walk or eat. He was dragged
from place to place by the police. When he was sent to the state hospital his body was covered with bruises, and he was very emaciated
and mute. At the state hospital it was not possible to get any information from him, and he had to be tube fed for quite a while. As far as
could be ascertained, he had lost almost 60 pounds in weight. At the
time Cal was returned to the county jail and sent to the clinic, his face
was sunken, his eyes stared straight forward, his hair had been cut almost to the point of being shaven, and he looked emaciated. He
spoke in a very hollow tone with no emotion whatever. However,
he was now able to eat, and he could converse though in a very lim-

ited fashion. He seemed aware of the purpose of the examination but said that he was very disinterested in whatever might happen to him. He did not want his attorney to use any type of psychiatric defense. Nevertheless, at the urging of his attorney he agreed to this examination. He did seem a bit intellectually challenged by the IQ test but nevertheless did not seem able to think out even the most simple intellectual problems. He was aware of his intellectual failures and did seem moderately bothered by the fact that he did not know things or could not solve things or could not remember how to do things he was sure he was once able to do. His responses to the IQ and other psychological tests were generally vague and often inappropriate. However, none of his responses were exceedingly bizarre or morbid. Many of his responses strongly suggested that he might have suffered some brain injury. On further questioning, he admitted that he had once eaten half of a Belladonna root and had been dreadfully ill for many days.

At the trial several months later, Cal seemed to have reconstituted a little bit more. His speaking voice was not quite as hollow, and he had a little more emotion in his voice as he described the details of the crime for the jury for what must have been the 100th time. He showed considerable emotion when he saw his mother present at the trial. He clasped her to him and wept with her. The reports of the psychological and psychiatric examinations were given to the court and were highly contested by the prosecuting attorney. Apparently, the report was almost totally ignored by the jury who found Cal guilty of murder in the first degree. He was sentenced to life imprisonment without hope of parole.

Questions for Cal B.

1. At the time of his appointment with the psychologist Cal was under indictment for murder. Consider what effects this might have had on:

    a. Cal's memory for recent events

    b. Cal's memory for early life events

    c. Cal's willingness to reveal signs of psychopathology.

To what extent is it possible to obtain valid estimates of psychopathological states under these circumstances?

2. Despite many arguments back and forth, a defense of insanity in the courts still relies on the M'Naughton rule. This rule specifies that "at the time of committing the act, the party accused was labouring under such a defect of reason, from disease of the mind, as not to know the nature and quality of the act he was doing, or if he did know it, that he did not know he was doing what was wrong" (Weihofen, 1933, p. 28).

To what extent did the psychologist's tests and interviews suggest that Cal was insane in this *legal* sense?

Defend your answer in terms of the following issues:

    a. What "disease of the mind" did Cal manifest? What psychiatric diagnosis supports this conclusion?

    b. It has never been decided which "diseases of the mind" qualify as legal insanity. Which psychiatric disorders, in your opinion, might qualify in the legal sense as "diseases of the mind" and which do not?

3. Cal was *not* judged legally insane by the jury. What are your feelings concerning his imprisonment, with all the implications that he was legally responsible for his actions in the murders?

4. Looking at the sparse background factors available on Cal, what seem to have been his strengths and weaknesses during his teenage years?

5. Looking at his college years, what frustrations and disappointments did he experience? How did he deal with these disappointments?

6. Are there any factors in Cal's life history which might predispose him to

    a. extensive psychoactive drug use

    b. involvement with a charismatic leader

    c. the commitment of severely antisocial acts?

7. A key issue in the drug abuse area is whether continued and sustained use of psychoactive drugs (marijuana, amphetamines, LSD) produce profound changes in personality, judgment, and ethical sense.

    a. What evidence can you find in the literature or in your reading on this issue?

    b. To what extent do these writings predict the progressive behavioral trends noted in Cal B. after he left college?

8. Insofar as drug use played a part in his behavior, which drug

might have produced a possible psychotic reaction with associated brain damage? In brief, how do you explain how a young man with this All-American background ends up with a life sentence for mass murder?

References

ACORD, L. D., & BARKER, D. D. Hallucinogenic drugs and cerebral deficit. *The Journal of Nervous and Mental Diseases*, 1973, **156**: 281–283.

BLACKER, K. H. Aggression and the chronic use of LSD. *American Journal of Psychiatry*, 1968, **123**: 97–107.

DAVIS, F., & MUNOZ, L. Heads and freaks: patterns and meanings of drug use among hippies. *Journal of Health and Social Behavior*, 1968, **9**: 156–164.

GLASS, G. S. Psychedelic drugs, stress, and the ego. *The Journal of Nervous and Mental Disease*, 1973, **156**: 232–241.

GOLDSTEIN, A. S. *The insanity defense*. New Haven: Yale University Press, 1967.

JONES, A. P. Personality and the value differences related to use of LSD-25. *International Journal of the Addictions*, 1973, **8**: 549–557.

SZASZ, T. S., *Law, liberty and psychiatry*. New York: Collier, 1971, Pp. 123–145.

WEIHOFEN, H. Insanity as a defense in criminal law. New York: The Commonwealth Fund, 1933.

THE CASE OF JONATHAN B.

Cup of Failure

Mr. B. arrived at the sanatorium shortly after midnight, stuporously drunk. He was an extremely obese man, and the alcohol made his normally pudgy face even more puffy and reddened his pale complexion. The formal dress suit which he was wearing seemed too small for his elephantine figure, and it was disheveled and muddy. He collapsed in a chair, bent over with his face in his hands, breathing heavily and audibly, almost as if sobbing. When the psychiatrist approached him, Mr. B. indicated with a wave of his hand that the doctor should talk to his wife, who was standing beside him. Mrs. B. was a tall, slim, gray-haired woman, neatly but modestly dressed in a dark brown suit. She spoke softly but there was considerable tension in her voice and her face had a harried expression.

Mrs. B. explained that earlier in the afternoon her husband had telephoned to say that he would not be home for dinner but was joining some of his friends and would go directly on to work. A violinist, he had been playing at an afternoon tea and was scheduled to play in the symphony that evening. She was quite uneasy about his phone call as his enunciation was slurred and she feared he had been drinking; however, she did not mention her apprehension to her husband as he had repeatedly told her that the reason he got drunk was because she nagged him. Several hours later, one of his colleagues called to advise her that Mr. B. was too drunk to play with the symphony that night. Because she was engaged at that moment in preparing their two pre-school boys for bed, she tried to get her husband's friend to put him in a taxi and send him home, but the concert was about to start. Although she was reluctant to reveal the situation to her mother-in-law, she was forced to call upon her to care for the boys while she herself went after her husband. She found him pleading with the concert master to be permitted to join the orchestra and was very embarrassed by the concert master's gruff order to "get this drunk out of here." Mrs. B. began to cry as she reported this incident; then, drying her tears, she apologized for losing control of her emotions.

At first Mrs. B. said that her husband had been drinking to excess "for the past three or four months" but then immediately corrected herself: "for the past several years." Even before they were married, five years previously, she was disturbed by the frequency with which he seemed to "have to have a drink." Before they would leave on a date, he would have one or two "quick ones," another before dinner or a show, and after the show, he rushed to the nearest bar. On their dates, he seldom became completely inebriated, but at cocktail parties or other social gatherings he usually ended up stupefied and incoherent. Afterwards he would be most apologetic. Whenever she tried to get him to limit his drinking, he kidded her about the fact that she was a social worker and complained that she was "trying to reform him." Indeed, if she remonstrated, he seemed to drink even more desperately—as if to spite her.

After they were married, Mrs. B. was dismayed to discover that Jonathan often had a drink beside him during the day and constantly throughout the evening. She estimated that as long as she had known him he had consumed at least a pint of whiskey a day. Thus, she had consciously admitted, at least to herself, that her husband was already an alcoholic at age twenty-five, when she married him. Her immediate impulse to help him was frustrated by his adamant refusal to recognize that any problem existed. Aware that his alcoholism might continue unabated, and possibly increase in severity, she feared that if she made an issue of it, her marriage would be endangered. Not only was she deeply in love with her new husband but, as she described herself, she was a "plain Jane" who had always been a "wallflower" and who, at age thirty-five had despaired of marrying until she met Jonathan. Although this dilemma continued to disturb her for the ensuing five years of her marriage, it was abated at least on the surface by the fact that his excessive drinking did not markedly interfere with their home life or, until recently, with his job. Even when drunk, Jonathan was a most amiable, easygoing person, who "never" lost his temper nor let things upset him. She described him as an affectionate and understanding person who "always made me feel wonderful even if I were blue," and "I hated myself if I

were critical of him or angry at him." Everyone "loved" him and seldom did anyone remark on his drinking.

Up until about six months before, Jonathan had usually been able
to get to work, although at times considerably under the influence
of alcohol. With increasing frequency in the past few months, Mrs.
B. had been forced to call the orchestra or his other employers to
report that he was "sick." His colleagues were aware of his increasing
alcoholism, and Mrs. B. felt sure that when he was "sick" it was
common knowledge that he was really inebriated. The previous
summer the orchestra had made a tour to Europe, and Mrs. B. was
very apprehensive that while away from home he might drink even
more and possibly lose his position with the orchestra. However, his
colleagues protected him when he did become drunk, and he was
able to make the tour and return without incident. Upon the orchestra's return, one of his best friends came to him and advised him
to seek psychiatric help. Mr. B. angrily told his friend to mind his
own business and broke off the friendship. Mrs. B. had tried her best
to keep her husband's parents unaware of his condition because
"it would break his mother's heart." However, she was pretty sure
that they had some idea of the extent of his drinking even though
it was never openly discussed.

In subsequent interviews, Mrs. B. recalled that her husband began
drinking most heavily about two years ago shortly after the couple
had moved out of the home of her in-laws. She regarded her mother-
and father-in-law as "the most wonderful people in the world"; she
"really adored them" and had no complaints against them. Nevertheless, after residing in their home for the first three years of her marriage, she became increasingly determined to set up a home of their
own. For some time, she had urged her husband to find them separate
living quarters, pleading that she wished more independence and
privacy. Jonathan had agreed but had made no move toward leaving
his parents' home. When she insisted more strongly, he demurred
on the grounds that their income was not great enough to obtain
the kind of home he wanted for her. She saw that their older child,
then almost three, made her aging in-laws uncomfortable with his
hyperactivity and added this as ammunition in her arguments with
her husband. Their problem was aggravated by the fact that this
was just after World War II and housing was very scarce. Finally
she herself went out and rented an old but roomy apartment which

was priced above their limited budget. In contrast with their previous quarters with Mr. B.'s parents, the new apartment was physically less comfortable and more shabby, but Mrs. B. felt a lessening of emotional tension. She had long realized that her husband was very dependent upon and under the domination of his parents, and she had hoped that the move away from them might lessen this childhood bond and intensify their marital tie. Mr. B., however, continued to visit his parents at least daily, sometimes twice a day. Mrs. B. was quick to point out that she felt that her in-laws in no way attempted to interfere with their marriage or with her management of the children. She had hoped that, once they moved away from Mr. B.'s parents, her husband would be less restless and more inclined to spend some time with her and the children. However, he continued to be unable to sit down around the house, always seemed to have something he *had* to do, or to feel a need to be "on the go." She was puzzled by his restlessness and tension and even though they seldom quarreled, she wondered if there was something wrong with their marriage.

The increased rent was only part of a rapidly increasing cost of living which the B.'s had not faced before. They had made only token contributions toward the family budget while living with Mr. B.'s parents. Mrs. B. had her master's degree in social work and for the decade prior to her marriage had been employed full-time as a medical social worker. She would have preferred to have stayed home and cared for her family but the new financial burden forced her to find a part-time job and put the children in a nursery school for half a day. She admitted that once she was back at work she enjoyed her job and realized that she had been bored with housework and baby care. Mr. B.'s income from his position with the symphony had always had to be augmented by giving private music lessons or by playing at weddings and other social events. As is true with even the most accomplished musicians, he continued to practice many hours of the day and his income was further reduced by such expenses as the cost of music lessons for himself, union dues, the care of his formal clothes, and so forth. Mrs. B. felt she might have managed on their combined earnings, but Mr. B., without telling his wife, got an additional job selling vacuum cleaners from door to door. Their working schedules left absolutely no time for any social life and, indeed, precious little time for relaxing together at home. Mr. B. defended his drinking by saying that "his occasional drink with the boys" after a concert was his only form of relaxation. Mrs. B. privately felt hurt, jealous, and angry that Mr. B. should spend any spare hours away from her and the children. Once, when she could no longer control her feelings and mentioned them to her husband, he became silent and guilty-looking and spent the rest of the evening getting quietly drunk at home. She in turn felt quite guilty that she had made any demands upon him since she realized that he had so few pleasures of his own. She tried to make extra efforts to make life comfortable for him at home; she made sure that she was at home whenever he was free, and that he had no obligations or things to do around the house. She tried to wait on him hand and foot. She sought to cook his favorite dishes, but she was never much of a cook and had done none of the cooking while they were living with his mother. Mr. B. never criticized his wife's cooking and, indeed, was quite appreciative of it, but Mrs. B. regarded her cooking as quite inferior to that of her mother-in-law who was "a natural-born" cook.

Though the B.'s had never discussed their sexual relationship between themselves, they each separately admitted to the psychiatrist that they felt their sexual relations had not been as satisfactory to them as they had wished. Each felt guilty that they might not be sexually satisfying to their partner. Although the B.'s had had one or two mutually satisfactory sexual experiences prior to marriage, their sexual relationships after marriage were less frequent and less satisfactory than either wished. Mrs. B. regarded herself as not too physically attractive and possibly sexually inhibited. Prior to her marriage she had often felt that she might not be sexually attractive to men and wondered if she could satisfy her husband sexually. She had never had any prior sexual relationships and had always felt somewhat uneasy and guilty regarding the topic of sex. She found that she reached sexual climax much more slowly than her husband and consequently felt both unsatisfied and inadequate. Mr. B. likewise had no premarital sexual experience other than masturbation. Although intellectually he knew that masturbation was a "natural part of adolescence," he did feel increasingly uneasy when this "habit" did not entirely abate following his marriage. He felt disappointed about their heterosexual relationship, admitting sadly that it did not seem much different from his masturbation. Jonathan realized that his

wife was seldom satisfied even though she had never mentioned it
to him. Both of them admitted that they would rather the other take
the initiative in love making, each saying that they did not feel right
imposing their impulses on the other person. More often than not, it
was Mrs. B. who was the sexual aggressor, which made her feel
angry at her husband and guilty over her own aggression. While
living under Mr. B.'s parental roof, each felt queasy about having
sexual relations, as though his parents might be aware and disapproving—even though in discussing this point each admitted that
such a feeling was irrational for married adults, especially as the
elder B.'s had never been disapproving of anything. Furthermore,
neither of them felt very inclined to have sexual relations during and
immediately after Mrs. B.'s pregnancies which had occupied almost
two of the five years of their marriage. During the year prior to
Mr. B.'s hospitalization, their sexual relationship had dwindled to
almost nothing. Mr. B. was often too tired or too drunk. Mrs. B. likewise was usually fatigued or too angry. She would lie awake beside
her snoring hulk of a husband, feeling both frustrated and guilty.
In the morning she would be tired and sleepy, using all of her energy
to control her feelings of irritability. Mr. B. sensed his wife's frustration, felt inadequate in that he was not satisfying to her, but felt
dominated by her and resentful over the guilt she aroused in him.

Prior History. Jonathan B., age thirty, was born and reared in the
same Atlantic coast metropolis where he then resided, and where
his parents and his grandparents had lived most of their lives. His
great-grandfather had been a court musician and composer in two
different German principalities in the early nineteenth century. His
grandfather, who had emigrated from Germany to the United States
as a boy, founded a music publishing house and was noted in the
community as an outstanding cellist. Jonathan's own father was an
internationally famous violin teacher who tutored several of the
major concert violinists of his time as well as most of the violin section of the symphony orchestra of the city. The elder Mr. B. shared
in the profits from the family publishing firm and his income from
his teaching provided more than a comfortable living for the family
during Jonathan's childhood years. Most of the other immediate relatives and friends were also musicians and the house was continually

filled with music and with talk about music. Although Jonathan was never told that he was expected to become a musician, music for the B. family was an exclusive way of life. Furthermore, Jonathan was the only child of the eldest son, and for many years the only grandson. Therefore, he was not only the subject of considerable attention and expectation but also of multiple if gentle correction and admonition. His parents were in their early thirties when they married and it was ten years before he was born. His uncles and aunts likewise married later than usual. Jonathan at one point speculated why this might have been so; he thought it was perhaps because they spent so much time developing their careers as musicians, but later he recognized that his grandmother played the role of "queen mother" who dominated her husband and all her children and kept them tied to her as long as possible. Daily visits by his father to his grandmother were mandatory until the day of her death. Usually Jonathan and his mother accompanied his father on these visits; illness was the only excuse for absence. Jonathan sensed that perhaps his mother might have resented this bond between her husband and his mother for the relationship between Jonathan's mother and his paternal grandmother was always very cold and formal; but his mother never said anything in his presence to indicate her displeasure. Yet, he remembered hurried whispered discussions between his parents whenever it was necessary for him and his mother to remain at home.

Jonathan knew nothing of the conditions of his birth, for "my parents never discussed such things." However, he was a sickly child who as far back as he could remember, suffered from one minor illness after another. The family physician, a gruff old man, frequently told the parents in front of Jonathan that there was "nothing much wrong with the boy," prescribed a "hardier life," and accused Jonathan's mother of spoiling him. Jonathan's many colds, fevers, and asthmatic breathing were treated with a variety of home remedies prescribed by his grandmother and aunts. His earliest years were spent largely indoors, usually in his own or the parental bedroom, both because he had to stay out of the way of his father and his pupils and because the fireplace in his parents' bedroom was one of the warmer spots of the house. Propped up on pillows in his parents' bed, surrounded by toys and books, he was waited upon and fed by his mother. He had no playmates before he entered school, and, even after he began to go to school, he seldom invited another child to his own home. He was treated as an adult by nearly everyone and his conversation and attitudes were adult. A precocious child, he learned to read several years before he started school, both in English and German. He was reading music and playing the violin and piano by the time he was six, and was familiar with most of the major instruments of the orchestra by the time he was twelve. Although religion was seldom discussed in his home, his parents were fairly faithful Catholics; thus Jonathan was sent to a parochial boys' school. He was always a top scholar and was graduated from high school at the age of sixteen. He completed two years in a Catholic university and was encouraged by several of his professors to continue but by this time, music had become so important to him that he decided to discontinue further academic training and devote himself entirely to becoming a polished musician.

Jonathan was subject to the military draft on his eighteenth birthday in 1943. However, because of his obesity and his history of continuous illnesses, he was deferred. Although he had no desire to join the military service, he often felt uneasy because he was one of the few men of his age who remained a civilian. His deferment added to his impression that "I really never was like other men." His embarrassment over his failure to meet the military's physical standards was later enhanced by the fact that his wife had served for two years with the Women's Auxiliary Corps.

Jonathan regarded both of his parents as very kindly, generous, and affectionate people. He expressed deep reverence for his father whom he described as a tall, stately man of grave demeanor, who always appeared old to Jonathan since he was white-haired at the time of Jonathan's birth. Yet despite the bond of affection between Jonathan and his father, these characteristics of his father made it difficult for Jonathan ever to ask questions of him, to discuss much with him other than music, or, in Jonathan's teen-age years, to question or rebel against anything that his father said or did. Furthermore, his father never made any open demands upon Jonathan; rather Jonathan knew what was expected of him and what his father's opinions were without his father ever putting them in words. Jonathan's mother was fairly quiet and busied herself continually with waiting on her husband and her son. She took considerable pride in her immaculate house and in the largesse of rich foods which were served continuously throughout the day and evening. Because Jonathan was sickly and pale, extra food was constantly urged upon him and, as a consequence, he was always obese. If his mother was not stuffing him, his grandmother was. Beer or wine was always served to guests as they entered the house. Jonathan's father usually joined his guests in a drink, but Jonathan never saw his father overindulge. Indeed, his parents made discreet frowns of disapproval at anyone who showed even the slightest sign of being inebriated.

In the all-boy school which he attended as a teen-ager, Jonathan had no opportunity to meet the opposite sex. His companions often discussed their dates and talked about girls, but Jonathan was not "on the in" of any of the groups of boys in his class. He remembered being very curious about sex and listening to the conversation of other boys, but was too bashful to ask any direct questions. Indeed, even at the time of his hospitalization, he considered himself sexually naïve. Only after his marriage did he find out some of the "facts of life" in discussion with his wife or from some of the books which she had. The other boys at school teased him unmercifully about his obesity and always told him that no girl would ever take a second look at him because he was too fat. After he started college his grandmother and aunts began a campaign of finding girls for him, but he was always too shy and reserved and could not carry on any conversation after the introduction. He disliked the girls who were aggressive and telephoned him with invitations to parties which he rarely accepted. The others, he recalled, were either "unmitigated gigglers" or "were as shy as I was."

As had been true with nearly every girl he had ever met, his introduction to his wife was arranged by Jonathan's grandmother. The future Mrs. B. had been reared abroad, the daughter of Protestant missionaries who were old friends of Jonathan's grandmother. She had been returned to the United States to complete her college and professional training and then had come to work in a social agency in this city where she was born. Jonathan found his wife to be different from any of the other girls; she was self-assured but not openly aggressive. She was interested in him and his work but made no demands upon him. He recalled that he was surprised to find himself calling her for a dinner date after their first introduction and equally surprised to find that she accepted it. He liked and envied her independent way of life and her social graciousness. He felt relaxed with her as he did with no other person and increasingly sought her company. His grandmother let him know in no uncertain terms that she disapproved of his attention to a non-Catholic girl. On the other hand, he was very happy that his wife and mother struck it off excellently from the beginning. He felt his father also approved of their marriage. When he proposed to his wife, he had no idea of where or how they might live, but, he admitted, it had never occurred to him that he might live elsewhere than under his parental roof. He realized later that his wife had many times suggested that they make plans for finding their own apartment after their wedding, but he ignored these hints, giving his limited income as an excuse. He denied that he was conscious of any tension between him and his wife during the years they lived with his parents and did not really understand why she finally insisted they move.

Jonathan often played in quartets and small orchestral groups with his family and their adult friends even when he was a child. His career as a professional musician began shortly after he finished high school. He received his seat in the symphony on his twenty-first birthday as a birthday gift from the symphony conductor, an old friend of the family. By this time, he was devoting nearly every minute of his waking life to music, even more than many of his fellow orchestra members, and he rose rapidly in the hierarchy of the orchestra to the second highest position, i.e. next to the concert master himself. In discussing his music he said that he regarded himself as certainly technically above average and probably fairly talented but that he had always felt in his own mind that he lacked something that would otherwise make him a great musician. He regarded his own playing as being so technically perfect as to be lacking in feeling. He felt that many of his colleagues, especially those who were jealous of his position in the orchestra, held similar views of his playing. He explained that in a symphony orchestra, where every chair was another mark in the hierarchy of one's worth and status, there existed a tense and constant rivalry. He knew that many of his colleagues believed that he had reached his position largely through the influence of his father, and Jonathan himself wondered if this were not true. At times, he grew very weary of the constant bickering within the orchestra, of the drudgery of day-long

rehearsals and the evening and Saturday and Sunday concerts, all
for a paltry subsistence. He was disgusted because it was necessary
to supplement his income by "fiddling" at social events or "by trying to force music down the throats of rich young brats." Increasingly, his professional life began to pall, and music no longer was the
wonderfully exhilarating emotional experience of his childhood. Although he had few acquaintances outside the field of music, he occasionally met other adults who seemed to enjoy their work, and he
felt envious of them. The idea that he might enjoy doing something
else crept into his mind with increasing frequency. He became depressed whenever he thought of how very limited his existence was;
yet he regarded himself not only as ill-prepared but probably inadequate to any other way of life. He had never before discussed these
feelings with anyone else. To have even hinted at this subject with
his parents would have been unthinkable and, he feared, would have
hurt them deeply. He did not mention his self-doubts to his wife
because to do so would have seemed an admission of weakness to
her. He already felt that she was far more efficient and worldly-wise
than he; she was not only able to manage their private affairs but
as a professional social worker made a living at managing the affairs
of others.

Course in Treatment. Mr. B. remained in the sanitarium only a few
days following his hospitalization. He and his wife accepted the
advice of the psychiatrist that he enter into psychotherapy twice
weekly and that she attend a psychotherapeutic group consisting of
women whose husbands were alcoholic. During the first several
months of treatment, Mr. B. abstained from any use of alcohol. He
came faithfully to his treatment hours and discussed much of his
history and present situation with considerable feeling and seeming
insight. He did this, however, with the air of a person making a
confession, believing that once he had described all of his background he would be forgiven. When confronted with this behavior
by his therapist, he was very puzzled and denied it, pointing out that
he had done nothing for which he might feel guilty and need for-
giveness. On the other hand, he agreed that he blamed no one other
than himself for his situation. Under questioning he admitted he

resented the psychiatrist's interpretation but immediately apologized, saying that he hoped the psychiatrist would not feel that he was ungrateful. More and more, it became clear that in some way he expected the doctor to "do something for him." Thereafter, without mentioning it to his doctor, he began to drink again. Several times his wife called the psychiatrist to report that her husband was inebriated and to ask that the doctor "do something." Mr. B. denied his drinking and complained with considerable anger that his wife was overly suspicious. Twice during the ensuing four months it was necessary to hospitalize him for several days. Each time he was depressed and remorseful. The psychiatric treatment rapidly drained the B.'s savings, and, although the fees were markedly reduced, they grew farther and farther behind in meeting their bills. The situation was discussed with the B.'s jointly and the possibility that they might continue in treatment with the same therapist in a public clinic was explored with them. However, before this plan could be instituted, Mr. B. disappeared. Mrs. B. continued in private treatment, paying her own way. She revealed that she had become more and more open in her disapproval of her husband's behavior and in expression of some of her feelings of frustration and hostility. She felt very guilty that she might have driven her husband away from her. He returned ill and out of funds approximately three months later. He rejected further psychiatric care but accepted the psychiatrist's prescription of antibuse, a drug which makes a person nauseous when they consume alcohol. Mrs. B. continued in group psychotherapy for another year.

At the conclusion of her treatment, she had resolved some of her own guilt about Jonathan's behavior; she no longer felt obligated to wait on him or cover up for him. She remained cautious about criticizing him but in general felt more free in expressing her feelings toward him. Their sexual relations became more enjoyable and more frequent. She discussed openly with him her need for a professional career of her own, and both of them seemed less guilty over the fact that she provided almost half of their income. He regained his seat with the orchestra and, continuing to use the antibuse, refrained entirely from alcohol. However, he often became much more openly irritable, depressed, and restless. Three years later, he suffered several coronary attacks, which finally resulted in his death at age thirty-five.

Questions for Jonathan B.

1. According to your textbook, what are the criteria for classifying a person as an alcoholic? Which of these behaviors does Jonathan manifest and which are not present?

2. How would you characterize Jonathan's attitude toward his drinking? What classic mechanisms of defense are implied in these attitudes?

3. Alcoholics Anonymous, a private organization for the treatment of alcoholism, requires that a person admit that he is an alcoholic before a group of members before they accept him for treatment. Can you see the rationale for this procedure from your answers to the previous questions?

4. Frequently a pattern of psychopathology becomes easier to understand when we look in detail at the matrix of interpersonal relationships in which it exists. Characterize in detail, the nature of Jonathan's current relationships with the following figures:

    a. his wife

    b. his mother

    c. his father

What common pattern exists in these relationships?

5. Attempt to describe how these relationships might have grown out of Jonathan's early family environment? In your answer, consider, among other things:

    a. the behavior which Jonathan's parents expected of him and rewarded him for

    b. the role of music in Jonathan's background and development

    c. the role of illnesses in Jonathan's early years

6. Some psychologists have emphasized the fact that healthy psychological development requires that an individual master a graded series of developmental tasks. What developmental tasks did Jonathan fail to master and why did this mastery fail to occur? What effects did these failures in mastery have upon Jonathan's

    a. interpersonal relationships

    b. ability to handle later stress, personal and professional

7. Jonathan obviously had a limited background in sexual matters. Do you see Jonathan's sexual problem as a separate conflict or does it appear to be another manifestation of some other core problem?

8. Can you understand, after exploring Jonathan's early history and interpersonal relationships, why his wife-to-be was particularly attractive to him? What aspects of his wife's behavior appeared not to threaten Jonathan and, in turn, fit in with his needs?

9. Can you raise some hypotheses indicating why Jonathan developed alcoholism rather than, say, a phobic reaction or obsessive neurosis? What relation might there be between Jonathan's alcoholism and his somatic symptoms, i.e. his childhood illnesses, his obesity, and his final coronary attack?

10. In psychoanalytic theory, Jonathan's personality would be classified as "oral." What evidence would support this classification? In what ways is such a classification scientifically helpful and in what ways is it of limited usefulness?

References

CONGER, J. J. The effect of alcohol on conflict behavior in the albino rat. *Quarterly Journal of Alcohol Studies*, 1951, **12**: Issue 1.

McCORD, W. Some current theories of alcoholism: a longitudinal evaluation. *Quarterly Journal of Alcohol Studies*, 1959, **20**: 727–749.

ROSEN, A. C. A comparative study of alcoholics and psychiatric patients with the MMPI. *Quarterly Journal of Alcohol Studies*, 1960, **21**: 253–266.

ZWERLING, I., & ROSEMBAUM, M. Alcoholic addiction and personality. ARIETI, S. (Ed.) *American handbook of psychiatry*, New York: Basic Books, 1959, Pp. 623–644.

THE CASE OF SALLY D.*

The Fight for Life

Sally D. was a markedly overweight woman whose face, although rather plain, seemed somewhat younger than that of a person of fifty-six, perhaps because of her close-cropped, sandy-colored hair. She frequently appeared in a black, cotton, semi-sack style dress and her attire in general was loose, scanty, and careless if not sloppy. Out of doors she wore sandals and at home went barefoot.

She gave the impression of being constantly active, either moving about the room or accompanying her rapid speech with a variety of gestures. Her voice was memorable because of its peculiarly penetrating quality, particularly when she laughed, which was often.

As she related her history Sally constantly submitted detailed descriptions of situations, lost track of topics she had just initiated, and was carried away in tirades against doctors, former acquaintances, and other figures from her past life against whom she apparently still held painful grudges. Photograph albums were brought out to illustrate and clarify many of the events which were related. Sally had been in psychotherapy for over a year at the time this history was accumulated, having originally requested treatment because she had contemplated suicide.

Childhood. Sally's childhood was spent in a large house in a small western town where her father was a wealthy lumber baron. Her grandparents were all native Americans and, on the father's side, extremely wealthy. Her father's father owned several banks and a

* Unlike many of the cases in this book, Sally D.'s case history was not taken in a clinical setting but emerged in the course of a laboratory exercise in psychological testing by one of our students. Thus, why psychotherapy was terminated is not known.

lumber company and was "worth several millions." Sally's father managed to retain a good deal of this wealth and, although he later suffered several financial reverses, at the time of her birth "had almost a million."

Sally was preceded by three sisters four, six, and seven years older. Her birth in 1898 was accompanied by that of a twin brother. Sally described her father as "a short man . . . quiet most of the time, but he had a *terrific* temper. He ran everything and mother did everything to suit him." Her mother was a "wonderful person, very athletic, and with an exaggerated sense of duty. She never did what she wanted to do, but always did what was proper. She never had a chance to think about herself. She was short too, on the squatty side, and very loud like I am."

Sally could remember nothing of her childhood before the age of eight. At that time she was an active athletic youngster who "went around more with boys than with girls; I suppose because of my twin brother . . . I don't know." Her recollections of this period begin with memories of sex-play with her brother and numerous neighborhood children: "they liked to use me because I enjoyed it so much." Her sisters, however, did not participate in these games. At about this time Sally's uncle, who had been having marital difficulties, began to seduce her regularly . . . "and from then on I had quite a sex life." In regard to more formal sex education Sally stated, "We didn't know too much . . . you mentioned somebody having a baby and you got slapped, so I couldn't ask my mother questions. I had to have other ways of finding out things."

Although she was very much attached to her sisters and especially to her twin brother, often they would not play with her. Sometimes her mother would intervene, but "I was always a nuisance. My brother would say: 'Does she always have to follow me around everywhere?' . . . The poor guy." He preferred the company of the next oldest sister who was "something of a tomboy." Nevertheless, she frequently comforted her brother against his fear of the dark. Her siblings were all successful in school and skipped grades; however, Sally passed only "because the teachers couldn't control me." At that time Sally was "always naughty . . . had a vivid imagination and used to tell horrible tales; I don't remember what they were . . . about things happening at home. I usually got half-killed, beaten up every day by mother." Sally also suffered from asthma and hives: "sometimes my feet would swell up so badly that my brother would have to bring me home from school on a sled." Her asthma continued to afflict her seasonally until she moved to California in 1925. On the other hand she had no serious illnesses and thought of the hives and asthma as "just annoying things." She described herself during this phase (about age 12) as "an athlete, scraggly, scrawny, no-account, no-good kid." Although she "can never remember having had affection from anyone in the family," some of her happiest memories were of the outdoor life in a remote, wooded, lakeside area where her father owned a large, rustic, vacation house. Here she went sailing, canoeing, swimming, and horseback riding. She recalled with great pleasure that every evening the whole family would gather on the porch overlooking the lake and watch the sunset.

Adolescence. Sally's adolescence was "nothing but one orgy of sex . . . that's the horrible part of it . . . I had intercourse with practically every boy or man I knew." She also maintained her interest in outdoor sports throughout this period. However, from the age of fourteen to twenty-two one of Sally's major interests was a Jewish boy, Lawrence. At the age of sixteen she became pregnant by him and wanted to get married. Unfortunately, her father, who was rabidly anti-Semitic, objected, and when he found out that Sally was pregnant he insisted that she have an abortion . . . "I would have had twins." The father also went to Lawrence's parents and threatened them with a pistol. Sally believed that he must have been drunk at the time. After that scene, marriage seemed out of the question, but the relationship with Lawrence continued in a sporadic and clandestine manner for about six years. Sally never stopped thinking of Lawrence with affection and always felt that her life would have been totally different had she been permitted to marry him and give birth to the twins.

Sally's twin brother was shot and killed in a hunting accident on his seventeenth birthday. He had been determined to join the army but his parents had refused to permit it. Sally felt that in some obscure way her parents were responsible for his death, and also that he had abandoned her: "He died just when I needed him most."

At seventeen, during the First World War, Sally worked for a while as a nurse, having obtained this position by falsifying her age and qualifications. Later in the year her family sent her to a private girls' school in New York. The school did not grant a high school diploma, a situation which has "stymied me ever since," and for which she blamed her parents throughout her life.

At eighteen Sally again became pregnant by Lawrence and again had an abortion. This was followed by a "nervous breakdown." "I was terribly upset because I couldn't get married . . . I wanted babies terribly; as far as I was concerned, all women were for was to have babies." Following her breakdown Sally's mother refused to let her stay at home. Sally wanted to go back to New York, so her father supplied the money for the trip. While living there her roommate introduced her to Phil, and although she hadn't wanted to go out with anybody, she saw Phil frequently and soon became pregnant again. Another abortion was carried out followed by another "nervous breakdown." At this point Sally began treatment with a psychiatrist "who had studied under Freud." This doctor, "thought I was bad all the way through," and advised a hysterectomy to reduce Sally's sexual drive. When she rejected the operation the doctor advised that she be placed in a sanatorium. Both Sally and her family were opposed to this, but a compromise was agreed upon and she was sent to an Episcopalian retreat in New Jersey. Here she lived for several months among the nuns in an environment without mirrors. Her sister "just about died" when she visited Sally. "It was a horrible place, but a gorgeous place."

Adulthood. Following her stay at the retreat, Sally did considerable traveling between her home and New York. She spent several semesters. at a junior college and resumed her affair with Lawrence. In 1920 she again moved to New York, where she began seeing Jack, "an old friend who knew all about me." Although she wasn't in love with him they were married and moved to Nevada, where Jack had a position as a mining engineer. Unfortunately, Jack became seriously ill shortly after their arrival at the small mining town where he was to work and had to be hospitalized. Sally lived all alone in a little shack. She recalls the bedroom being full of snow so that she almost froze to death, and that she let in all the stray dogs and cats in the neighborhood to help keep her warm. Jack's recovery was followed by a series of strikes at the mine. Their financial situation deteriorated still further and Jack began to drink heavily. Sally's weight had increased to three hundred pounds in spite of their lack of funds for food. Jack continued to drink heavily and at one point had an attack of delerium tremens. The couple next moved to Montana, but Jack's illness returned and became worse so they returned to the Far West to live near Sally's family.

During the summer following their return Sally worked as a lifeguard. While on this job she met Bill, also a lifeguard, with whom she engaged in an affair because "Jack never did me any good sexually." During a trip to Chicago with Bill, Sally had intercourse with several of Bill's friends, and another pregnancy resulted. This time no abortion was performed and Sally's first child, Keith, was born. A year or so later, another child was born, Laura, who could definitely be attributed to Bill. By this time Sally's relationship with her husband had become quite stormy. When Jack threatened to shoot both Sally and himself she left him, taking the five-month-old Laura and Keith with her. Since she had no job she soon had to place the children with a community shelter. After several months she was able to secure a good paying job through her father's influence, but had again become pregnant. At this point her father visited her and decided to take her and her children back home with him. Another abortion was performed, but it was only partially successful; Sally had been pregnant with twins again. A tubal pregnancy occurred and Sally had to undergo several operations.

In 1925, Sally's divorce from Jack was final. The following year her father gave her $1000 so that she could move to California. There she quickly secured a job as a swimming instructor at a private club. While working there she formed an attachment to Phil, a young man who had never held a steady job and who was unemployed at the time. After a pregnancy, an abortion, and another pregnancy Sally and Phil decided to get married. Phil had promised to get a job before the marriage, but it was over a year before he was able to do so. Meanwhile a third child, Tim, was born. Following Tim's birth Sally "had one abortion after another . . . I aborted four pairs of twins altogether." Phil didn't want any more babies because Sally was "horrible to live with when pregnant." They had been living on money sent by Sally's father until 1933 when financial reverses forced him to discontinue his support. Bills mounted up quickly and the couple had to borrow a considerable sum. One day Phil told her that they were "all through . . . he no longer wanted to live with a fat old woman with three kids." Sally "couldn't get over him" and "wept for a year," but nevertheless got into her car with the children and drove across the country to Michigan.

During the trip Keith became ill with appendicitis, Laura's stomach was upset, and Tim had tonsillitis. Sally, in desperation, went to the police in an effort to locate Phil's brother, whom she had never met, but with whom she had corresponded. With the police's help she located her brother-in-law's house. When he arrived home from work he found her there with her three sick children. He and his pregnant wife were "wonderful" to Sally although they had never met her; she stayed with them for several months.

In the ensuing period Sally made many trips, but couldn't be happy anywhere. She made attempts to reconcile with Phil, "but it didn't work out." Returning to California with her children, she found a place with two teen-age boys. Although she slept on the floor and the house had no lights, gas, or hot water, she regards this as a happy period. "We had lots of fun; we even had a sailboat that one of the boys found." She managed to make some money by taking in washing for truck drivers, collected food that had been discarded by wholesalers and cooked it in the fireplace.

Then, just as she had acquired some furniture and rented an apartment with all the usual conveniences, her son Keith came down with polio. Sally's description of this period was related angrily. She refused to permit the doctor to take Keith to the county hospital because "conditions were horrible there, he would never have lived . . . the doctors were all sick . . . they tied kids to the beds." In the period of deprivation that followed Sally contacted a number of welfare agencies and once sat in a welfare office until the police came, because they wouldn't give her a job.

However, by the time the children were out of grade school, Sally had again been able to improve her status and was living in a large house in a good neighborhood. Since then she had had a variety of jobs: taught swimming and managed the laundry at a dude ranch, done practical nursing, supervised a girl scout troop, worked at various aircraft plants, was a telephone operator, and drove a school bus. She had maintained her interest in travel and took trips all over the country with her children.

Sally remained sexually active throughout her life. Her partners in the latter period were usually younger men, although she had several lesbian experiences which left her unsatisfied. She estimated she had had eighteen abortions. She stated that within the last three or four years she had become increasingly "depressed, tired of fighting," and had attempted suicide. The attempt followed the conclusion of an affair with a young medical student. She then entered psychoanalysis because her father's will was being settled and "if I died my children would not receive any money and that's all I'll have to give them." She hoped also that analysis would solve her weight problem which she felt to be psychogenic.

Asked to describe herself at the time the history was taken, Sally said: "I'm a fat, blowsy blonde covered with blubber. A loud, brash sort of creature . . . I'm everything I would like not to be. I'd like to be a nice, quiet, intellectual. Instead I'm a boob . . . my own worst enemy."

Epilogue. Several months after relating her history Sally's father's will was settled and Sally was able to see that the money was distributed between her three children. After this matter was disposed of, Sally found herself becoming progressively more despondent. Her life seemed to have little meaning any more and she felt that she was rapidly losing her ability to snap back from each adversity of her life. One day, after her children had been placed with a baby-sitter for the weekend, Sally drove to an isolated mountain area where she rented a cabin. That evening, Sally filled the bathtub with water, climbed into it, and swallowed fifty barbiturate pills. She was found the next morning floating in the tub, dead.

Questions for Sally D.

1. From the brief description of Sally's early life, what hypotheses can you raise about which of Sally's basic needs were not satisfied in her early family relationships? List the need or needs which you feel were not adequately gratified and describe the reason for the failure of gratification (overindulgence, deprivation, traumatic training, and so forth).

2. What modes of behavior did Sally adopt in her interpersonal re-

lationships to compensate for her frustrated needs? Are these behaviors covered by some of the conventional terms used to describe psychological defense mechanisms? If so, what are some of the terms that describe Sally's reaction patterns?

3. In your estimation, does your answer to question 2 explain Sally's pattern of sexual behavior? In what way does it provide an explanation? What other hypotheses do you find necessary to explain Sally's sexual pattern?

4. Evidently it was terribly important to Sally to have children. How can you account for the intensity of this need?

5. Sally evidently had a tendency toward overeating and obesity. What hypotheses can you raise which might provide an explanation for *both* Sally's sexual promiscuity and her overeating? (*Hint:* Assume the operation of a single need system with different manifestations and see how far this takes you.)

6. Sally evidently had a large reservoir of energy to resist repeated psychological and physical stress. What clinical disorder, in its acute state, is characterized by high energy, loudness, overeating, and a flight of ideas? Does Sally manifest a mild form of this clinical disorder or do you see her as manifesting a totally different reaction pattern? Justify your answer.

7. What role did Sally's energy and high activity appear to play in keeping Sally's anxiety level within livable bounds?

8. Describe the events which were going on in Sally's life at the time that she committed suicide. Contrast these events with the state of Sally's life over the previous twenty years. What hypotheses can you raise to account for the fact that Sally committed suicide when events were as they were?

9. It is frequently argued that a profound mood of depression coupled with intense guilt feelings predisposes a person to consider suicide as a solution to her problems.

   a. Do we see any suggestions of consciously experienced depression in Sally at the time that she committed suicide?

   b. Do we see any indications of long-term defenses against depression which were beginning to fail at the time of the suicide?

10. The reading list below includes a number of theories of suicide. Do any of these theories seem to cover Sally's situation? If so, which one does seem to fit?

References

BRUCH, H. Psychiatric aspects of obesity. *Psychiatry*, 1947, **10**: 273–281.

FARBEROW, N. L. Personality patterns of suicidal mental patients. *Genetic Psychology Monographs*, 1950, **42**: 3–79.

FARBEROW, N. L., & SHNEIDMAN, E. *The cry for help.* New York: McGraw-Hill, 1961. Of particular interest in understanding the present case: Chap. 5, The assessment of self-destructive potentiality, and Chaps. 12–19, in which various experts, representing different psychological points of view, attempt a theoretical explanation of suicide.

HENDIN, H. Psychodynamic and motivational factors in suicide. *Psychiatric Quarterly*, 1951, **25**: 672–678.

THE CASE OF PHILIP H.

The Bottom of the Stairs

Philip H. appeared at a psychological clinic in the spring of the year expressing a desperate need for help with his problem. He was, at forty-five, a man with little or no purpose in life, bright and well-educated—yet marked by a severe sexual deviancy. Philip was a child molester who had spent most of his adult years deriving his primary sexual gratification from relations with young adolescent boys. Although Philip had followed this practice for over twenty-five years, his first conflict with law enforcement authorities occurred only two years previously when he was arrested for molesting a young boy in a movie theater. Following this arrest, Philip was committed to a state hospital for sexual deviants where he received group therapy as well as various forms of occupational therapy. At the time of his discharge, Philip was considered to have been a model patient—bright, insightful, and co-operative, and one who had apparently conquered his problem. It was obvious from talking to Philip that this hospitalization had had a profound and shocking effect upon him. For many years Philip had been able to maintain the fiction that there was nothing wrong in his sexual behavior. Indeed, he had built up a complex set of rationalizations for his behavior, built upon the premise that he was actually providing needed love and affection for the boys. His encounter with the judicial and hospital system seriously challenged this distorted self-conception.

Philip arrived at the clinic a frightened man, on the surface superficially eager to be co-operative, but still reserving judgment about whether or not he wanted to change his ways. In appearance, he was of average height, thin and tense looking, and dressed quite shabbily. Yet he affected an air of dignity and intelligence which was hard to reconcile with his appearance. He stated at the outset, with apparent pride, that he was a "sexual psychopath." However, as he spoke these words, the sense of shame which he felt about coming to a clinic was more evident than this superficial bravado. As he talked, it became obvious that Philip was a well-educated person who was pedantic in his speech and placed a great value upon his intellectual achievements. An underlying mood of tension and hostility also was present in Philip's behavior. He fidgeted a great deal during the interview and mentioned that he was struggling against a blinding headache which started that morning.

Background and Early History. Philip was born in a large metropolitan area on the eastern seaboard of the United States, the next to youngest in a family of four children, all girls but himself. His father was a large vigorous man who ran a tavern. Philip admired him but had little contact with him. His father was away much of the time and when he was home there were many family problems which kept him busy. Philip recalled that when he was young, he was thin and scrawny and wished that he was larger and more like his father in physique. He was unable to remember anything about his mother. She died in childbirth with his younger sister when Philip was only four years old. Philip did recall his mother's death and the drastic effects which followed with considerable emotion. Following her death Philip was cared for by a series of foster parents whose modes of discipline and affection varied widely. After two years, Philip's father remarried and he was taken back into his father's home. Although he was apprehensive about this move, his fears were quickly dispelled when he met his stepmother, Rosemary. Rosemary, a warm, affectionate person, made efforts to make Philip and his sisters feel that they had a real home once again. Philip recalled the next two years as the happiest of his life. The family was again a unit and although Philip still was unable to get as close to his father as he would have liked, he was happy with Rosemary. This idyllic period ended dramatically and drastically when Rosemary suddenly became ill and died. Following this second devasting experience, Philip was sent to live with an aunt and uncle on a farm in New England. He stated that his aunt and uncle were very kind to him and made every effort to raise him as their own child. He was raised with a cousin who was close to him in age. Philip found the small-town life very pleasant and friendly. He attended grade school there between his eighth and tenth years and was a very good student. During this period, he recalled the beginning of his interest in sex, and also recalled that when he was ten, he and his cousin would spend many hours playing in the barn and the hayloft. During one of these periods the boys talked of sex and exhibited themselves to each other. Philip found himself very excited during the experience and pressed his cousin to let him fondle his sexual organs. His cousin reluctantly agreed and Philip found the experience very pleasurable. On a number of different occasions following this experience Philip tried to have sexual experiences with his cousin, but the cousin became more and more reluctant to participate until finally he refused altogether.

When Philip was ten, his father remarried once again and asked that Philip return home. Philip left his aunt and uncle reluctantly to face a new stepmother and a father whom he had seen only infrequently during the previous three years. Unlike Rosemary, Sally G., his new stepmother, was a cold, ambitious woman whom Philip disliked intensely from their first meeting. Philip found himself in constant conflict with her. She insisted that Philip wear fancy clothes so that he frequently was more elaborately dressed than the other boys, which made it difficult for him to make friends. Sally also was very strict with Philip. Whenever anything was missing or broken about the house, Philip was automatically accused and punished. Although Philip pleaded with his father to intervene with Sally, his father expressed a sense of helplessness in dealing with her. Sally had very strict rules about studying and insisted that Philip return home immediately after school to do his lessons. Many afternoons Philip passed other boys playing in the street and longed to play with them, but Sally insisted that weekday afternoons were for studying and not for play.

During this period, Philip's father began to drink heavily. While he previously had a reputation for consuming his own product at work, he gradually began to drink more and more at home. Philip recalled that on numerous occasions, his father drank himself into a stupor by early afternoon. When Philip was fourteen, his father became quite ill with liver trouble and was confined to bed. The illness took a progressively downward course and within six months he was dead. Philip recalled his father's death as a tremendous blow. Since the family was Catholic, a priest was called in to administer the last rites. After the rites were administered, Philip asked the priest if his father was going to heaven, and the priest replied that his father had not been a good man and would probably end in Hell. Philip was furious at the priest for this and vowed that from that day onward that he would have nothing further to do with the Church, a vow which he assiduously kept over the years.

Following his father's death Philip continued to live with his stepmother and an uncle who moved in with them. The uncle evidently took over the financial responsibility for Philip, and was reluctant to spend money on him. Philip remembered the next three years as very bitter ones in which he felt alone in a hostile home. He felt that he was a financial burden on the family and that they were basically not interested in him. Throughout this time, there was constant pressure on him to leave school and go to work, pressure which he successfully resisted until he graduated from high school.

It was during his last year of high school that Philip met Elizabeth, a girl who lived nearby who was very attractive but who walked with a slight limp. Philip fell madly in love with Elizabeth and felt that possibly her deformity might make her more likely to be interested in a man like himself. He mentally put Elizabeth on a pedestal, worshiped her, and never dared to approach her sexually, feeling that this might destroy the relationship. Shortly before graduating from high school, Philip asked Elizabeth to marry him. She refused on the basis that they were too young to marry, and Philip felt crushed. He recalled thinking at the time that this was the last time that he was going to have anything to do with women. From this point on, Philip turned progressively to homosexual outlets for sexual gratification.

It was the middle of the depression of the 'thirties when Philip left high school and he found it impossible to get a job. He left the big city and roamed from town to town as an itinerant construction worker. He evidently picked up some surveying knowledge and was able to get work. Philip mentioned that he rarely stayed for very long on any one job despite the fact that his bosses were always satisfied with him and wanted him to stay. He mentioned that once a job was going well, he felt an unexplainable need to leave. Philip felt that he was always looking for something and felt that it lay just around the next bend. But, just what he was looking for was hard to say. All he could verbalize was that once his part on a job was completed and he no longer felt essential, he had to leave.

This pattern of drifting from job to job continued throughout the depression and until the beginning of World War II. At this time, Philip was drafted into the army as a private and within a few months of basic training was shipped overseas and stationed in Hawaii. Philip rose rapidly in army ranks and was evidently a very successful soldier, so successful that by the end of the war he had reached the rank of first lieutenant. Philip was evidently quite happy during this period and did not often engage in homosexual activity. From time to time, when tension built up, he sought relief with a young boy, but these occasions were rarer than they had been in civilian life.

It was during this period that Philip met the woman who was later to become his wife. Each Sunday he visited the home of a local woman, considerably older than himself, who invited him and his buddy over for dinner. Philip spent most of his time with the older woman while his friend dated the woman's younger friend, Evelyn. Philip mentioned that he enjoyed his relations with this older woman as it provided him with feminine companionship without any possibility of sexual relations. It was during this period that Philip was surprised to receive a letter from Elizabeth. In the letter, Elizabeth indicated that she expected him to marry her when he returned from the war. He found this implication very disturbing and resented the fact that Elizabeth was proposing to him instead of him to her. In a moment of combined rage and panic, Philip called Evelyn, the buddy's girl friend with whom he had had little contact and asked her to marry him. Much to his surprise and chagrin, Evelyn accepted and they were married two days later. Philip left for the battle area shortly thereafter and saw little of Evelyn except for a few brief furloughs. However, during these furloughs, they engaged in sexual relations and Evelyn became pregnant and over the subsequent two years bore two children.

Following the war, Philip returned to the United States where he enrolled in college under the G.I. Bill. He reluctantly brought Evelyn to the mainland and they set up house. From the outset the marriage was not a happy one. Philip did not want to be married and the constant threat of heterosexual relations stood over him. He tried to avoid sexual relations as much as possible and responded only to her direct requests for intercourse. This he found disturbing also, as he felt that he should be the aggressor and not the passive member of the family. Philip resented any requests that Evelyn made on him to do anything around the house and constantly tried to teach her to be self-reliant and to fix things herself. During this period he engaged in frequent sex play with young boys, and gradually his wife became aware from some campus gossip that something was wrong.

Despite the disordered marital relationship, Philip had phenomenal success in his academic work. He was a straight A student and was well-regarded by all his professors. Evidently, he was successful in keeping his sexual deviancy from the attention of his teachers and fellow students. At the time of graduation, he accepted a good job with an advertising agency in a large western city. He went ahead to make plans for housing, and planned to have his family follow him west. However within two days after arriving in the new city, he received a letter from Evelyn's lawyer indicating that a suit for divorce had been filed. He wrote a letter to Evelyn asking what was behind this action, but when no reply was received he decided that possibly it was all for the best and dropped the matter. It was around this time that Philip started frequenting certain movie houses in town which were rumored to be hangouts for homosexuals. It was in one of these movie houses that he was arrested for engaging in sexual relations with a sixteen-year-old boy.

Although throughout his life, Philip had had sexual relations with boys, he was not attracted to all types of boys or boys of all ages. The boys had to be of "good build" and smaller than Philip, usually between twelve and sixteen years of age. There were some adult men that he found sexually attractive, usually Mexican or Negro of slight build, whom he felt were inferior to him. In all his sexual contacts, he felt it necessary to feel superior to his partner. He never felt attracted to white adult males. At various times, in an effort to break out of his antisocial action, Philip tried consciously to become a true homosexual who focused exclusively upon adults. He found these attempts futile as he did not know how to approach adult homosexuals and often felt rejected by them. Also, sexual relations with an adult male did not satisfy him in the way contact with younger males did. In describing his sexual contacts, Philip emphasized time and again his desire not to harm the boys in any way. He approached them cautiously, never forcing his attention, and trying desperately to get some sign of willingness from the boy before making any approach. He also emphasized how important it was to him not to be rejected by his prospective sex partner. He had to be sure that the boy was interested in him sexually; he developed a complex set of maneuvers desiged to avoid rejection and at the same time to test the potential partner's interest in him.

In describing his relations with the boys, Philip emphasized the tender feelings he felt for them during and after the sex act. He wanted to do something for them and frequently bought them clothes and books. He hated furtive, one-time relations and frequently would try to establish a long-term relationship with a boy. Interestingly, after such a relationship was established, he lost interest in the sexual side and found it fully satisfying just to spend time with the boy and to take him places.

From time to time, Philip would attempt to tell the interviewer how he felt while having sexual relations with a boy. He described a sensation almost mystical in quality, of fusing with the young boy in the midst of sexual relations. He stated that when he was holding a young boy he felt a sense of identity with him and could not distinguish between himself as a person and the boy as a person and frequently felt that he was the boy, and his own personality failed to exist. The interviewer who saw Philip could not help but feel as he heard these descriptions, despite the repugnance of the act, a pathetic, love-starved quality about Philip as he talked of these contacts.

Course in Treatment. Philip was accepted into psychotherapy with misgivings on the part of the clinic staff. His age and general lack of insight argued against a successful outcome. Philip was seen on a once-a-week basis. Initially, he was very defensive, talked pedantically about himself and his past, and typically tried to present the picture of a perfectly co-operative patient. After a while, he began to manifest various signs of dependence upon the therapist and was continually concerned as to whether the therapist would be present for the next meeting. Philip gradually became less defensive and as he did so, he became more willing to explore his past, particularly as it bore upon his sexual deviancy. It was obvious from reports that Philip brought in that his behavior with others, particularly on his job, was undergoing a marked change for the better. However, he reported little or no change in the intensity of his sexual desires for young boys. At one critical point, Philip indicated that he would like to give up his perverted way of expressing his sexual desires, but one thing made it difficult for him to do so. From his vantage point, these sexual experiences were the only pleasures he experienced in his life and he seriously challenged the therapist to guarantee him that some other substitute source of pleasure would be available to him if he gave up his perversion. Time and again, he said to the therapist, "You're trying to take away from me the only pleasure I've ever had in life. Can you guarantee that some other pleasure will exist for me, after I give this one up?" At the height of dealing with Philip's feelings about giving up his perversion, a most unfortunate experience occurred; Philip's therapist was forced to leave the city because of serious illness in his family and it was necessary for him to suspend therapy for a month. This matter was discussed with Philip and he showed no particular concern about it and a date was set five weeks later for the next appointment. Philip kept that appointment but expressed his intention to terminate his therapy. When pressed for his reasons he said that during the period that his therapist was gone, he noticed a subtle change in his ability to control his sexual experiences. While previously he felt that these impulses were under his control, he now experienced them as obsessive thoughts totally outside the range of conscious control. He found that he could think of nothing else but finding young boys and was so pre-occupied that he could do little else. This shift in the way that he experienced his sexual impulses frightened Philip intensely and was the major reason that he reported wanting to leave therapy. His therapist tried to explain to Philip the implications of his actions —that another contact with the law was inevitable, this time with a longer sentence. Philip agreed that this was a horrible, yet likely, prospect, but was so disturbed that "anything is better than this hell of therapy." Before leaving, Philip mentioned a dream which he had the night before. In this dream, a recurring one which dated back to childhood, he was about to be hung. However, in the past he was always able to slip out of the rope before the trap door was sprung. Now, however, his therapist was the hangman and Philip had the feeling that he was no longer able to slip out of the noose; he was terrified as he stood at the top of the stairs and when the trap door was sprung he fell down to the bottom of the stairs. As he was falling he thought in his dream, "I don't care if I die, but I hope I don't hurt myself when I hit the bottom of the stairs."

All further efforts by the therapist were futile. Philip left the clinic and never returned. To this day nothing is known of his sexual adjustment.

Questions for Philip H.

1. Describe the experiences which Philip had with his mother and mother figures prior to reaching adulthood.
2. What common core do you see in all or most of these relationships in terms of
    a. their duration
    b. their emotional quality
    c. their mode of cessation
3. What basic needs were frustrated in most of these relationships and what effect did this frustration appear to have upon
    a. Philip's self-concept
    b. Philip's attitudes toward women
    c. Philip's general comfort with other people, regardless of their sex
4. From the brief description given in the case concerning Philip's relationship with his father, what inferences can you draw about the following:
    a. Philip's closeness with his father
    b. Philip's sense of adequacy as a man as compared with his father
5. Summarize from your previous answers:
    a. Philip's attitudes toward women
    b. Philip's attitude toward men
    c. Philip's attitudes toward himself
6. Does this summary in question 5 aid in explaining the following events in Philip's later life? If so, how can they account for them?
    a. Philip's preference for boys between fourteen and sixteen years of age who had to be smaller than himself
    b. Philip's anxiety when Elizabeth intimated that they might marry when he returned from the war
    c. Philip's attitude toward his wife
7. Philip tells us two interesting things about his job behavior prior to World War II. First, that he moved from job to job as soon as he felt that his job was accomplished. Second, that he constantly felt

that he was looking for something which might turn up in the next city.

> *a.* What motivation or motivations appear to underly this restless, longing behavior?
>
> *b.* Do you see any relationship between this motivation and Philip's sexual behavior? If so, what sort of relationship do you see?

8. *a.* What hypotheses can you raise to account for the fact that Philip, despite numerous conscious attempts to focus on adult males as the source of sexual gratification, was unable to achieve the same gratification with older men? (*Hint:* This question might be best answered in reverse. First, try to understand which of Philip's needs were met with young boys and then attempt to understand why grown men could not meet these needs.) Reread Philip's description of how he felt during sexual relations with his adolescent partners before answering this question.

> *b.* What psychological mechanisms, which you may have read or heard about, are useful in understanding Philip's attraction to adolescent boys? In what way are these mechanisms helpful in understanding this case?

9. Philip never returned to therapy after his therapist was unavoidably called out of town. From your understanding of Philip, how do you account for this reaction?

10. What are some theories which have been offered to explain the etiology of homosexuality? Do any of these theories apply to Philip?

References

BRANCALE, R., ELLIS, A., & DOORBAR, RUTH. Psychiatric and psychological investigations of convicted sex offenders: a summary report. *American Journal of Psychiatry*, 1952, **109**: 17–21.

FREUD, S. Instincts and their vicissitudes. In *Collected papers of Sigmund Freud*. Vol. 4. New York: Basic Books, 1959. Pp. 60–83.

GREENSPAN, H., & CAMPBELL, J. D. The homosexual as a personality type. *American Journal of Psychiatry*, 1945. **101**: 682–689.

HARLOW, H. F. The nature of love. *American Psychologist*, 1958, **13**: 673–685.

KARPMAN, B. *The sexual offender and his offenses*. New York: Julian Press, 1954. Pp. 104–106.

THE CASE OF KITTY G.

Who'll Feed a Bad Girl?

After repeated warnings from the school nurse that her son, Pete, was becoming uncontrollably hyperactive in the classroom, Mrs. G. reluctantly brought him to the psychiatric clinic. At first Mrs. G. denied having any problems other than Pete. However, in the middle of the initial interview she broke down and wept, saying that she considered herself "hopeless" but that perhaps something could at least be done for her son. She readily admitted to being very depressed much of the time. During these periods of depression she felt helpless, alone, and unwanted. She brooded guiltily over her past, regarding her "sins" as unforgivable. She had frequent premonitions that God would punish her or that she might die. On several occasions she had seriously considered suicide, although she had made no actual attempts.

Despite being seventy pounds overweight, Mrs. G. was a pretty woman, with a fair complexion and light brown hair, and a childlike, winsome smile. Indeed, at times the interviewer thought that he was talking to a teenager rather than a 26-year-old housewife because of the glib manner in which she spoke and her girlish poses. She usually had on a well-worn, faded housedress, but she was neat, clean, and well-groomed. In between her occasional outbursts of tears and the depression which clouded her face, she often smiled and kidded in a flirtatious manner with the interviewer. She could discuss freely her current troubles, but after she began her general descriptions of her feelings of unworthiness and sin, Mrs. G. bit her lip and became silent. Finally she blurted out that she was afraid the interviewer would regard her as "a no-good tramp" and would have nothing more to do with her.

It seemed to Mrs. G. that she could remember very few happy periods in her life, but at least she had always managed to scrape by financially. For several years, Mr. G. had not been steadily employed, the family was deeply in debt, the rent was in arrears, and there was little food in the house. About three months ago, her husband deserted her, telling her that he was going to live with another woman with whom he had been consorting for the past year. They had a violent quarrel during which he struck her. Declaring that she was a "fat pig" for whom he had no further use, he stalked from the house. Mrs. G. ran after him but he drove off, leaving her screaming in the street. For several days, she sat immobilized in their tiny two-room apartment, moaning and crying. Pete, age eight, and his brother, Raymond, age six, who had been shut in their room, remained there, also crying, until finally overcome with hunger, they escaped to beg a meal from a neighbor. The neighbor fed and comforted the boys, but Mrs. G. rejected her further offers of help. Finally the neighbor was able to rouse Mrs. G. sufficiently to get her to obtain a food and rent allowance from the county welfare bureau. A warrant for failure to support was issued by the district attorney against her husband.

During the next three months Mrs. G. did little but sit around the house, care for her children, and eat. Considerably overweight when her husband left, she gained thirty additional pounds. Mr. G. began to visit the family about once a week. Sometimes he would bring a little money, but he always would demand sexual relations with Kitty. She usually complied with his demands, hoping to induce him to return. Mr. G. had made daily demands for sexual satisfaction throughout their marriage. Kitty had never been able to enjoy their sexual relations and now his advances revolted her. His visits often ended in screaming violent fights. Twice the neighbors called the police, although no arrests were made. After these quarrels Mrs. G. would sit for hours, staring into space, leaving the children to fend for themselves. Whenever the children made demands, she became irritable and she would strike out at them. Then, guilty over her outburst, she would weep with them. Pete, in particular, seemed to annoy her with every action. He always seemed to be the one who spilled his food, left his toys strewn about, refused to go to bed, or failed to come home promptly from school. In contrast, Raymond made extra efforts to please her, in effect telling his brother, "Look what a good boy I am." This served to enrage Pete, who would run out of the house and remain away for hours while Kitty roamed the streets looking for him.

Mrs. G.'s application for psychiatric help was also motivated, at least indirectly, by two other current situations. First, the county welfare department had threatened to terminate financial aid in order to force her to go to work. She argued that she was needed at home by her two boys, but the welfare office demanded that she accept their plan to have the boys cared for during the day at a public nursery. Kitty felt emotionally unable to work and hoped that the clinic would attest to this fact.

Second, about a week previously, Kitty had allowed a completely strange man to walk her home from the bus and to stay overnight with her. She continued to have sexual relations with him for the duration of the week; moreover, for the first time in her life sex was satisfying to her. She guessed that he was twenty years her senior, gray-haired, well-dressed and, in her opinion, handsome, although not exactly her romantic ideal. Most of all, she found him a kindly and reassuring person who was attentive to the boys. He bought them all food although he did not give her any money. Otherwise, she knew nothing about him, not even his last name! She appeared very guilty about this relationship and called herself "a prostitute," but she made no effort to send him away. In addition to this illicit relationship, she later revealed that several nights after her husband had left she had sexual relations with the husband of the neighbor who had helped her out initially. This incident made her feel even more guilty and it was soon after this that she began to have premonitions that she might die suddenly. Nominally a Catholic, she had not attended church for many years. On several occasions she had wanted very much to receive absolution through confession, but she could not bring herself to enter the confessional booth. Once she attended mass but halfway through the service, Kitty began to cry and ran from the church. She tried praying at home but found that she was unable to say her prayers.

Past History. Kitty G. was the fifth of nine children, born and reared in the slums of a metropolitan Atlantic seaport. She described her family as "shanty Irish." Her father was a chronic alcoholic who occasionally worked as a longshoreman, but during the depression of the 1930's, when she was a child, the family lived mainly on relief. Occasionally her mother was able to earn some extra money doing housework at various homes. Her mother cautioned the children not to talk about the mother's earnings for fear that the relief worker would find out and cut them off from welfare funds. They lived in a crowded, third-story, cold-water flat, which had no heat except the kitchen stove. The children slept in one room—she and her sisters crowded in one bed and her brothers shared another. The children were approximately two years apart; in Kitty's memory, her mother was always pregnant or just recovering from childbirth. Kitty regarded herself as her father's favorite, even though she was often ashamed of him when he appeared drunk in public, often in broad daylight. The other children teased and jeered at her. Late at night, if her father had not returned home, Kitty would usually volunteer to search for him and to persuade him to come home. Her mother continually upbraided her husband for his failure to support them. When she berated him for his alcoholism, he would retaliate by heading for the nearest bar. Kitty recalled that often she would find her mother crying while carrying out her household duties; other times, her mother would sit at the kitchen table with her head buried in her arms. Her mother was devoutly religious and insisted that the children attend mass regularly and learn their catechism. Kitty believed that her mother's religious faith and insistence upon moral standards in the home helped to keep them out of trouble. Kitty could not remember that any of her brothers and sisters were ever in trouble with the law, although many of the neighborhood children were delinquent.

When Kitty was approximately eleven, her father disappeared, and for the following three years, the two oldest sons supported the family until they married. It was during these years that Kitty became increasingly disobedient, both at home and at school. She became impudent to her mother, accusing her of being responsible for the father's desertion. When Kitty related this, she became tearful. She said that even as a child she had felt extremely guilty after her outbursts against her mother; she realized that her mother had made many sacrifices, not only for the family but for Kitty in particular. Her mother had often stinted on her own needs in order that Kitty could be well-dressed. Other times, although Kitty never knew of it until afterwards, her mother denied herself supper so that the children could eat.

Although she was unhappy, Kitty did not become a serious behavior problem until after her puberty. About the time of her twelfth birthday, she had her first menstrual period; she was quite frightened for all she knew about menstruation was that her older sister had suffered continual cramps. Her mother gave her no explanation other than how to care for herself hygienically, adding the cryptic warning that she should have nothing to do with boys. Kitty began to be increasingly truant from school. At the suggestion of a welfare worker she was placed in a home in a rural area outside the city. Here she was extremely lonely, wept frequently, and felt that her mother had rejected her completely. After approximately six weeks she ran away and found her way back home. Her mother was ill and did not force her return to the foster home. She continued to be truant at school and began to run around with an older group. She had her first heterosexual experience when she was thirteen when a friend of her older brother forced himself on her in the basement of their tenement. She was frightened, angry, and guilty. She would have liked to confess to someone but there was no one she felt she could turn to. Soon afterwards she began to submit regularly to the sexual demands of the older boys in the gang.

Kitty was sixteen when she met her husband, who was five years her senior. She said, without boasting, that at that time, she was still slim but "with a good figure," was a good dancer, and one of the more popular girls in her "gang." Ramon, a handsome, dark-complexioned Mexican, was especially attractive because he had the things "every girl wanted." He owned a "souped-up" car, was a "flashy dresser," and always seemed to have spending money. At the time she met him he had just been released from the state reformatory after serving a year's sentence for car theft. Three months after they started going together, she discovered that she was pregnant. When he refused to marry her she appealed to his mother, who forced him into the marriage. She described her mother-in-law as an extremely dominating person who attempted in every way possible to control Ramon's life. She was a widow, Ramon her only son. Kitty spoke no Spanish and her mother-in-law very little English. Consequently Kitty often felt left out when Ramon and his mother conversed. Increasingly Kitty became jealous and angry as her mother-in-law hovered over her husband, trying to control their every action.

At this time, Kitty's mother made the surprising announcement that she was planning to remarry. Concurrently, Kitty's father returned and tried to persuade Kitty to live with him and to take care of him. Her reaction to these various strains was very similar to her current behavior, i.e. she sat alone for hours, crying, and she stuffed herself with food. She believes that it was as a consequence of these stresses that she miscarried. Because of their religion the couple used no contraceptives; yet despite her husband's constant sexual demands, she did not immediately become pregnant again. During this time Ramon was often unemployed and the couple was supported by his mother, who was now living with them. Her mother-in-law made constant reference to the fact that Kitty was not yet pregnant; she intimated that this was God's punishment for Kitty's promiscuous behavior prior to her marriage. After they had been married for approximately two years, Ramon suddenly deserted Kitty and went to live with another woman.

Kitty then moved in with her father; at this time he was "on the wagon" through the help of Alcoholics Anonymous. Kitty considered the following two years as the only happy period in her entire life. Her father was able to work; he made a fair living and they had a decent place to live. They enjoyed going out together, and they even went to dances. However, her husband and mother-in-law tried to make her life miserable—chiefly by parading the husband's common-law wife and baby in front of her and by gossiping about her to all the neighbors. Apparently the common-law wife also found the mother-in-law difficult to live with for she disappeared one day, taking her child with her. Even before she left, Mr. G. occasionally visited Kitty and talked about a reconciliation. Finally, he came to live with her and her father. Fortunately, there was not enough room in the present apartment for the mother-in-law and the couple lived in relative peace until Pete was born. Subsequently, Kitty's father started to drink heavily again, and he and Mr. G. clashed frequently. Eventually, in an effort to separate from both sets of parents, the couple moved away to another large city. When the mother-in-law attempted again to move in with them, Kitty threatened to leave if Ramon would not send his mother away; on one occasion she grabbed her mother-in-law and might have strangled her had her husband not stopped her. She was pregnant with Raymond, and her husband, fearful that she might lose another child, convinced his mother to leave.

Kitty found that caring for two children was a constant chore. She received no help from Ramon; in fact he began to make many more demands upon her. He became exceedingly jealous of the time that she spent with the children. Many a quarrel ensued because he expected her to cater immediately to his demands, even if she happened to be caring for one of the children at the time. She usually acceded to his sexual demands, but still he complained that because she was merely submitting, she was not satisfying him. He often demanded intercourse during the daytime when the children were awake, but Kitty always was fearful that the children could hear and possibly observe them. He also insisted on increased sexual play, both before and after intercourse, and this Kitty regarded as perverse. She accused Ramon of seeing other women; he never denied this charge, but instead used it as a threat to compel her to accede to his demands. Although he was frequently unemployed, and they seldom had enough money for food or rent, he managed to be well-dressed and maintained a good car. It occurred to Kitty that he might be receiving income from some criminal activity, but she was afraid to mention her suspicions to him. Whenever she remarked on his clothes or his car, he became violently angry and threatened to leave. He constantly teased her about her increasing weight and taunted her that she was becoming ugly. His relationship with the children varied: at times he would boast about them to everyone; other times he would beat them for the slightest infraction. The boys became frightened of him; they would hide whenever he came home, but this only irritated him more. Often, Kitty wished that he would leave; yet at the same time she thought that if he did leave, then she would truly be left alone in the world. With the exception of one sister, who lived fifty miles away, her brothers and sisters were scattered across the country. Kitty had never had a close relationship with this sister and recently this sister had told Kitty that she would have nothing to do with her as long as she was living with Mr. G.

Course in Treatment. When Kitty told the welfare office that she was to be accepted for psychiatric treatment, the welfare worker telephoned the clinic and was advised that, although currently Kitty might not be able to find or maintain herself on a job, it was probably a good idea for the welfare office to continue to insist that economic independence be one of the ultimate aims for Kitty. The welfare office agreed not to remove Kitty from their rolls at this time. Peter was seen by another therapist in a playroom setting once a week. At the same time individual interviews were conducted with Kitty for approximately four months. Although she continued to have some crying spells, her depression lifted markedly. She became openly flirtatious with her therapist. She reported that although she had discontinued seeing the older stranger, she was becoming involved with another man whom she had met through one of her girl friends. She often requested extra interviews, but just as likely, she would fail to appear for her regular appointments. She showed little insight into her behavior and showed a tendency to blame everything on her husband. Because of her intense feelings of unworthiness and her feelings that no one would like her, it was decided that group psychotherapy might be the treatment of choice. The only group open to new members at that time in the clinic consisted of women, all older than Kitty, who also had problem children being treated at the clinic. Kitty was angry when she was moved from individual to group treatment, regarding this as another rejection. In the group she discussed little of her own problems, but made constant hints that she could tell the "ladies" things that would amaze them. Most of the older women came from middle-class backgrounds and were amazed when Kitty began to reveal her history of sexual promiscuity. She seemed to enjoy shocking them but she was mystified when, instead of rejecting her, they began to regard her with pity. In a maternal fashion they advised and scolded her. However, they never really rejected her and when she became increasingly guilty they supported her and pointed out that she probably was really punishing herself. After a year and a half of attending the group, Kitty suddenly announced that she had taken a factory job and would be unable to continue treatment. Some six months later she appeared at the clinic without an appointment to tell the therapist she was planning to marry again. She did not seem to have doubts about the marriage but merely wanted the therapist's congratulations. She had lost forty pounds, looked relaxed and happy, and reported that she was still employed in her factory job.

Questions for Kitty G.

1. When Kitty came to the clinic, she was under considerable external stress.

   a. Summarize and categorize her reactions to this stress.

   b. In what ways might these reactions be considered "normal," i.e. related realistically to her circumstances, and in what ways "neurotic," i.e. associated with personal, internal conflicts?

   c. What aspects of Kitty's past history facilitated the learning of these ways of reacting to stress?

   d. In particular, what other needs or drives appeared to have been reduced by overeating and indulging in sexual relations?

2. What socio-economic class does Kitty come from? In what ways was her behavior normative and in what ways deviant for that social class?

3. Describe Kitty's behavior as a mother. What factors in her early environment seemed to predispose her to react this way toward her children?

4. Kitty was quite promiscuous sexually, but claimed not to enjoy sexual relations at all. How can these apparently contradictory facts be reconciled? What might have been the reasons that Kitty later was able to enjoy sex with the older stranger?

5. Although a welfare bureau and a district attorney's office commonly are faced with cases similar to Kitty's, such cases are rarely referred to mental hygiene clinics or other sources of psychological treatment. Even when so referred, they are often regarded as unpromising.

   a. What might be some of the reasons such cases are not referred (aside from the unavailability of treatment facilities)?

   b. Why might psychotherapists regard such cases as difficult to treat?

   c. Hollingshead and Redlich argue that one of the reasons that persons from Kitty's socio-economic group are often not referred nor treated lies in the class differences between the patient and the professional worker. Which of the reasons you have listed in your answers a and b might be associated with such differences in social class attitudes? What other inter-class differences might be present in such cases?

d. What factors in Kitty's case made her *more* likely to be referred and accepted for treatment?

e. To what extent do you feel compassion for Kitty and a desire to help her out of her difficulties? To what extent did you find Kitty's situation foreign to you? Why do you think that you feel as you do?

6. *a.* In addition to the personal problems represented in this case, what social problems do such persons present to the community?

b. In what ways are such social problems perpetuated from one generation to another in these families?

c. What facilities in the community might be utilized to *prevent* such problems?

d. What agencies, other than psychological treatment clinics, might be used in rehabilitation of such individuals and families? (In your answers to these questions cite examples from Kitty's case.)

References

BOWLBY, J. *Child care and the growth of love.* London: Pelican Books, 1953. Read the whole book if possible, but particularly Chaps. 2–6 and 7–9.

BAAM, I. Psychic factors in obesity; observations in over 1,000 cases, *Archives of Pediatrics,* 1950, **67**: 543–552.

ERIKSEN, E. H. Growth and crises of the "healthy personality." In *Personality in nature, society and culture,* Kluckhohn, Murray, and Schneider (Eds.) New York: Knopf, 1955.

GREEN, A. "The cult of personality" and sexual relations. In *The family,* Bell, N. W., and Vogel, E. (Eds.) Glencoe, Ill.: The Free Press, 1960.

HOLLINGSHEAD, A., & REDLICH, F. *Social class and mental illness,* New York: John Wiley, 1958. Chaps. 3, 4, 11, 12.

PART V PSYCHIATRIC REACTIONS IN ADULTHOOD

THE CASE OF "BUDDY" A.

The Attainment of Nirvana

Buddy's admission to the psychiatric ward of the county hospital was precipitated by the following events, which took place several hours earlier. He informed his mother that it would be necessary to sacrifice her in order for him to "attain Nirvana"; he threw her to the floor and, with his knee on her chest, began choking her. After a violent struggle she was finally able to free herself and fled, screaming for the police. Buddy left the house and wandered about the streets. When the police located him he surrendered without protest.

His entrance into the hospital emergency room was most dramatic: a huge, muscular man, he strode across the lobby, dragging behind him the two policemen to whom he was handcuffed. He was clad only in a filthy towel wrapped around his waist. His unkempt hair reached his shoulders and a massive beard covered most of his face. His body, hair, and beard were caked with dirt, and blood flowed from the scratches inflicted by his mother. Barely visible was the elaborate tattoo of a battleship across his chest; his arms were also decorated by a tattoo of a reverse swastika and of a heart-and-dagger. He voluntarily seated himself on a bench at the admission desk, forcing the officers also to sit. Aside from the glassy stare of his eyes, his face was expressionless. He paid no attention to questions addressed to him and said nothing to anyone. Staring at the ceiling he occasionally mumbled indistinctly to himself.

Released from the handcuffs, he allowed himself to be led to the general admitting ward where, for the next four hours, he squatted on his haunches at the foot of his bed, his head bowed as he muttered to himself. Several times the nursing attendants tried to get him to shower and dress in preparation for a physical examination. Finally, two of them attempted to lift him to his feet, hoping to lead him to the shower, at which time he savagely attacked them and began destroying the furniture and bedding. Forcibly restrained and put in a separate room, he continued briefly to pound on the walls before he finally settled back into his buddha-like squat on the floor and resumed his trance-like appearance.

Later in the evening he appeared in the door of his cell and asked for a cigarette, whereupon the attending psychiatrist came to see him and brought him cigarettes. He was eager to talk but seemed somewhat confused. He was not sure where he was or how he got there. He did remember the assault on his mother, an act which he said he regretted but had felt compelled to commit because of what the "voice" had told him. He said that for several years he had regularly heard voices telling him what to do, although in the past year, since he had been studying religions of the Far East, the voices had been less frequent. In a rambling confused fashion he attempted to explain his need to find "unity with nature" and "a higher level of enlightenment," referring vaguely to Yoga, Zen, and the Bhagavad-Gita. He apologized for being "incommunicado" earlier in the day, explaining that he was being "bombarded with knowledge." Increasingly preoccupied with expounding his philosophy, he became unable to discuss anything else. Near the end of the hour when asked again if he knew where he was, he was able to respond correctly. He was also oriented as to the date, and was even aware of the time of day. When asked about such facts as his age and occupation, he again launched into a philosophic discussion of the unimportance of such information, saying that he felt ageless and that his life was devoted to the problem of "self-realization and enlightenment." Shortly thereafter, he gave his age as twenty-three, said he usually worked as a dishwasher but had been unemployed for approximately a year and a half, except for occasional employment at a coffee house.

This question reminded him that he had not eaten for the past twenty-four hours. Told that it would be necessary for him to bathe and dress before he would be given food, he complied. During his bath he again got into an altercation with the nurse's aides, cursed them loudly and threatened them with bodily harm, but calmed down after a few minutes and apologized to them for his outburst. He put on a hospital gown but refused shoes and stockings. Since it was near midnight, a dinner had to be ordered from the employees' kitchen and there was a slight delay. He accepted the meal silently but after eating, again became violently angry, throwing the dishes and shouting vulgar threats. Although Buddy could not say what it was that upset him, the nurses guessed that he had overheard them discussing their difficulty in obtaining food for him. Heavy doses of a combination of psychotropic drugs were prescribed, which quieted him, and he did not repeat any of his violent and destructive behavior during the next eight days in the county hospital receiving ward.

At the request of the social worker, Buddy's mother and sister came to the hospital for interviews several times during the ensuing week. Still very fearful, they did not visit Buddy. However, he did not appear perturbed, and requested only that they bring some of his books and other possessions from home. He spent his time peacefully reading his books on occult religion, and practicing his Yoga exercises. He graciously permitted his contemplations to be interrupted twice daily for psychiatric interviews and even seemed to enjoy talking about himself and his ideas. Although the tranquilizers made him drowsy and inert, his conversation was much more lucid than when he first arrived at the hospital and his thought processes did not seem slowed down or quite as confused.

Mrs. A.'s heavily lined face and dry blotched complexion made Buddy's mother appear at least ten years older than her stated age of forty-seven. An obvious wig of a reddish-brown hue grotesquely capped her tiny figure, contrasting oddly with her drab and shabby clothes. Her tremulous voice and downcast expression suggested considerable depression. She kept repeating such phrases as "I don't know what I've done to deserve all this," or "God knows I've tried, I've tried." At times she gave bits of information pertinent to Buddy's current illness and childhood, but on the whole she was not really able to give a comprehensive history in anything approaching a chronological order. Buddy's sister, Trudy, was built more along the lines of her brother, almost six feet tall, raw-boned, yet not exactly lacking in attractiveness. She was better dressed than her mother and seemed to pay at least average attention to her appearance. During the first two interviews she accompanied her mother and occasionally attempted to clarify her mother's rambling account of Buddy's history. On the third interview the sister seemed markedly under the influence of alcohol and contributed little to the discussion. Mrs. A. was seen for two further interviews, but her daughter did not appear again at the hospital.

In Buddy's memory his emotional disturbance began during adolescence when, in his words, he was "a very mixed-up kid." However, he regarded himself as having matured considerably over the past two years since he began the study of religion. He attributed much of his aberrant behavior as an adolescent to the fact that he had once or twice smoked marijuana. It was during a period of drug intoxication that he first heard voices telling him that he was Christ. Later, without the drug, he again conferred with these voices to be reassured that he should take up the study of religion and that this would be the answer he was seeking. As his conversations with these voices progressed, he began to see visions of holy figures from different religions floating before his eyes. In thinking over his attempt to murder his mother, Buddy realized he might have misinterpreted a command from the voices. Or he thought possibly this attack was caused by an experiment with peyote, even though his use of this drug had occurred several months previously.

Buddy's mother was also unable to give a coherent picture of the immediate events surrounding Buddy's murderous outburst. Seemingly unable to stick to the immediate event, she kept interjecting disconnected vague references to her troubles, past and present. From what she did say, and from what her daughter added, it appeared that Buddy had been a worry to her during his adolescence, but she was not really concerned about his "mind" until approximately two years ago, after he returned home from military service. At that time he seemed moody and restless and easily irritated. Often, he would absent himself from the house or would refuse to speak to anyone for several days at a time, seemingly wrapped up in his own thoughts. His irregular sleeping and eating particularly worried Mrs. A. Employed briefly on several different jobs, he found nothing to interest him. Mrs. A. knew little of Buddy's activities away from home, but her daughter added disparagingly that "he hung around a bunch of bums and 'beatniks'." At first Mrs. A. and her daughter thought little of Buddy's interest in religion as he had always been an avid reader and was always "off on some kick or other."

Over the past year Buddy had become even more morose. He was easily angered into violent outbursts, sometimes smashing furniture to the point of injuring himself, and often threatening his mother with violence on the slightest provocation. "He had always been a hard boy to control," Mrs. A. said sadly, "but now you don't dare say anything to him." For the past year he had not even bothered to seek unemployment insurance benefits and was entirely dependent on his mother. (His sister lived by herself in another part of town.) When he was not reading, Buddy devoted himself to his Yoga exercises. As he usually paraded around the house and yard wearing only his sandals and a towel, the neighbors had protested several times and the police had been called twice to investigate. Each time Mrs. A. had taken pains to keep Buddy away from the door as she was afraid he would become embroiled in an altercation with the police.

Past History. Mrs. A. lost both her parents during the influenza epidemic of World War I, when she was still an infant, and was reared in a series of foster homes. Her last set of foster parents forced her to quit school after the eighth grade in order to work in their delicatessen. Throughout her childhood she had felt like a cast-off, unwanted and lonely, and as an adolescent she was also withdrawn and friendless, deprived of any kind of social or family life. To add to her misery, she suffered an endocrinological defect which left her completely bald. When she was seventeen her foster parents arranged a marriage for her with Otto A. Sr., Buddy's father. Although he was twenty years her senior and a stranger, she accepted the marriage without question, since in the past her life had always been arranged for her. At the time she had at least a faint hope that someone wanted her and would care for her. She learned indirectly that Mr. A.'s parents, then deceased, had emigrated from Germany and raised a large family, but she met none of them. Other than this, she knew nothing about her husband's background or his personal life. She was not even sure how he earned his living or spent his time when away from home. A minor political "ward-heeler" in a Midwestern metropolis, Mr. A. always seemed to have plenty of money but no definite means of earning a livelihood. Mrs. A. thought it probable that he had made most of his money illegally during Prohibition. Although he provided his family with at least the bare essentials, he showed no affection or regard for either his wife or children. Whenever the slightest demand was made on him, he became angrily abusive, frightening them into submission. Mrs. A. wondered why he ever married, since he was seldom home and seemed to have little need for a wife, either as companion or sexual partner. Buddy himself spoke of his father more fondly, but his recollections were vague. He recalled two occasions when his father had thought to bring him a birthday present, but had no other definite memories of his father. Buddy seemed proud of the fact that he resembled his father physically.

Buddy was born six years after his parents' marriage, four years after Trudy's birth. Mrs. A. skipped over the details of Buddy's birth and early development, remarking only, "Buddy was a very sweet baby and never gave me any trouble." Later in the interviews, she described him as "being quite a handful after he learned to walk . . . he grew very fast and was always too big for me to manage." . . . "He had quite a temper and there wasn't anything you could do when he threw a tantrum." Mrs. A. believed that one of the sources of Buddy's problems throughout his life was the fact that he had no father to discipline him or teach him self-control. On the other hand, she insisted that during his early childhood, Buddy was usually "a pretty good boy" or, at least, got into no serious trouble either at home or at school.

His health was, in general, excellent—except for the fact that he was bald, since he suffered from the same endocrinological defect as his mother. Mrs. A. used to be concerned about the effect Buddy's baldness might have upon him, but, so far as she could remember he had never been bothered by it. His sister agreed, but said that this was only because Buddy would "beat the tar out of any kid who so much as looked at him cross-eyed." Apparently, even as a child Buddy towered over other children. An above-average student, he enjoyed going to school. His athletic prowess commanded respect among his companions, not to mention his ability to cow them into submission if they were critical of him. According to his sister he was the "kingpin of the school" throughout his grade-school years.

For reasons she could not explain, Mrs. A. decided, when Buddy was about eleven, to leave her husband and move to southern California. She did not admit to the children that she was separating from her husband, but told them instead that he had a job elsewhere and would join them soon. For several years he continued to send her money, which she invested in several apartment houses. However, for the past decade she had not heard from her husband. Buddy and his sister would occasionally ask after their father, but since they had seen so little of him in their childhood, it did not seem to Mrs. A. that his absence made any difference to them. Buddy, who could not recall this period of his life, said only that he knew his father "always had been a bum and probably still was." In any case, Mrs. A. was more concerned with Trudy, then thirteen, who had run away from home several times, traveled with a "fast" crowd, and was in frequent conflict with the law for truancy and being loose on the streets late at night. Whenever Mrs. A. attempted to confront her daughter with her behavior, Trudy became truculently defiant and Mrs. A. wept helplessly. Buddy also recalled these scenes, mentioning that he remembered being left at home at night, lonely and scared, while his mother went out to look for his sister. At fifteen, Trudy was finally placed by the court in a foster home where she remained until she finished high school. Since then her adjustment has been, at best, marginal, marked by several marriages and increasing alcoholism.

Buddy's adolescent problems followed shortly upon Trudy's. Not long after the family moved to Los Angeles, Mrs. A. became determined to do something about Buddy's baldness and took him to a physician, who began hormone treatments which proved quite effective. About the time Buddy turned thirteen a light fuzz of red hair appeared across the top of his head and shortly afterwards on other parts of his body in normal fashion. However, Buddy seemed to resent intensely the hormone treatments and the resulting hair growth. At school he was no longer able to beat back every taunter and, indeed, seemed to feel he had nothing to fight about. Having moved from a school where he had been a physical and social leader, he now had to take a back seat. He was often in trouble with the school authorities for fighting. Now the other youngsters shunned him. In recalling this period of life Buddy associated the growth of his hair with a sense of failure and inadequacy, for which he blamed his mother. Once he shaved his head bald again, but his hair returned thicker and longer than ever before. He gradually became more and more of an isolate, "hating myself and everyone else too."

During his later teens he seemed to make a brief effort to break away from this social isolation. He joined with one and then another of the delinquent groups at high school, engaging in behavior which seemed specifically aimed at defying the school authorities. According to Trudy, Buddy had dressed in black leather coat and tight jeans, and sported a "duck-tail" haircut; he swaggered about, insolent to adults, much to the dismay of his mother. Buddy himself recalled that he had tried to act like a "big shot," but later discovered that this was not the "true way to self-realization." He admitted that he had become so attached to and so admired one of the gang leaders that he actually had "a crush on him" and tried to imitate his idol, submitting to everything that he was asked to do. However, the gang leader seemed to take particular pleasure in embarrassing Buddy by ordering him to carry out either difficult or silly tasks. For example, the only time Buddy really was in trouble with the law, other than for truancy, was when he was commanded by the gang leader to "strip" (steal exterior accessories) a car—which turned out to be a police car. Buddy was promptly apprehended and the gang thought this a great joke. On his own Buddy would think up "crazy stunts" which sometimes amused his peers but more often confirmed their opinion that he was an "oddball." Not sure they could trust him, the gang excluded Buddy from their group sexual activities and much of their other asocial behavior, which made him feel very much of an outsider. Even before this he had begun to worry about his sexual adequacy; from age thirteen on he had been masturbating several times a day, with elaborate daydreams of sexual prowess. Discovered once by the gang, he was forced to masturbate in front of them while they roared in laughter, especially because he was unable to maintain an erection.

Buddy's educational achievement was at best erratic. He made barely passing marks in most of his subjects, but occasionally he would become fascinated with some particular topic and would be among the top in his class for a semester. His teachers were surprised by the display of miscellaneous knowledge derived from his extensive reading, or when they received a satisfactory paper after he had done absolutely no work in class. Even his performance on intelligence tests varied so extremely that one school counselor sought to refer him to the school guidance clinic; however, due to a long waiting list, he never received attention. His surly and defiant attitude toward teachers and school authorities became so extreme that he was suspended from school several times during his junior and senior years. As he grew increasingly disgusted with school, his attendence became more and more irregular; approximately three months before the time he might have been graduated, he dropped out of high school altogether. His mother had always supplied him with petty cash on his demand, so Buddy had never had to work. However, his expenses were small since he never dated. After he quit high school he sat around the house doing little except watching TV and eating constantly. He gained so much weight that his mother became worried. As she recalled her concern, during the interview, she sighed and remarked, "Whenever Buddy starts something there is no stopping him; he seems to have no control over himself."

Shortly after his eighteenth birthday, Buddy was drafted into the military service. Even before he had completed his basic training he had been reprimanded twice by "company courts-martial" for minor infractions of army regulations. Although Buddy pleaded ignorance, these rules were common knowledge to every soldier. After approximately six months' service he was convicted of the use of narcotics and sentenced to a dishonorable discharge plus a year's hard labor in the military prison. Buddy admitted that he had previously tried smoking marijuana as a "joke" with the gang, but maintained that this incident in the army was a single occasion when in his loneliness he sought the company of young men similar to those he had known in high school. The other men fled when the military police appeared, leaving Buddy in possession of the marijuana cigarettes. In the military prison Buddy was screened by a psychiatrist, who, Buddy believed, had recommended to the military courts that his sentence be commuted. After four months in prison he was dishonorably discharged from the service. Upon return to civilian life Buddy was unable to obtain a job because of his lack of education and experience. The nature of his military discharge deprived him of his veteran's rights to further education. Furthermore, when prospective employers asked about his military service he became evasive and left without making further application for employment. He rapidly came to believe that everyone knew about his military conviction and imprisonment. He therefore returned to his former behavior of sitting around the house with nothing to do or wandering aimlessly about the streets. His mother and sister, concerned about his behavior, hired an attorney who agreed that the sentence had been unusually harsh for a crime which in civilian life would be a misdemeanor. However, the attorney was unable to effect any reversal of the court-martial sentence.

Depressed and bitter, Buddy withdrew in silence from all social contacts, even with his family. Though Mrs. A. and Trudy were concerned, they did not know how to comfort him and were hurt when he ignored their overtures.

When he began his bizarre religious practices his family became even more uneasy, but since he seemed to find surcease from his troubles they avoided disturbing him. Even when Buddy began to talk with his "voices" and to lie around the house almost naked, masturbating openly in the living room, Mrs. A. tried to maintain an air of composure, hoping he suddenly would "come back to his old sweet self." When she finally admitted to Trudy how frightened she was by Buddy's outbursts of violence, Trudy tried to convince her to take him to a psychiatrist. Overhearing them, Buddy threatened to kill them and himself if they interfered with his freedom in any way. Cowed by his belligerence, they had despaired of taking any action, until the incident occurred which led to Buddy's hospitalization.

Disposition and Treatment. At the end of eight days of observation in the county hospital, the staff recommended to the courts that Buddy be committed to the state hospital. The psychiatrist was able to convince Buddy that he should go to the hospital as a "voluntary" patient, which avoided legal procedure. Buddy's mother and the police dropped all criminal charges against him. About a week later, Buddy reappeared at the outpatient section of the county hospital asking to see the psychiatrist to whom he had talked previously. He waited around many hours until that particular doctor was free. He explained that he could not peacefully practice his religion behind hospital walls and so had signed himself out against medical advice. However, he wanted to let this doctor know since he respected the doctor's opinion. It appeared also that Buddy was very afraid that he might be given electric shock treatment. After talking to him for several hours the psychiatrist permitted Buddy to return home with the promise that he would return on appointment. Buddy did not keep the appointment, but did reappear without an appointment several days later. He continued to appear, sometimes on appointment although more often without. Most of his discussion with the psychiatrist concerned his current adjustment at home. He was able to move away from home to a boarding house, which was arranged for him by the clinic social worker. He found a job as a dishwasher, which he held for two or three weeks, but thereafter shifted from one menial job to another over approximately a year's period. The psychiatrist insisted that if Buddy could not keep appointments with him that at least Buddy should come to see him or telephone him when any crisis arose. Several times Buddy called him at night for long telephone conversations without apparent reason, but at such times he usually seemed panicky or depressed. After approximately a year Buddy became considerably depressed and finally admitted that he again had an urge to kill someone. He voluntarily returned to the state hospital, where he remained for approximately two years, at which time he was discharged as being "in remission." Over the next several years Buddy contacted his psychiatrist at the county hospital only twice. Both times he came on the pretext of seeking advice about some change in his living situation, but really seemed to need the assurance that assistance was available whenever he might need it. On neither occasion did he appear unusually depressed. He remained emotionally and socially isolated but appeared to have dropped his religious fanaticism and other bizarre behavior and, in general, was less overtly disturbed. When last heard from, he was continuing his marginal existence outside the hospital, maintaining himself away from home through intermittent employment at unskilled jobs.

Questions for "Buddy" A.

1. List Buddy's symptoms and behavior at the time that he was first brought to the hospital. What clinical diagnosis best fits Buddy's behavior? Defend your answer.

2. Trace Buddy's social development since childhood. Recount what you see in terms of the following:

    a. the quality of relationships with his mother and father

    b. the quality of his relationships with friends of the same sex

    c. the quality of his relationships with members of the opposite sex

3. In later years, Buddy evinced an interest in certain Far Eastern religions:

    a. What are some of the fundamental concepts of Yoga and the Buddhist religions?

b. In the light of your answers to the above, why might some of these concepts have been perceived by Buddy as a possible source of relief for his anxieties about his (1) relations with members of his own sex; (2) relations with members of the opposite sex; (3) masturbation?

4. Read the Phillips and Rodnick and the Garmezy articles listed in the references.

a. According to the criteria advanced by Phillips, would you classify Buddy as a "*good* pre-morbid" or a "*poor* pre-morbid"?

b. To what extent do Rodnick and Garmezy's descriptions of family organization for each pre-morbid group fit Buddy's family constellation?

5. How would you characterize Buddy's relationship with his father? What effect did this relationship appear to have in Buddy's concept of himself as a man?

6. Can you see any relation between your answer to question 5 above and some of Buddy's psychotic symptoms (i.e. his feeling that he was Jesus Christ; his attempt to kill his mother to achieve Nirvana)?

7. Surprisingly, Buddy reacted very unfavorably to the successful treatment of his endocrine disorder. How can you account for this reaction? (*Hint:* Consider the gratifications which his affliction provided Buddy earlier in his life, and the age at which the successful treatment occurred.)

8. During his most disturbed period, Buddy showed some profound disturbances in his thinking. This thinking has been termed pseudological by some writers. For example, one bit of psychotic thinking has been reconstructed in syllogistic form as follows:

George Washington was a man

I am a man

Therefore, I am George Washington

Attempt, following the above example, a reconstruction of the syllogism underlying Buddy's conclusion that in order to achieve Nirvana he had to kill his mother.

9. From what you know of psychology, how can you account for the fact that thinking, as it exists in the psychotic, can go so awry? Attempt an explanation either from a learning theory or psychoanalytic theory of the thinking disturbance shown by Buddy.

10. Make an estimation of the likelihood that Buddy will return to a

mental hospital at some time in his life. Base your estimate on statistical figures or factors that point to a return of psychotic symptoms after a first episode and not upon a personal judgment. (*Hint:* See Phillip's article, ref. 3.)

References

ARIETI, S. *Interpretation of schizophrenia*. New York: Robert Brunner, 1955. P. 192.

CAMERON, N. Deterioration and regression in schizophrenic thinking. *Journal of Abnormal and Social Psychology*, 1939, **34**: 265–270.

PHILLIPS, L. Case history data and prognosis in schizophrenia. *Journal of Nervous and Mental Disorders*, 1953, **117**: 515–525.

RODNICK, E. T., & GARMEZY, N. An experimental approach to the study of motivation in schizophrenia. In JONES, M. R. (Ed.) *Nebraska Symposium on Motivation*. Lincoln: Univer. of Nebraska Press, 1957. Pp. 109–183.

SULLIVAN, H. S. *The interpersonal theory of psychiatry*. New York: W. W. Norton & Co., 1953. Pp. 325–327.

THE CASE OF DR. McD.

The Lonely Sex

Dr. McD., a 54-year-old, white, unmarried physician, was originally admitted to the Veterans' Administration hospital in 1954. A major in the army reserve, Dr. McD. had re-entered active service in the Korean conflict as a lieutenant colonel. Soon after he had been placed in command of an overseas hospital, the War Department in Washington began to receive letters directly from him complaining of graft in both the American and Korean forces. Since these letters did not come through the usual "channels," an investigator from the Inspector General's office was assigned to his hospital. When evidence of this alleged graft was requested of Dr. McD., he presented the investigator with boxes containing slips of paper, most of which appeared to be laundry receipts or old prescriptions from his home town pharmacy. In addition, Dr McD. made rash accusations against many of his fellow officers and the United Nations command, intimating that many of the high command in Korea were actually on the side of the Communists. On the advice of the base psychiatrist, Dr. McD. was hospitalized in a psychiatric ward and given a medical discharge with the recommendation that he be immediately hospitalized in a veterans' hospital.

Although Dr. McD. protested what he regarded as the extreme injustice of this move, he did accept the hospitalization. At the time of this first admission to the V.A. hospital, Dr. McD. explained to the admitting physician that he regarded the entire war as a conflict between Christianity and Judaism and had accepted the hospitalization only because he felt he could better report to the proper authorities what he regarded as the machinations of Jewish psychiatry against the government.

At this time, Dr. McD. remained in the hospital approximately five months. However, he never assumed the role of a patient but continued to behave as a physician on the staff of a hospital. Thus, he refused to discuss any of his private life with any of the staff. Although at first he openly expressed his opinions regarding graft in Korea and the nature of the war, he gradually ceased to mention these ideas and subsequently denied them. Since he had been a fairly prominent physician in a nearby city, and a clinical instructor at the university, he succeeded in awing some of the younger staff, who found themselves being queried about their knowledge of medicine, defending themselves rather than investigating the patient's case. His overt and snide anti-Semitism also angered many of the staff members, both Jewish and Gentile. Many of the staff had had brief professional contact with him, but no one knew much about his personal life. As far back as anyone could remember, Dr. McD. had been regarded as an eccentric lone wolf. He never confided in anyone and seldom consulted with any of his colleagues on any case unless invited to do so by them. He never hesitated to air his views about psychiatry; he was quite critical of its tenets and enjoyed mocking psychiatry and psychiatrists to their faces. He said several times at public meetings that he regarded psychiatry as an extension of the Jewish faith. Only because of his brilliant record as a research worker and as a diagnostician had he been granted professional status within the medical community.

Dr. McD.'s ability to buffalo the hospital staff was furthered by his appearance and demeanor. Although a slightly built, gray-haired man, he had an erect military posture, and as he sat stiffly upright, his hands gripping the arms of the chair, he seemed to command the situation. His rimless spectacles and his tiny gray moustache seemed to add to the severity of his countenance. He was always impeccably dressed in his military uniform, with his brass buttons gleaming, and his shoes highly polished. (Hospital regulations prohibiting the wearing of military uniforms had been relaxed in this case, since Dr. McD. had brought no other clothes with him and he adamantly refused to wear hospital clothes.) Despite his grim appearance, he was always polite and overtly pleasant, albeit his smile seemed forced and artificial. He spoke slowly and precisely, in a modulated voice, even when expressing his most violent opinions or strongest protests against being hospitalized. Although he made what seemed to be rash accusations against other people, he remained overtly calm and reasonable.

Throughout this initial hospitalization, his attitude and behavior continued to annoy and upset the staff. He ordered the nurses and medical attendants about in an authoritative manner, to which they often responded in complaint fashion before they realized who was giving the commands. On several occasions he seated himself in the doctors' offices when no one was present and made notes in other patients' charts, prescribing medicine or other medical procedures. Because the hospital was large and many of the staff new, his orders were sometimes carried out. On most occasions his orders and prescriptions were innocuous or even appropriate. However, he also made bizarre entries into the chart which had nothing to do with the patient, such as the following:

3:00 a.m. Heard shots being fired at the back fence. This is obviously another case of failure on the part of the hospital administration. 5:00 a.m. I could not locate the body. 9:00 a.m. Freshly burned refuse in back of building 504. Contains what must be human bones. The administration has gotten rid of the evidence.

For the most part Dr. McD. was allowed full range of the hospital grounds. However, it was twice necessary to place him on a locked ward. Typically, he merely raged or threw objects such as shoes at patients whom he claimed were insulting him, but once he wrestled a much larger patient to the floor and was attempting to strangle him when attendants came into the room. Later he laughed off this incident as the kind of thing one might expect when one tried to protect oneself from psychotic patients. His second outburst occurred when the attending psychiatrist attempted to inquire into his sexual adjustment. Dr. McD. calmly responded that he believed his sexual adjustment was beyond question. He suggested that the psychiatrist might be sexually maladjusted since he knew that psychiatrists were particularly "sexually minded," and he had expected them to bring this question up. The same evening following this interview the patient disappeared from the ward and did not return until after midnight. When he returned he raged up and down the ward, disturbing everyone and finally had to be forcibly restrained and put in a private room for the night. The next morning he denied that his behavior had been in any way unusual, claiming that the night staff always made such accusations against him.

During the admission staff conference, a month after Dr. McD.

was admitted to the hospital, the staff discussed the patient's behavior, the difficulties which they had encountered in interviewing him and finding out anything of his background, and their own reactions of frustration and anger in response to his resistance, his arrogance, and his prejudiced social attitude. Under the circumstances, it was agreed that direct exploration of the patient's anxieties and personal life was futile, but that continued detailed notes on his behavior by the psychiatric nursing staff would be helpful in planning hospital management. It was decided to accord him the deference and respect which his status as a senior member of the medical profession would be granted, but to avoid, in as kindly a manner as possible, carrying out his orders and to prevent his gaining access to medical charts. Because of his difficulties with other patients, he was given a private but unlocked room. This approach to Dr. McD. was reinforced by the clinical director who invited Dr. McD. to his office "for a chat," asking whether there was anything else he needed and offering his personal attention should Dr. McD. have any requests. At the same time, the director explained to him that under the circumstances, it would not be possible for him to practice medicine without a formal appointment to the staff, much as they appreciated his efforts. Dr. McD. accepted this explanation in what appeared to be a most co-operative and understanding attitude. However, when the clinical director requested permission to meet with the patient's sister (his only living relative), Dr. McD. demurred, explaining that she was elderly and had been ill.

During the ensuing months, Dr. McD.'s stay in the hospital was without incident. He accepted even the usual frustrations of daily hospital routine with an imperturbable nonchalance. He avoided all contact with other patients, remaining by himself in his room, or pacing the perimeter of the hospital grounds alone. He made no effort to order the nurses around, although his sharp commanding voice continued to snap them to attention from time to time. He greeted the medical staff in a friendly manner, stopping them to exchange the time of day or to discuss articles he had been reading in his professional journals or in the medical library, to which the director had granted him access. After four months he requested permission from the director to visit his sister, which was granted. After the second such visit, he informed the director that he believed he had "served his time" and was ready to leave the hospital. The director agreed to consider his request, but expressed the hope that, as his patient, Dr. McD. would accept his medical opinion. The next day, Dr. McD. was more demanding, and when the director recommended to him that he remain in the hospital, Dr. McD. argued that he was not legally committed and therefore could leave of his own volition. Agreeing that Dr. McD. had voluntarily committed himself, the director pointed out that if Dr. McD. left, it would be "against medical advice," and encouraged him to consider the matter further. Nevertheless, Dr. McD. immediately signed the formal papers requesting release from the hospital and, after the legally required wait of three days, he returned to his home.

Thirteen months later, Dr. McD. was involuntarily recommitted by the Superior Court on the petition of his sister. At the time of this readmission, Dr. McD. denied vigorously that there was anything wrong with him, and averred that his hospitalization was a plot by his sister and the government. Dr. McD.'s sister alleged that during this year his behavior had become increasingly bizarre, culminating in an attack on his Japanese houseboy, whom Dr. McD. accused of plotting to attack him in the near future.

After returning home from his initial hospitalization, Dr. McD. attempted to resume his practice as an internist. However, he found that many of his patients had transferred to other physicians and did not return to him. Dr. McD. felt very bitter about this and blamed his colleagues for stealing his old patients and for refusing to refer new patients to him. Many of his colleagues were shocked by these accusations and reacted to them by not referring any new patients to him. When Dr. Mc.D. was fortunate enough to get a new patient on his own, his gruff manner and his insistence in inquiring in detail into the patient's social and sexual adjustment, even when appropriate, frequently drove these new patients away. He spent many hours sitting alone in his apartment and claimed to be working on a new book which "would revolutionize medicine." However, his houseboy reported that Dr. McD. did not appear to be doing any writing, but seemed instead to spend a great deal of time playing with his model railroad, his telescope, or just sitting by the hour staring into space. Although not previously a religious man, Dr. McD. began to attend church services regularly, often stopping at the door to argue about the sermon with the minister. He often attended other church meetings including those of the board of the church. At these meetings he criticized the behavior of the board members, intimating that they were not good Christians. He also became involved in one petty complaint after another against his landlord, and, when the landlord attempted to break his lease, Dr. McD. took him into court on three different counts regarding the care of the building. During the month prior to his readmission to the hospital, Dr. McD. had called the police fifteen times regarding what he felt to be suspicious looking characters who were entering the lobby of his apartment house or strolling through the neighborhood streets. He could not make any definite complaints against any of these people nor could he identify any of them, but he became quite irritated when the police pointed out that they could not investigate further without some direct evidence or charges.

Although he had not physically attacked anyone prior to his attempted assault on his houseboy, Dr. McD. had recently purchased two new revolvers. He had been in contact with his sister only twice during the year, but on both occasions had mentioned in passing that she should not be surprised if he were found dead within a year.

Upon admission to the hospital, Dr. McD. vigorously denied that he had attacked his houseboy but rather accused the houseboy of being a thief and a sexual pervert. He further claimed that instead of wanting to harm his houseboy he had tried to protect and befriend "this fellow" for the twenty years that he had worked for him. Dr. McD. claimed that the houseboy had threatened him because he had advised the houseboy's fiancée of what he regarded as the houseboy's alleged character defects. At other times, Dr. McD. defended his behavior as an effort to prevent the houseboy from making an unsatisfactory marriage. The patient was also very critical of the houseboy's fiancée, claiming that she was merely after the houseboy's money.

At the time of this readmission, Dr. McD.'s sister visited the hospital, and, in interviews with the psychiatric social worker, further information concerning his early development and background were obtained. His houseboy was also interviewed. In addition, a member of the medical staff recalled that he had attended the same private high school as Dr. McD. for two years, and was able to shed some light on Dr. McD.'s adjustment as an adolescent.

Prior History. Dr. McD. was born and reared in the city in which he was currently practicing medicine. His father, a prominent physician, had married late in life to a widow, then also in her forties, who had an eighteen-year-old daughter from her previous marriage. His father died when Dr. McD. was four years old, leaving him with a very comfortable inheritance and a trust fund which financed all of his schooling. Dr. McD.'s mother died two years later leaving him in the care of his sister then aged twenty-six. As far as his sister could remember, his early training and development had otherwise been uneventful. Their mother had been sickly and her brother had been under the care of various housekeepers in the home. Dr. McD.'s sister had been in a boarding school during the patient's early childhood. After she was given guardianship of Dr. McD., she placed him in a boarding school and seldom saw him except on holidays. As far as she knew, Dr. McD. adjusted well in this school, always made top grades, and was a well behaved and polite little boy. During the summer periods he was usually sent to camp. He seldom spent as much as a week in her home during the holidays.

Dr. McD. graduated with full honors from a private high school at age sixteen. The staff physician who had attended high school with him recalled that Dr. McD. had demanded and been granted many special privileges at the school which were not ordinarily accorded the other boys. The other boys were jealous of him, teased him, and refused to include him in their cliques. They identified him with the headmaster, a gruff disciplinarian who seemed to protect him, and felt that he tattled on them to the headmaster. At one time, Dr. McD. had the nickname in the school of "the little head." One of the privileges granted the patient by the headmaster was a private room, allegedly because the patient refused to dress or bathe in front of the other boys. The patient did not participate in any of the school's sports activities or other extra-curricular activities and the boys thus considered him a "sissy." There was considerable sexual curiosity and homosexual play among the other boys in the school from which the patient was specifically excluded because it was thought that he would report them to school authorities. One incident the staff physician recalled specifically: the boys had discovered that Dr. McD. was on the toilet and would not come out while they were present. They accused him of masturbating and stood guard over him for several hours until the situation was broken up by one of the teachers. In reminiscing further, the staff physician was of the opinion that possibly the headmaster may not have been as cold and distant as the boys regarded him, and that perhaps he had taken pity on the patient because of the treatment accorded him by the other boys. Possibly this pity was motivated by the fact that Dr. McD. was an orphan. It was reported that one Christmas Dr. McD. could not go to his sister's home because the family was ill, and the headmaster suggested to several of the other boys' parents that they invite him to their homes for the holiday. Since no one accepted this suggestion, the patient spent Christmas with the headmaster and his wife which only furthered the boys' impression that the patient was a "pet." Because the patient was a brilliant student, the teachers praised and rewarded him, adding to the jealousy of the other boys.

Following graduation Dr. McD. went on to the university to take his premedical training. He finished this undergraduate training in two and a half years rather than the usual three. Since he was six months too young to be admitted to medical school, he was sent abroad for a period of travel by himself. During this year abroad, he attempted to look up relatives in the country in which his mother had been born and was quite disgusted and upset to find these relatives living in a ghetto. Although he mentioned this to his sister upon his return from Europe, he acted and spoke as if he were unaware that his mother was Jewish.

On returning to this country, he entered medical school where he was again a top student in his class. Dr. McD. spent his summers at the medical school on research scholarships. During these medical school years Dr. McD. lived at a boarding house near the university in a room by himself. He had almost no social life as a student and lived as an isolate, spending most of his time either in the laboratory or in his own room. His sister and several older women members of the family frequently invited Dr. McD. to come to their houses or saw that he got frequent invitations to parties, which he usually attended and at which he seemed to enjoy himself. His sister and the other women attempted to pair him off with many of the young ladies in their social group, and although he went along on theater parties and other affairs, he never followed through with their hopes that he would continue to date one of these girls on a steady basis Indeed, Dr. McD. seemed amused by his sister's efforts to get him "hooked up" with some girl, and he once informed her that he was determined to outwit her and her friends in their plans for him. In a cynical fashion, which gradually began to alienate other people, Dr. McD. informed his brother-in-law, and other married men of his acquaintance, that he would never marry any girl who was not a virgin, and that, furthermore, his medical training and experience had led him to believe that there were few, if any, women over the age of twelve who were virgins. Dr. McD. also took every opportunity possible to make fun of married life and to argue for the joys of celibacy.

Outside of medicine, Dr. McD.'s only enduring interest was in railroading. He had read many books on the topic and built a large and elaborate model railroad in his apartment. He had a similar fascination with astronomy; on his balcony were mounted several powerful telescopes. His fellow medical students kidded him when they discovered that these telescopes could be trained at the windows of the nurses' home at the medical school down the block. Dr. McD. took this kidding good-naturedly, but pointed out that it was his fellow students who had thought of this use of the telescope.

After being graduated *cum laude* from medical school, Dr. McD. was immediately admitted to an internship at the same university, and thereafter, a residency in internal medicine. He continued to pursue his research interests during his residency and completed a study on the functioning of the kidney which was regarded as revolutionary and was widely quoted in medical textbooks. The year after he finished his residency, he authored a text on the office practice of internal medicine which was so well received that it became a standard work in that field.

Following the completion of his residency Dr. McD. engaged in the private practice of internal medicine. He was moderately successful and his life went along in a comparatively uneventful fashion until the outbreak of World War II. No one was aware why Dr. McD. was not immediately called up for duty at the outbreak of World War II. The colleagues who disliked him voiced the opinion that he had been rejected on psychiatric grounds. However, while staying at home, Dr. McD. became extremely busy since he was one of the few physicians left in his community. He was appointed Acting Assistant Medical Director at one of the large hospitals. Shortly before the end of the war Dr. McD. was given an appointment as captain in the U.S. Army and served briefly at a military hospital nearby. During the physical examination, when first admitted to the veterans' hospital, Dr. McD. was asked about a surgical scar on his scrotum. He mentioned that he had had an operation for an undescended testicle in 1944. He at first denied that there was any special purpose for this operation at that particular time, but later mentioned that this physical abnormality was the reason he had been denied a commission in the service earlier. Apparently the surgery corrected this abnormality and he was accepted in the service in 1944. As far as could be determined, Dr. McD.'s year of service in World War II was uneventful, and he showed none of the unusual behavior which he manifested during his Korean period of duty. After World War II, Dr. McD. continued in the military reserve, attending all reserve meetings faithfully and going on brief periods of active duty every summer. He rose to the rank of major and entered active duty at the onset of the Korean war with the rank of lieutenant colonel. Dr. McD. seemed very proud of his military activities and rank and wore his uniform at every possible opportunity.

Course in the Hospital During Second Admission. On readmission to the veterans' hospital, Dr. McD. was found to be in good physical health. He denied any history of illness or injury and did not recall having even any of the usual childhood diseases. He claimed to keep himself in good health by walking. The examination by the admitting psychiatrist revealed that the patient was "well-oriented as to time, place, and person" and that except for his ideas concerning the nature of the war and the reasons for his hospitalization, appeared to be able to reason logically. Various tests of intelligence and abstract reasoning indicated that Dr. McD. was of superior intelligence and, in general, showed no obvious deterioration of his thought processes. The psychologist noted, however, that while the patient seemed to reason well enough, his logic was defective in that he often argued on the basis of false premises. Emotionally, Dr. McD. showed no overt anxiety or depression. On the ward and around the hospital, except for the occasional outbursts mentioned above, Dr. McD. was well-behaved and co-operative. Although a patient, Dr. McD. continued to play the role of a physician and behaved toward other patients as he might if he were a member of the hospital staff.

Since Dr. McD. was so reluctant to discuss his personal life and seemed so defensive about it, he was not considered a favorable candidate for individual psychotherapy. One attempt was made to include him in a psychotherapeutic group but once again he took the role of the physician rather than the patient, and interviewed the other patients in the group rather than talk about himself. When the other patients challenged his attitude, Dr. McD. failed to appear at any future group meetings. Although generally aloof, Dr. McD. did seem to form some sort of continuing relationship with a student psychologist assigned to study his case. The student had been advised by his supervisor of Dr. McD.'s defensiveness and was cautioned not to attempt any direct inquiry into the patient's personal life. It was emphasized that the student should attempt to form some kind of relationship with Dr. McD. and to merely listen to him. Dr. McD. permitted the student to accompany him on his walks around the hospital and regaled him with his attitudes about the war, medicine, psychiatry, and the details and history of railroads in the United States. However, the student's curiosity and impatience grew from week to week and finally one day, in a pause during their daily walk, the student haltingly inquired about one small aspect of Dr. McD.'s personal life. Dr. McD. turned to the student and said in a stern but friendly fashion, "Young man, I am an old and lonely man, and there is nothing you can do about it."

Dr. McD. continued to reside in the hospital and it was the opinion of the psychiatric staff that he will probably remain there for the rest of his life.

Questions for Dr. McD.

1. The hospital notes on Dr. McD. indicated that he was not visibly anxious and could discuss his accusations against others in a calm and detached manner. How can we reconcile the fact that Dr. McD. was so disturbed psychologically with his apparent lack of overt discomfort?

2. What anxieties are present in Dr. McD., although not directly observable? Suggest a theoretical formulation which permits the existence of anxiety and no overt manifestations of anxiety operating concurrently.

3. Taking a long term view of Dr. McD.'s life, what are the personality traits which seem to herald the form of his later disorder?

4. What kinds of approach-avoidance conflicts appear to underlie the learning of the traits suggested in your answer to question 3?

5. What were the conditions in Dr. McD.'s early life that appeared particularly conducive to the learning of the conflicts listed in question 4 above?

6. What psychological defenses did Dr. McD. learn to use in reducing anxiety?

7. Obviously these defenses eventually resulted in a psychotic reaction rather than a neurotic one. Can you explain why the more serious reaction (psychosis) pattern occurred rather than the less serious one (neurosis)?

8. One popular theory of Dr. McD.'s disorder (that offered by Freud) emphasizes the central role of latent homosexuality. Do you see any evidence in Dr. McD. of homosexual trends, latent or otherwise?

9. How can you account for the following:
   a. Dr. McD.'s celibacy
   b. Dr. McD.'s enjoyment of the army role
   c. Dr. McD.'s need to maintain the role of the physician even when hospitalized

10. Do the results of the psychological examination fit with the usual criteria for diagnosing a person as paranoid schizophrenic? If not, what diagnosis also might be said to cover Dr. McD.'s' pattern of symptoms?

11. Dr. McD. expressed openly his religious prejudice and in general his behavior might be called "authoritarian." Compare this case with those reported by Maria Levinson in *The Authoritarian Personality* (see reference below). In what way does Dr. McD. fit the characteristics of the authoritarian personality, and in what ways is he different?

References

CAMERON, N. The paranoid pseudo-community. *American Journal of Sociology*, 1943, **49**: 32–38.

FROMM-REICHMAN, F. Loneliness. *Psychiatry*, 1959, **22**: 1–15.

LEVINSON, MARIA. Psychological ill health in relation to potential fascism: a study of psychiatric clinic patients. In ADORNO, T. W., FRENKEL-BRUNSWIK, E., LEVINSON, D., & SANFORD, R. N. *The authoritarian personality*. New York: Harper and Bros., 1950. Pp. 891–970.

OVESY, L. Pseudo homosexuality, the paranoid mechanism and paranoia. *Psychiatry*, 1955, **18**: 163–173. (Also reprinted in REED, C. R., ALEXANDER, I. E., & TOMPKINS, S. S., *Psychopathology*, Cambridge: Harvard Univer. Press, 1958. Chap. 25.)

PHILLIPS, L. Case history data and prognosis in schizophrenia. *Journal of Nervous and Mental Diseases*, 1953, **117**: 515–525.

SEITZ, P. Infantile experience and adult behavior in animal subjects. II, Age of separation from the mother and adult behavior in the cat. *Psychosomatic Medicine*, 1959, **21**: 353–378.

THE CASE OF MARLA T.

The Dance on the Precipice

Marla T.'s entrance into the hospital's reception room was most flamboyant. A petite but plump woman, in her early thirties, she was garishly clad in a sleeveless sheath dress of a silver-colored metallic cloth and wore elbow length gloves of the same material. A pair of elaborate and gaudy earrings dangled below her platinum-blonde hair, which was cut in a Dutch bob. Her make-up was so heavy that she looked ready to appear on stage. However, this layer of cosmetics failed to hide the "crow's feet" around her eyes; very near-sighted, she peered through the thick lenses of her plain, dark-rimmed glasses—which contrasted starkly with her otherwise ostentatious costume. Since Marla and her husband arrived about noon, her dress and appearance seemed even more bizarre. Somewhere between her car and the hospital door, she had kicked off her shoes, which her husband was carrying. As she entered the hospital door, she was talking rapidly in a loud, raucous voice, and continued to chatter incessantly for the next hour to anyone and everyone. Her husband was an immense, dark-complexioned, handsome Negro, who was dressed much more modestly in dark sport clothes. He said very little, except to attempt periodically to quiet her and to suggest that she listen to the doctor.

In the initial interview, Marla insisted that everything was "copacetic" (a slang term from World War II, meaning "in smooth running order"). She saw no reason that she should enter the hospital but then agreed that "perhaps" she could use some rest. Her husband was "perfectly wonderful to be so concerned about my health," and if he thought she should be hospitalized, she certainly was willing to "do anything to please him." She was "very delighted" with the condition of the hospital grounds and with the "handsome" doctors. She was sure that she would get the rest that her husband thought she needed. However, she was equally sure that she probably would be home either that evening or the next morning. Marla kept demanding that her husband check through her overnight bag to make sure that she had all the things she needed. Repeatedly she sought reassurance that he would visit her that evening, and pleaded with the doctor to admit her husband with her. However, she avoided the questions of the admitting physician, saying only that she felt perfectly all right. She immediately changed the topic when any specific questions were asked. Marla talked very rapidly, skipping from one topic to another with apparent ease. She read out loud the diplomas on the doctor's wall, mentioned persons she knew who had attended the university where the doctor got his degree, and went on to tell the personal history of these people, the towns from which they had come, other people she had known there, how this was related to her feelings about world politics, particularly the problem of racial segregation in the United States. She went on to tell how she had been engaged for the past week, almost night and day, in programs dealing with the abolition of segregation. Any attempts to question her about her other behavior or her life in general were answered briefly and politely, but she quickly came back to her ideas on how to solve the problems of race prejudice. Her husband sat by silently, with a pained expression on his face. As Marla became increasingly incoherent she was given a heavy sedative, which she accepted without question, and was led into another room with the suggestion that she should take a brief nap. She continued to talk to an accompanying nurse for almost another hour before the sedation took effect.

Mr. T. reported that the behavior which his wife demonstrated had come on rather gradually, over the past six weeks. He described her as usually a garrulous and sociable person whom everybody liked. She was always "on the go," and was considered the "life of the party." Over the past six weeks, however, she had become increasingly involved in several allied organizations that were conducting active programs to combat race prejudice. She went to one meeting after another, participated in parades and demonstrations, and seemed to be able to talk or think about little else. Marla's husband had become increasingly embarrassed by the loudness of her voice, as had others who spent any time in her company. She had gotten herself onto a TV program, and argued in an angry and abusive fashion with the moderator. Marla had spent one night in jail after fighting with the police, in a scuffle which occurred in a demonstration picket line. For the past four days she had eaten very little, slept only sporadically, and had not taken off her dress, the one she was wearing when she came to the hospital. Her general appearance had also changed; she usually dressed much more modestly and wore little or no make-up.

As far as her husband knew she had never had such passionate devotion to any cause. Usually she was much more calm and level-headed. She transacted a great deal of the financial side of his work, often traveling about the country selling the modern artistic jewelery which he made. Indeed, she had built his art hobby into a thriving business. Only twice in their two years of marriage had he been concerned about her emotional adjustment. Once on her return from a selling trip, seeming very tired and unusually quiet, she had gone to bed immediately and slept for well over forty-eight hours. He had discovered later that she had taken a heavy dose of sleeping pills. Another time she had frightened him when, after a late party, she had climbed atop a twelve-foot wall overlooking the ocean and proceeded to dance the length of the wall, threatening to jump into the water. When he expressed his concern she said it was all a joke.

Mr. T. could offer little information about his wife's background, as she had told him only of intermittent parts of her life. They had met a little over two years before in one of the organizations fighting race prejudice. Soon afterward they began living together in a common-law marriage, which Mr. T. felt has been essentially very happy and satisfying to both. Her ability to create a business out of his artistic work had enabled him to quit his job as a truck driver and devote himself entirely to his art, and to return to his college education. Several times he had urged his wife to legalize their marriage, but she had put this off, joking that if they became legally married they would not be acceptable in the artists' colony in which they lived. Asked what he had hoped might be added to the marriage by legalizing it, he sheepishly admitted that he would like to have children, although he quickly assured the interviewer that he realized that neither their economic nor their social situation was very amenable to raising of children.

The past summer his thirteen-year-old niece had been left in their care, which delighted his wife. Marla and his niece had become very close. Marla had devoted considerable energy to seeing that the girl was entertained, and spent a great deal of their budget in buying her clothes. She was disappointed when the niece returned to her own family at the end of the summer. This had raised Mr. T.'s hopes that she might want children, but he had not reintroduced the topic with her.

Asked specifically about their sexual relationships, he said that they were usually quite gratifying to him, and he supposed to her. Regarding her current sexual adjustment, Mrs. T. said only that "everything is wonderful; my husband is a wonderful lover," and refused to discuss the matter further. Mr. T. knew that Mrs. T. used a diaphragm, but had never discussed the matter of contraceptives with her, and he denied that he felt any need to discuss it. He did remark that during her menstrual period she seemed excessively irritable, and would either completely reject any sexual advances on his part, or demand repeated intercourse.

On further inquiry he agreed that, although she was generally an affectionate and warm-hearted person, she also could be very irritable and difficult to please at times. While she was always trying to do something for other people, it always had to be *her* way of doing it, and often she seemed to be doing things for others whether or not they wanted anything done for them. During the preceding weeks several of the organizations to which she belonged had at first suggested to her that she take it easy, and finally the leader of one organization had told her to stay away from their meetings entirely. She was very hurt and wept for days after the quarrel with this organization president, but finally resolved her tears by deciding that this man was emotionally disturbed and that she could help the organization best by not irritating him further. Even before her present disturbance, however, she frequently cooked fancy dishes for the neighbors, which she insisted her husband take to them, even though the neighbors protested that they did not need her gifts of food. Marla was always bringing someone home to dinner or for a drink. Marla's husband denied that either of them used alcohol at all, although they kept some alcoholic beverages in their home to serve guests. The couple lived in a one-room studio in a community largely inhabited by artists and writers.

Past History. Marla's past history was pieced together from further statements by the patient and her husband, and by a subsequent interview with the patient's grandmother, Mrs. H. An only child, Marla was reared chiefly by her maternal grandmother, as her parents had separated shortly before her birth. Marla's father never reappeared, and her mother, who was secretary for a prominent politician in Washington, left Marla entirely in the care of her grandmother before Marla was a year old. Marla remembered her mother chiefly as a stranger who visited the home at less than six-month intervals. Her earliest memory of her mother was of a large heavily perfumed fur coat in which Marla buried her head and cried. At other times her mother would greet her at the door and grasp her in her arms, and Marla would wiggle out and run into the other room crying. The grandmother remembered Marla as a very happy and pretty child. She ate well, according to the grandmother, and gained weight very rapidly, and was always a heavy-set child. The grandmother could not remember exactly when Marla learned to walk or talk, but believed that there was nothing unusual about her development during infancy. She did remember that Marla continued to be fed from the bottle until she was almost three years of age, but the grandmother did not regard this as anything unusual. She said, defensively, that she had fed Marla baby foods and solid foods at the same time that Marla was also carrying the bottle around. Asked about Marla's toilet-training, the grandmother claimed that Marla had always been a very clean child, and that she had been successful in toilet-training Marla before she was a year old. Mrs. H.'s only child had been Marla's mother, and Mr. H. had died five years before Marla's birth. The child and grandmother lived in a large, old house near the center of town.

About the only outward evidence of emotional disturbance in Marla's early childhood was her social isolation. Her grandmother enrolled Marla in a parochial school, believing it would provide "better discipline for the child," although she could not say why she thought Marla needed any special discipline. Marla denied any definite memory of her early school years, saying only that she made fair grades and "got along well" with the sisters and the students. Her grandmother reported that at times Marla seemed very unhappy, and was called "fatso" by the other children because of her mild obesity. She had little in common with the other children; she was not a member of their social clique at the school, nor did she associate with the children outside of school. She had almost no friends in her neighborhood, which was largely inhabited by older people, with no young children. Marla spent many hours playing by herself, especially with her puppets. From early childhood, she showed evidence of artistic taste—if not artistic talent—and was skillful and interested in various handicrafts. Her grandmother taught her to sew and, using sewing scraps, she constructed a large collection of elaborate hand-puppets, including costumes from many nations, fairy-book characters, and a royal family. Her favorite, however, was a rag-doll "orphan," the central character in Marla's chief puppet play. In this play the orphan, after having been abused by bad step-parents, was rescued by the prince, and it was then discovered that the orphan was really royalty.

Mrs. H. praised Marla for her being a well-behaved and helpful child who voluntarily helped with the housework and who was always obedient. Mrs. H. was convinced that Marla's disturbance began about age thirteen, when Marla's mother returned. Marla's mother had been married and divorced twice in the interim, had lost her job in Washington, and returned home broke and unmarried. Quarreling broke out between Marla and her mother almost immediately. Marla was critical of her mother's dress and her mother's habits. Her mother always wore fine clothes and went out a great deal, dating various men. At home Marla's mother slept till noon, then spent most of the afternoon grooming herself at home or at the beauty shop. Marla felt that her mother's attention to her dress and grooming was "sinful." At the same time Marla's mother made fun of Marla for quoting religious dicta on behavior, and called her "a little prissy." She blamed the grandmother for Marla's overweight, and insisted that Marla be put on a diet. She removed Marla from the parochial school, and put her in public school. Instead of the simple uniforms which Marla had been wearing, her mother bought her fancy clothes and Marla felt out of place in the public school with her silk dresses and patent leather shoes.

Once, when quite inebriated, Marla's mother described in detail her sexual exploits with her boy friend the night before. Mrs. H. then insisted that her daughter leave the house and have nothing more to do with them. The mother responded that if she left she was taking Marla with her. This quarrel, which lasted for twenty-four hours, was climaxed by Marla, who ran away from home. She was picked up by the police two hundred miles away from home, in a motel with two sailors. Mrs. H. reported that she had given Marla no sexual instruction at all, other than on the use of feminine hygiene during her menstrual period. Marla had started developing secondary sexual characteristics at about age eleven, and her first menstrual period was a month before her twelfth birthday. The grandmother denied that Marla had shown any interest in boys up to this time whatsoever and had never so much as been on a date. Marla admitted that she had spent the night in the motel with the sailors, but refused to divulge to the grandmother whether or not she had had any sexual relations with them. Marla, in giving her own history, did not mention this episode, but stated rather that she had engaged in sexual play with both girls and boys from about age eight on, and had had her first heterosexual experience with a neighbor boy when she was about ten.

Shortly after this episode Marla's mother remarried and took Marla to live with her. Marla would have preferred to stay with her grandmother, but she was also excited by the idea of having a stepfather. "I adored him the first time I met him." He treated her as a little adult, brought her presents when he came on dates with her mother, and teased her about her developing figure and attractiveness. Marla was very excited over the prospect of her mother's marriage to this man and was thus extremely disappointed when they went out of town to get married. After her mother's marriage, however, Marla saw little of her stepfather; he worked the "swing shift" in a wartime industry, departing for work before she returned from school and not awakening in the morning before she left the house. Even his day off occurred in the middle of the week, rather than on the weekend.

Marla remembered her mother at this time as being excessively strict and concerned with Marla's social behavior. Marla began to meet boys at the public high school and to go to parties and dates; she had sexual affairs with several boys. Her mother was very suspicious of her, and kept accusing her of being sexually loose. After about a year of frequent quarrels with her mother she left her mother's home when her mother accused her of attempting to seduce her stepfather, which Marla hotly denied. Mrs. H., who seemed unaware of Marla's sexual behavior, described Marla at age sixteen as being a very beautiful and attractive girl, having lost much of the excess weight of her childhood. Mrs. H. was very proud of the fact that many boys were attracted to Marla and had great hopes that Marla would make a successful marriage to a rich and ambitious young man. She thus encouraged Marla's dating and spent a great deal of money in helping Marla buy clothes and go to the beauty shop. Despite the fact that Marla was out on a date almost every night and for long weekend parties during high school, she succeeded in graduating from high school with high honors. She had developed an interest in writing, and won a state poetry writing contest. Graduating from high school before she was eighteen, she received a scholarship to the local university.

When Marla entered the university, she became enamored of a slightly older woman graduate student and moved into her apartment, where she quickly became involved in a very intense, overt homosexual relationship. This relationship lasted about three months, at which time Marla began to demonstrate many of the symptoms she showed at the time of the present hospitalization. Her grandmother remembered that Marla upon returning home talked incessantly and was unable to sleep. She recited poetry by the hour, speaking in blank verse. The grandmother believed that her behavior was associated with the heavy use of alcohol, although Marla denied this. This incident was climaxed when Marla ran out of the house in excitement and was hit by a truck in the street. She was badly injured, and it was believed for a while that she would be crippled for life. She was returned in a wheelchair to her grandmother's home, and the grandmother proceeded to nurse her and care for her like a baby. Marla remembers her grandmother rubbing her legs and helping her with the exercises prescribed by the orthopedist. Within the year Marla was able to get around on crutches, and the following year seemed almost entirely recovered. Current medical examination revealed scars of the orthopedic surgery, but there was no muscle or nerve loss.

Once Marla was able to be up and around she did not attempt to return to the university, but obtained various short-term jobs as a secretary. Marla herself reports that she was most interested in getting married, but never seemed to decide on any one man. She volunteered that she took great joy in seeing how quickly she could seduce every new man that she met. She also had one or two brief homosexual affairs. Mrs. H. reported that Marla often seemed to be at loose ends, and that she was fearful that Marla would never "amount to anything." By this, Mrs. H. meant that she hoped that Marla would return to her college education, and find either a good job or a rich husband, or both. At times Marla did engage in alcoholic bouts, which sometimes resulted in complete incapacitation for several days at a time. Mrs. H. was quite worried about Marla and tried to discourage her use of alcohol, but always nursed her back to health whenever she went on one of these binges. For the first time Marla began to quarrel with her grandmother, and to deride her old-fashioned ways. Mrs. H. was very hurt and blamed Marla's dissension on the alcohol.

Marla's interest in poetry, the fine arts, and music continued, and many of her friends were artists and writers. She became involved in various social movements, particularly in the organizations concerned with the amelioration of race prejudice. Much to her grandmother's dismay she had dated several Negroes prior to meeting her husband. Marla was very proud of her open-minded approach to sociological questions, and often engaged in prolonged arguments with people regarding the accepted institutions and prejudices of the community. It was after an extended and bitter quarrel with her grandmother, the subject of which neither could remember, that Marla went to live with her husband, Mr. T. Although Marla and her grandmother did not speak for almost three months following Marla's common-law marriage to Mr. T., thereafter Marla and her husband moved in with the grandmother and took over the house, with almost no objection on the part of the grandmother. At times the grandmother protested, saying that she was very ashamed to have a Negro in her home, which was in an all white community. Marla would become angry at her grandmother and curse at her in loud tones, telling her that she was narrow-minded and Godless, which hurt the grandmother very much. Finally, at the insistence of Mr. T., the couple moved away to their present studio, approximately six months ago. Marla continued to visit her grandmother occasionally, but always parted in a fit of anger. Their last contact was approximately six weeks before, at which time Marla swore she would never have anything more to do with her grandmother at all.

Course in Hospital. During the first week of hospitalization Marla required considerable sedation. However, she soon began to quiet down, and to follow the hospital routine. She would occasionally burst into tears and demand that the hospital get in touch with her husband, whom she said she missed dreadfully. During the second and third weeks she refused to eat and she sat at the window for hours on end, silent. This depression lifted spontaneously, however, and although still considerably quiescent she once more returned to joining in ward activities. At the end of five weeks she was allowed to go home on a visit, and upon her return seemed to be quite happy and at ease, but without the excitement she had shown on admission. The following week, after another home visit, her husband requested that she be discharged. She was put on a three months' trial home visit, at the end of which she was formally discharged from the hospital. In closing her case, the psychiatrist noted "prognosis is guarded."

During her hospitalization several interviews were conducted by the psychiatrist with Marla. She seemed eager to talk about her life, but kept denying that any such discussion had any bearing on her adjustment, or that she needed any type of psychotherapy. She brought her poetry with her, and made several attempts to write more poetry while in the hospital, but complained that she was unable to be creative at this time. Her poetry consisted of several volumes of handwritten pages of blank verse, which was largely incomprehensible. She smiled when the doctors asked her about the meaning of it, and explained that one had to know something about modern poetry to be able to understand it. The wording of the poetry was extremely morbid, and often overtly sexual. Many of the words referred to death and violent destruction or to the unhappiness of the world in general. At the doctor's request Mr. T. brought in some of Marla's published poems, which were only slightly more formal and comprehensible, and in which the themes of death and meaninglessness were prominent.

Questions for Marla T.

1. Cite the critical experiences and relationships in Marla's early life that provided a fertile ground for learning various conflicts.
2. What need (or needs) appear to have been particularly frustrated as a result of these experiences?

3. How did Marla learn to react to the frustration of these needs?

4. What additional conflicts appear to have been stimulated when Marla's mother returned home when Marla was thirteen?

5. How can we account for the fact that in spite of their poor relationship, Marla appears to have patterned a substantial part of her behavior after that of her mother?

6. Marla's sexual history is bizarre in many ways, yet it may be seen to be quite explicable when studied in some detail. First, try and explain Marla's motivation in running away with the two sailors at age thirteen.

7. How much of Marla's later sexual behavior might be seen as being based on the same motivation? Consider the following in your answer:

    a. Marla's promiscuity and enjoyment in seducing all men

    b. Marla's homosexual affair with the graduate student

    c. Marla's interest in dating men of other racial groups

8. How can we reconcile Marla's sexual looseness with the other side of her personality, namely the desire to help others, to give things to them, and to fight for the cause of minority groups?

9. Marla's first acutely excited episode occurred during her homosexual affair with the graduate student. Do we see any common features between that situation and the events preceding Marla's present breakdown?

10. Can you trace any relation between Marla's conflicts and the types of symptoms she developed during her acute episode, i.e. garish dress, excited talking, expansive feeling of well-being, and so forth?

References

CAMERON, D. E. Some relationships between excitement, depression and anxiety. *American Journal of Psychiatry*, 1945, **102**: 385–394.

CAMERON, N. The place of mania among the depressions from a biological standpoint. *Journal of Psychology*, 1942, **14**: 181–195.

GIBSON, R. W. The family background and early life experience of the manic-depressive patient. *Psychiatry*, 1958, **21**: 71–90. (Also reprinted in SARBIN, T. (Ed.) *Studies in behavior pathology*. New York: Holt, Rinehart, Winston, 1961. Pp. 210–228.

RENNIE, T. Prognosis in manic depressive psychoses. *American Journal of Psychiatry*, 1942, **98**: 801–814.

THE CASE OF LUCY Q.

A Woman's Work

Although Mrs. Q. had just passed her sixty-second birthday, her behavior and appearance gave the impression of marked physical and mental deterioration. She stumbled feebly up the steps of the state hospital, grasping at her daughter's arm for support, and had to be helped to a seat in the reception hall. Her wispy snow-white hair was sparse; her face was pinched and heavily wrinkled; and her blood vessels were visible through her pale, dry skin. Although dressed neatly in a little black bonnet and a relatively new pink wool suit, her clothes hung loosely on her tiny, thin frame. Apparently uncomfortable, she pulled nervously at her collar and blouse until scolded in a stage whisper by her daughter. In the office, she sat tensely on the edge of a chair, tremulous but tight-lipped, clutching at her purse.

Her daughter, Vicki, described Mrs. Q.'s condition and background to the doctor in front of her mother as if Mrs. Q. could not hear her, although later it proved that she had no hearing defect whatever. However, Mrs. Q. seemed either unaffected by or inattentive to anything her daughter said to the admitting physician. When the physician turned to Mrs. Q. and introduced himself, she smiled politely and shook his hand and asked anxiously if he had met her husband—despite the fact that her daughter had told the physician in Mrs. Q.'s presence only five minutes before that Mr. Q. had been dead for two years. Without waiting for an answer, Mrs. Q. went on to describe what a wonderful man her husband was and how sorry she was that he was not with her that day to meet the doctor. Asked how she felt about going into the hospital, Mrs. Q. grabbed her daughter's shoulder and began to weep. When her daughter pushed her away, Mrs. Q. sat back in her chair, looked very dejected, dabbed at her face with her handkerchief, and said bitterly,

"They hate me! They all hate me!" Her daughter also began to cry
and tried to reassure her mother, "We don't hate you, Mother, it's
all for your own good." She turned to the doctor and remarked, "I
was afraid she would make a scene." Mrs. Q. seemed to recover her
aplomb for a moment and retorted, "I'm not making a scene; you'll
have to excuse me, doctor; I haven't been feeling well and we must
leave now." Asked about her health, Mrs. Q. relaxed and told in detail of her many pains, her weakness, and especially her sensation
that something was eating away at her stomach and bowels.
Throughout her recitation of her physical miseries, she kept hinting
that none of her children understood or sympathized with her disa-
bilities. She seemed reassured for the moment by the doctor's statement that in the hospital she would receive the medical care, rest,
and attention she needed, but when the nurse came Mrs. Q. cried out
plaintively, "Where are you taking me? Where are you taking me?"

When examined several days later on the ward, Mrs. Q. appeared
even more deteriorated. Her daughter had brought no additional
clothes for her other than a nightgown. Mrs. Q.'s suit had been
stored in a locker and she was dressed in "hospital clothes," a faded
and ill-fitting house dress which drooped around her emaciated
body. In the interim, she had broken both her glasses and her dental
plate while washing up in the ward bathroom. Her toothless condition increased her appearance of severe aging. The nurse reported
that she had eaten little and seemed very depressed. She sat in a
chair in one corner of the room, not responding to anyone. She had
not voluntarily washed herself, and at the end of two days she was
given a shower bath by one of the nurses, to which she submitted
without question. She dozed at times during the day in her chair,
slept fitfully at night, and arose once or twice and wandered about the
hall muttering to herself until led back to bed.

She shuffled into the examining room in her hospital slippers and
stood rigidly in the doorway, pouting in anger. Introduced to another doctor, she protested, "You're not my doctor; I want to see *my*
doctor." Before the situation could again be explained to her, she
reassured herself with a declaration that her son was coming and
that everything would be all right. Again by inquiring about her
health the doctor was able to calm her, and she launched once more
into a recitation of her physical ills. Asked what medication and
treatment she had received, she replied that doctors and pills had

done her no good and explained that she found the greatest relief through "the power of prayer." Although born and reared a Catholic, she no longer had any use for the Catholic Church and had taken up "faith science." A brief mental examination was conducted, during which it was ascertained that she had no idea of the date or year. Although she could give her birth date correctly, she was not sure of her age. At one moment in the examination she recognized that she was in a hospital, but did not know the name of the hospital or why she was there; later she appeared to be confused as to exactly where she was. Her speech often trailed off and she would sit silent for a moment, seemingly collecting thoughts. Many of her remarks were irrelevant and she was difficult to follow as one idea seemed to float into the next in tangential fashion. At the end of the examination she repeated her hope that her son and daughter would come and take her home. Physical examination revealed an undernourished individual with mild signs of arteriosclerosis. There was a well-healed scar at the base of her throat, confirming the daughter's report that Mrs. Q. had had a goiter removed several years ago. There were also suggestions that she might be suffering from a mild kidney infection. Her gums were so deteriorated that the dentist wondered how she was able to utilize the dental plate, which had been ill fitting.

Past History. Since Mrs. Q. was unable to give a coherent account of her background, most of this information was obtained either from her daughter, Vicki, at the time of admission, or from her son, Steve, who made several visits within the next two weeks. Neither of these informants knew anything of Mrs. Q.'s birth and childhood development. She emigrated from Ireland to this country in her late teens. They believed that her parents died when she was quite young and that she had been reared by various older brothers and sisters. So far as they knew, she had no relatives in this country and never spoke of her kinfolk in Ireland. Steve remembered that his mother had spoken of "working out" before she emigrated, which he took to mean that she had been a servant girl in her early teens. Mrs. Q. had pointed out to them at one time the wealthy home where she had worked briefly before her marriage. She was barely twenty when she married their father, then a rookie patrolman in a small manufacturing city on the Atlantic coast. Vicki, their eldest, was born approximately a year after her parents married. Steve was approximately five years her junior, and there survived one other living child, Emily, who was six years younger than Steve. Vicki believed her mother was pregnant at least twice after she was born and before Steve was born but that there was only one live birth and this child died in its first year of life. Mrs. Q. was also pregnant twice between the middle and youngest child but both times suffered miscarriages. One other child was born after Emily, but it also died in infancy.

Both Vicki and Steve described their mother as an extremely hard-working, vigorous woman who devoted all her energies to her home and children. She scrubbed her house until it was "hospital clean." She hovered over her children's every move, constantly correcting them and threatening them with punishment from their father or from God if they did not obey her immediately. "We weren't afraid of our father," said Steve with a laugh, "because he was never home." Apparently they weren't afraid of God either, for they did not carry out their mother's wishes that they attend church. Steve had completed more religious training than his sisters but had rebelled against it in his adolescence; his mother was very disappointed that he did not become a priest.

Although Mrs. Q. never made any complaint against her husband even privately, her children realized when they became adults that she felt sorely mistreated by him. He expected her to wait on him hand and foot, never showed her any open affection, and gave her only the barest allowance on which to run the house. It was common gossip in the community that he was a "ladies' man," unfaithful to his wife. As the children grew older, Mrs. Q.'s patience with them grew shorter. She seemed to have little understanding of their social or emotional needs and they rebelled against her scolding and ignored her fears. Her husband labeled her a nag and laughed at the children's misdemeanors. Steve admitted that in his adolescence he was involved in several serious delinquencies and would have been sent to jail if his policeman father had not intervened for him. Vicki, in an act of rebellion, ran away and got married in her early teens, a marriage which was annulled shortly afterwards. However, her mother was furious, called her a slut, would not take her back in the house, and did not speak to her for several years. Emily also married soon after she left high school and moved to another part of the country. Neither Steve nor Vicki had seen much of her since and they did not believe that she had written her mother in years. They admitted with some guilt that they had never felt close to either their mother or father. As soon as they became adults they went their own ways, became involved in their own lives, and had only infrequent contact with their parents. Letters from their mother were replete with accounts of her physical suffering, but they were unsure of the nature of her illnesses. "She was the kind of person who enjoyed poor health." Vicki could not remember exactly when her mother had been operated on for the goiter.

About ten years prior to Mrs. Q.'s present hospitalization she had been very depressed and disturbed. Their father, who never wrote to them, had telephoned to ask their advice as to whether she needed "to be put away." Months before, in a sudden pique, she had stopped speaking to him. She remained in her room, often weeping to herself and neglecting her housework. More religious than ever before, she built a small shrine in her bedroom and frequently repeated her prayers. Steve visited her at this time and found her much as his father had described. In a long, involved, and not too coherent tale she confided to Steve that the neighbors were plotting against her and asked him to prevail on his father to get her a gun. When Mr. Q. demanded that Steve sign papers to commit his mother to the state hospital, Steve refused on the grounds that this was his father's responsibility. Mr. Q.'s excuse that any such action on his part might jeopardize his position on the police force seemed unreasonable to Steve. After a bitter argument with his father, Steve returned home, angry and guilty, having left his mother in the same situation in which he had found her.

In more recent contacts with their mother, Steve and Vicki found her emotional condition ameliorated, although she remained depressed and suspicious of everyone in general. Steve's wife, in an effort to make friends with her mother-in-law, made a long and tiring visit with their children only to find Mrs. Q. uninterested and weary. Vicki, about a year prior to her father's death, invited her parents to her home for Christmas. Mrs. Q.'s caustic criticism of Vicki's handling of her children and of her housekeeping had irritated Vicki intensely. She scarcely knew her father and found that she and her husband had little in common with him.

Mr. Q. had died suddenly of a heart attack within the first year

of his retirement from the police force. Steve and Vicki discovered
that he had taken his entire pension out in cash, and there was no
account of what had happened to his money. It also appeared that
he had heavily mortgaged their home. Mrs. Q. was of the opinion
that her husband had gambled heavily and lost a great deal. She
was financially destitute, depressed, and bitter. Both Vicki and Steve
lived in small houses which had no separate quarters for their
mother, and neither were at all eager to take her into their homes.
She was not at that time eligible for any type of old-age insurance
or public pension. Although Steve could ill afford any further expenses from his own modest salary, he attempted for almost a year
to make payments on the mortgage and to cover his mother's utili-
ties. Vicki agreed to furnish her mother's food and clothing. Mrs. Q.
shrugged her shoulders and looked away when informed of her
children's plans. Steve was able to keep up his end of the bargain
for approximately nine months at which time he lost his job. Vicki
had informed him that her mother continued to be depressed and
was not eating well. Most of all, Vicki was upset because Mrs. Q.,
neglecting her personal care, had become dirty and unkempt, in contrast to her previous obsession with cleanliness. Abandoning her
Catholicism, Mrs. Q. had become involved in a small religious sect
known as "Truth Science," to which, Vicki discovered, Mrs. Q. contributed much of her food and clothing allowance.

Steve and Vicki despaired of what to do with their mother. For
the next year she lived with each of them alternately. At Vicki's
home, she slept on a couch in the dining room, keeping her meager
belongings in the guest closet in the front hall. She was annoyed
and impatient with Vicki's teen-age children and was constantly correcting them. She complained of the noise of the television, only to
demand her own programs. Because she only washed and changed
her clothes when Vicki pressed her, she was often unpresentable,
which embarrassed Vicki in front of her friends. At Steve's home,
Steve's wife gave her mother-in-law their bedroom while she and
Steve slept in the living room. Mrs. Q. was a little happier here, but
her complaints and corrections of Steve's behavior and of Steve's
young children sorely strained their tolerance. As Mrs. Q.'s mental
confusion and depression increased, both of her children realized
they could no longer care for her.

Treatment and Disposition. Mrs. Q. was put on an immediate "total push" program of rehabilitation, aimed at her physical, social, and emotional needs. Medications were prescribed to slow down the process of her arteriosclerosis and to clear up her kidney infection. New dental plates and new glasses were fitted for her, with extra pairs in case one was broken. As the state did not supply the glasses cost free, Steve was very happy to carry this expense, and Mrs. Q. was informed that her son was making this contribution. Vicki volunteered to take her mother shopping when she was advised of her mother's need for clothes. Placed on a ward where there were other ladies her age, Mrs. Q. was engaged in a busy program of occupational therapy. She learned to knit, at which she proved very adept. A beauty shop operator volunteered to teach the women patients to set one another's hair and manicure their nails. Mrs. Q. took a renewed pride in her personal grooming. She had no recreational interests whatever and could not be involved in the card games or other activities of the patients on the ward. She did enjoy, however, taking long walks with one of the psychiatric aides. First assigned a job helping to serve food on the ward, she later, on her own initiative, asked to be transferred to helping to feed the patients on the children's ward. Here she was allowed to do some cooking, making special treats for "her" children. The hospital was too distant from town for Vicki and Steve to visit their mother regularly, but, with the encouragement of the hospital social worker, occasionally they did take their mother to their homes. Her weight returned to near normal and she ceased mentioning her illnesses and seemed much more cheerful and a little less confused. One of the other women patients on her ward, also born and reared in Ireland, attached herself to Mrs. Q. and enjoyed exchanging childhood memories. When Mrs. Q.'s friend was placed in a foster home, Mrs. Q. requested to be transferred there also. The foster home provided Mrs. Q. and her friend with a small kitchen where they could do some of their own cooking. They soon became popular as baby sitters throughout the neighborhood. Mrs. Q. seemed much less depressed and much better oriented to everyday affairs the last time she was visited by the field social worker.

Questions for Lucy Q.

1. List the symptoms which Lucy Q. expressed at the time of admission to the hospital classifying them into
   a. emotional features
   b. intellectual features

2. Which of these symptoms are known to be the psychological consequences of arteriosclerosis? Which are not?

3. If you have listed some symptoms to the second part of question 2, indicate what diagnostic category could subsume these additional features.

4. There are certain ideas about herself which Lucy manifests which are more or less characteristic of mental disorders in advanced years. What are these ideas? How can you account, on a psychological basis, for the prominence of these symptoms in people of advanced age?

5. Ordinarily, mental illness, even when it has an organic component, reflects the long-standing personality adjustment of the individual to stress. What evidence do we see in Lucy for pathological modes of adjustment over her adult life-span?

6. Which of the pathological modes of adjustment remained intact during Lucy's illness and which yielded to other, more regressive, behavior patterns?

7. From your answers to questions 5 and 7, speculate as to which drives or emotions Lucy was striving to keep out of awareness during her pre-illness period of life.

8. What factors existed in Lucy's environment which placed unusual stress upon her ability to master her environment?
   a. 10 years previously
   b. at the time of the present illness

9. What role did Lucy's relationship with her husband appear to play in her two illnesses?

10. How can you account for the fact that Lucy's relationship with her children deteriorated over the years? What effect did this alienation from her children have upon her self-concept?

11. a. What specific things were done to Lucy during her stay in the hospital?
    b. What psychological needs did they satisfy for Lucy which

evidently permitted her to reintegrate her personality during this period?

12. What are some specific psychological problems unique to the fifth and sixth decade of life?

13. Using your answer to question 12 as a base, attempt to account for the fact that the modal pattern of abnormal behavior in the late adult years is depression?

References

BUSSE, E. Psychopathology. In BIRREN, J. (Ed.) *Handbook of aging and the individual.* Chicago: Univer. of Chicago Press, 1959.

DAVIS, D., WEISS, J. M. A., GILDEA, E. F., & MENSH, I. Psychiatric problems of later life. II. Clinical syndromes. *American Practitioner, Diagnosis and Treatment,* 1959, 10: 61–65.

FERRARO, A. Psychoses with cerebral arteriosclerosis. In ARIETI, S. (Ed.) *American handbook of psychiatry.* New York: Basic Books, 1959. Pp. 1080–1086.

RECHTSCHAFFEN, A., et al. An intensive treatment program for state hospital geriatric patients. *Geriatrics,* 1954, 28–36.

REISMAN, D. Some clinical and cultural aspects of aging. *Selected essays from individualism reconsidered.* New York: Doubleday Anchor Books, 1955. Pp. 164–173.

PART VI CASE PARODY

THE CASE OF CHRISTOPHER K.

"The Brothers Karamazov"

Christopher K. came to the clinic, complaining of frequent attacks of measles. He claimed to have no other symptoms or difficulties. His doctor had found no medical basis for the measles and had advised that Christopher seek psychiatric help.

Christopher was a well-dressed man of 21, with dark brown hair that he wore rather longer than was the fashion, tied in a neat bun at the nape of the neck. He had a clear complexion, except for the red spots that covered his face, hands, and bare feet. He seemed to find it difficult to speak, and complained from time to time of a sore throat, and later from a headache. As he became more comfortable in the interview situation, he gradually fell asleep.

Prior History. Christopher was an only child until he was five years old, at which time his mother gave birth to a daughter, giving him a sister and making him a brother. He remembered being very fond of his sister, and giving her all his toys, and even his desserts at dinner time. This latter, however, only when his mother wasn't looking, since the sister was still an infant, unable to eat anything solid. He told about her death in a curiously detached manner, seemingly emotionlessly.

Christopher never knew who his father was. "Father," he used to ask him, "who are you?" However, his father would tell him to go out and play, without answering. Christopher reported having his first sexual experience at age 5, when he seduced the little girl next door, who was 4 years old. The girl's family was furious, since their daughter later turned out to be pregnant, and insisted on a wedding. He reported having terrible guilt feelings at this time, and shortly thereafter, joined the boy-scouts, seeking anonymity in uniform. "I was looking for somewhere I could *belong*," he said. He called this the happiest part of his life. However, two days after he joined, he was thrown out for stealing the treasury and running off with the den mother.

Course in Treatment. Shortly after the commencement of treatment, Mr. K.'s symptoms became worse. He complained of being tired out and dizzy and of ever-worsening headaches. He also became more and more hostile to the analyst, giving him less and less cooperation, until finally, he died.

Questions for Christopher K.

1. From your understanding of the case, what part did Christopher's sexual adjustment play in his life?
2. What part does sexual adjustment play in *your* life?
3. How was Christopher related to:
    a. his mother
    b. his father
    c. his sister?
4. What defense mechanism did Christopher put to use by dying?
5. How did this become manifest in his later life?

References

HAVSOME, T. The effect of Ibsen on contemporary drama. *Psychotic Quarterly Supplement,* 1962, **97**: 2–5.

KWITE, M. T. Palm reading among the Gururumba. *Schizophrenic Home Companion,* 1962, **97**: 2–5.

KILDARE, M. D. The black mass. *Archives of Generals,* 1962, **97**: 2–5.